A POTENT SPELL

Books by Janna Malamud Smith

Private Matters:
In Defense of the Personal Life

A Potent Spell:
Mother Love and the Power of Fear

A Potent Spell

MOTHER LOVE
AND THE
POWER OF FEAR

Janna Malamud Smith

Houghton Mifflin Company

BOSTON • NEW YORK

2003

For information about permission to reproduce selections from
this book, write to Permissions, Houghton Mifflin Company,
215 Park Avenue South, New York, New York 10003.

Visit our Web site: www.houghtonmifflinbooks.com.

Library of Congress Cataloging-in-Publication Data
Smith, Janna Malamud.
A potent spell : mother love and the power of fear / Janna
Malamud Smith.
p.   cm.
Includes bibliographical references and index.
ISBN 0-618-06349-8
1. Motherhood — Psychological aspects. 2. Mothers — Psychology.
3. Mothers. 4. Mother and child. I. Title.
HQ759 .S618 2002
306.8743'3 — dc21   2002027632

Book design by Victoria Hartman

Printed in the United States of America

VB 10 9 8 7 6 5 4 3 2 1

Quotes from "Home Burial" from *The Poetry of Robert Frost* edited by
Edward Connery Lathem, © 1958 by Robert Frost, © 1967 by Lesley Frost
Ballantine. Reprinted by permission of Henry Holt & Co., LLC.

For my mother,
Ann deChiara Malamud

CONTENTS

PART III: "A PAIN SO DURABLE"

ACKNOWLEDGMENTS

I WANT FIRST to express my warm gratitude to my agent, Miriam Altshuler; and to my editor, Janet Silver, whose willingness to read, comment on, and then reread and comment on the manuscript, rigorously and through many drafts, has been extraordinary. Without the efforts of both these women, I would not have written this book. Their vital engagement, by turns demanding and generous, has been a gift.

At Houghton Mifflin, I would also like to thank Gracie Doyle, Jayne Yaffe Kemp, Corrina Lesser, and Christina Smith.

Additionally I want to thank Jackie Bonenfant, Christopher Ann Corkery, Judith Edersheim, Diane Feeney, Mary Theresa Flanagan, Adele Gagne, Maggie Jackson, Sarah Kerr-Garraty, Sonya Larrieux, Nan Lee, Jan Lerbinger, Alison MacIver, Shirley McMahon, Paula Paris, Jeanne Strassburger, Anne White, and many other women for sharing their mothering stories.

For reading chapters or early drafts I thank Lisa Baker, Patricia Cantor, Michael T. Gilmore, Doris Kearns Goodwin, Richard Ryerson, Bennett Simon and Roberta Apfel, Shoshona Sokoloff, and Deborah Valenze.

I am indebted to the kind reference librarians at the Countway, Widener, Houghton, and Schlesinger libraries; and to the historians Philip Greven and Mary Beth Norton for generously answering e-mail inquiries.

I thank my friends and colleagues, especially those who have managed to overlook—or tolerate—the thankless aspects of befriending this writer.

Excessive hugs and kisses to our sons, Peter and Zack Smith, and a particular nod to them for pointlessly but raucously recalling—line by line—all those *Simpsons* episodes over dinner, thus preventing sensible conversation and quashing opportunities to parent responsibly.

Most of all, my love and gratitude to my husband, first reader and closest friend, David M. Smith.

Finally, I want to acknowledge a debt to the many feminists who have critiqued social and psychoanalytic views of women and mothers. When, in the late 1970s, I first read Jean Baker Miller's *Toward a New Psychology of Women* and Adrienne Rich's *Of Woman Born,* I felt my life and thinking change. Earlier I'd found my way to Kate Millet, and Germaine Greer. In fact, one of the sweetest pleasures of my adulthood has been witnessing the great river thaw, and women's ideas—as alternately brilliant and idiotic as men's—pour forth. Over the years, I have read with interest pieces by psychoanalytic writers like Jessica Benjamin, Nancy Chodorow, Helene Cixious, Jane Gallop, Judith Herman, Luce Irigaray, Juliet Mitchell, and Ethel Person. Additionally, I admire and have learned much from the writings of feminist social critics, including Barbara Ehrenreich, Betty Friedan, bell hooks, and Katha Pollitt.

Oh, what a power is motherhood, possessing
A potent spell. All women alike fight fiercely for a child.

— Euripides, *Iphigenia at Aulis*

Yet someone had loved him, borne him in her arms and in her heart. But for her the race of the world would have trampled him under foot, a squashed boneless snail. She had loved his weak watery blood drained from her own. Was that then real? The only true thing in life?

— James Joyce, *Ulysses*

Introduction

GROWING UP, I did not think a lot about becoming a mother. I played with dolls sometimes, and remember two particularly. The first, a brown-skinned boy infant, was my favorite. The other, a white, chestnut-haired creature named Bella, appeared one year at Christmas complete with a shoebox of outfits sewn by my grandmother. My best friend had a Barbie and Ken, who, as we grew older, kept us busy planning scenes of their sexual undoing, followed by guilt-exculpating marriage.

When doll play got boring, Kokie, our Siamese cat, could be dressed in an old sleeveless undershirt and stuffed into a small carriage on her back, her black legs jutting out of the blanket and visible above the sides. She would protest but never bite, and usually allowed the ruse to continue for a half minute before she bolted. I can still hear the strangulated gargling sound she made attempting to meow as I squirted milk from the doll bottle into her mouth. She was the infant stand-in on whom I practiced.

But in spite of a native instinct, and unlike many of my friends in the small town in Oregon in which we lived in the 1950s, I did not dream longingly of becoming a mother. In retrospect, this seems particularly odd since mothering was the only adult possibility I could see for married women. Looking back half a century later, it is difficult to convey the iron curtain that surrounded women and blocked opportunity. In our small town a widowed woman could work as a secretary; a single woman, newlywed, or divorcée might teach elementary school, practice as a nurse, or can vegetables in the local factory; but my mother's friends, married with children, stayed home. Except for one woman who taught college English, I can remember none of them in an ambitious or lucrative job. If there were other exceptions, the era's sanctions made me snow-blind, and I did not register what my eyes saw.

The grade-school library had a shelf of brown-covered biographies of American heroes—among them Wild Bill Hickok, Abraham Lincoln, Davy Crockett. Out of maybe thirty-five, two or three were about women—none of whom had children. I dismissed Clara Barton and Florence Nightingale because—portrayed in those days primarily as self-sacrificers extraordinaire—they were unbearable. Only Annie Oakley did serviceable duty. In retrospect, it seems somewhere between amusing and pathetic that a stage performer with a rifle became my image of female autonomy, but so it was. (I remember singing with a friend tunes from *Annie Get Your Gun,* bellowing together with Ethel Merman the musical's quintessential, contradictory, Freudian chant for 1950s females, "No, ya can't get a man with a gunnnn!!") Overall, the outcome of my reading was to confirm an impression that no biography paid attention to mothers, and, conversely, that no woman with a public role had children.

Born a dozen years earlier, I might have glimpsed Eleanor Roosevelt breaking "first lady" conventions, or a nation of mothers driving rivets into destroyer hulls. But by the mid-1950s that reality had vanished, erased and left as flat and blank as our clean schoolroom chalkboards at the end of the day. Women were to stay home with children. Mothering was everything. In truth, mothering was devalued as often as honored, and women were portrayed as beautiful fools.

It was still taken for granted in the 1950s and 1960s that women were inferior. At the local college, girls were called "co-eds" and were assumed to have come for husbands—though, strangely, the male students were never said to be in search of wives. Biology was destiny. Emotion kept females from thinking clearly. Irrationality cycled like fertility, and peaked in the days leading up to menstruation. Meanwhile, menstruation was not a word anyone mentioned. Scan the horizon as I might, I could find no trace of a respected, assertive public woman, certainly not one with children.

From my little-girl perspective, mothers in our small town lived as mostly cheerful servants. I didn't have those words then, but I think from early on I had the feeling. Wherever I looked, I saw mothers putting their husbands' dinners on the table and scraping their plates when they finished. I saw them washing and ironing their husband's shirts, picking up after them, running their errands, turning to them for money or a night out . . . cleaning, weeding, shopping, mending, and supervising children.

Between chores and chauffeuring duties, they spent long afternoons talking. I listened as they recounted sorrows and complaints amid the neighborhood news, but I also heard much that spoke of contentment. Why not? After teen years in the Depression and early adulthoods worrying about brothers and lovers fighting in World War II, this postwar world must have seemed Edenic. Few among my parents' friends had money, but life was good. The men had jobs. Families could afford to buy small houses and secondhand cars. Neighbors helped pick one another's fruit trees, and afterward made plum jam, or apple butter, or ladled cooked pears and cherries into Mason jars. The landscape—rolling fields surrounded by stands of huge, dark green Douglas fir trees—was gorgeous; the town was safe; the public schools orderly. The ghosts of immigrant forebears and war dead looked on in awe.

Lacking perspective, I could not make sense of the mothers' ways. No, that's not true: I took them and their position for granted. They were female reality. What perplexed me was my own reluctance to imagine a future in which I would take my place among them. I dreamed of kissing boys—and more—but had no interest in planning the obligatory wedding, or choosing a bassinet. I wanted adventure. I wanted to get on a horse and ride through the west, roping rogue cows and bad guys. At the end of a long day's work, I wanted to fall asleep on a bedroll under the stars. (A few years later, when we moved east, I was filled with melancholy over the loss of Oregon and the premature dismantling of my fantasy cowgirl world. The tame New England landscape with its pathetic deciduous trees and aging hills passed off as mountains, offended me. Not questioning my urgency, my mother kindly drove me twenty-five miles to a town in the next state, where a dingy store sold cowboy boots.)

Growing up, I did not think longingly about raising children because I could not reconcile the circumscribed lives of the neighborhood mothers with my eagerness to explore a larger world. I put away my conscious maternal wishes; figuring where the baby would fit on the saddle was too hard. We may grow to reject the limiting images in the old Dick and Jane readers, or Walt Disney's portrayal of the American family on 1950s television, or any of the other distortions the young of my generation were fed. But they remain in the mind, shading our sensibilities. In spite of ourselves, we absorb the culture's views.

Now the mother of two teenage boys, I think back and wonder how I could have hesitated so to approach the best part of my life. Nothing in my worries prepared me for the complete transforming joy of having children, nor for the way that the experience would shake my universe and rearrange all meanings so that the rest of life retreated into the background. And while these are not fresh observations, oddly, one experiences them as such. I think many women—but perhaps particularly ones who, like me, started out uncertain about how to reconcile child-rearing with other wishes—experience the pleasure, the anxiety, the enormous depth of feeling as an original discovery, as something surprising. The strange infant is in your arms. It breathes funny and your heart stops. Fear has become love's best friend. You are owned.

Once a mother attaches to an infant, whether before or after it is born to her or adopted; once she experiences that surge of overwhelming protective love and visceral affiliation, her life is transformed by the basic imperative of the relationship: children require care. I remember feeling puzzled lying in the hospital immediately after our first son was born. Although doctors and visitors came and went, the scrunch-faced alien stayed. Why did no one claim him? A quiet terror whispered, "You have acted irrevocably. Now you're stuck." As the exhaustion lifted, my feelings changed; tenderness and awe stirred, then flooded in. If a nurse removed him even briefly, I became uneasy. His life was in my hands; and my hands, my arms, my lips, flexed by new nerves, rearranged themselves in his service.

The primary, intimate labor of protection across time and societies has been assigned to mothers—with varying amounts of assistance provided by older children, fathers, other kin, and caretakers. As a friend, a neighbor, and in my work as a psychotherapist, I have spoken with many women about the electric storm inside a new mother as she begins caring for an infant—how tossed, twisted, ecstatic, and frightened, how completely changed she feels, how much more vulnerable. She has brought a new life into the world. Its well-being rests on every motion she makes, or so it seems.

My husband and I still laugh about our older son's first diaper change. Overwhelmed by his fragility, we were sure if we touched him wrong, he'd break. A hurried nurse had handed me a clean diaper and some wipes, then left. We gingerly unwrapped the breathing bundle and gently, oh so gently, started cleaning him up. We worked away with the exacting, nerve-wracking attention of novice curators assigned to polish a Bernini sculpture. Something priceless was in our care, and we could ruin it. What if we snapped off a piece?

You probably remember that meconium quite resembles tar. You no doubt know better than we did how newborns hate being unwrapped, and tend to wail when they feel cold air. We began to sweat. Finally, perhaps fifteen minutes later (it seemed like hours), we finished our labor. Our subject was still breathing; in fact, he had stopped crying and fallen asleep. Perhaps he'd simply gone into shock, having grasped the inept hands into which he'd been delivered. Meanwhile, we were both emotionally wrung out. But proud. A nurse came and wheeled our re-diapered baby away. My husband headed home. Maybe half an hour later the nurse stuck her head into the room, cranky. "Next time you put on a new diaper," she barked, "you have to wipe him clean first." I dissolved into helpless giggles. "But we did," I finally gasped. She scowled and departed. I'd been a mother less than a day, and already I was in trouble.

The worst clumsiness tends to pass. But a new, enlarged vulnerability remains. In fact, it settles in like a great hawk perched on your shoulders. Its talons grasp flesh whenever the sharp-eyed creature startles, and much makes it uneasy. Whether you talk to the mother of a newborn, or the mother of a twenty-five-year-old, she will tell you how her stomach knots and worry descends whenever she senses that a child's well-being is at risk. If she believes she has made a serious mistake, she feels worse than awful. Until you have children, one mother reflected when I interviewed her, "You don't think about what an impact you can make on someone else's life."[1]

This awareness translates into new feelings of responsibility. What I do decides whether this baby lives or dies, whether it thrives or suffers. Each choice I make matters. And the sum of my minute-by-minute decisions determines—or so as mothers we are repeatedly told—how my child fares in the world. Many moments are mundane: "No, you cannot watch that television program." Yet, in truth, all mothers sense, without dwelling on it, that they can make a life-and-death mistake of judgment at any time. We can say, "Yes, you can walk alone to your friend's house," when it will turn out that the correct answer was "No, cars run the stop sign at that corner too frequently. Let me walk with you."

Small decisions can have large consequences. This disjunction, paired with our intense sense of responsibility, puts us on edge. We worry. "Did he remember his asthma inhaler on the overnight wilderness hiking trip? I should have tried to phone the camp office again." Or, as one mother put it when she described reluctantly allowing her thirteen-year-old son to attend a rock concert with a friend because he so desperately wanted to go, "If a terrorist bombs the [concert hall], or if he gets trampled, I will spend the rest of my life hating myself for [my decision]."[2] Each week is packed with choices that likely will come out just fine, but . . .

Another mother tells me how frightened she felt, mistakenly believing that her seventeen-year-old daughter was out with other teenagers in a car on icy roads in the midst of an unexpected snowfall. The mother of an eleven-year-old recalls how a week earlier she left him home alone one day so she could go to her new job. (Her husband was unable to stay home.) The boy, who appeared to have a cold, turned out to have pneumonia. He recovered, but his mother felt miserable that she had not appreciated how ill he was.

Since having children, and after almost twenty-five years working as a clinical social worker and psychotherapist hearing about other mothers' experiences, I have realized that not only can you not understand mothers, but you cannot grasp the long, robust endurance of gender inequality without exploring the ways mothering affects women, heightening their sensitivity to varieties of threat, awakening new and more profound fears of loss, intensifying focus, and inexorably drawing them toward personal choices and accommodations that seem to enhance their children's safety.

Mothers' passionate concern with keeping beloved children alive is a central fact of life—so primary that it is taken for granted and mostly goes unnamed—just as when we mention daylight, we assume the sun. Each place and time, each society, jury-rigs ways of addressing and mediating maternal fears about the survival and well-being of children—yet often at a high price to mothers. And while this observation about maternal focus may seem obvious, its consequences—its place in understanding how mothers live in the world—has been largely overlooked, including by writers of history and psychology.

Such neglect is startling only if one forgets that until about thirty years ago, mothers and other women generally were considered irrelevant by historians. I was "educated" in grade school to believe that the only woman worthy of mention in the American Revolution was Betsy Ross, who sewed the flag. As a college senior in 1973 I took the first course my school taught in American women's history. Brainwashed in spite of myself by the university's devaluing of women (it could find few to employ and none to tenure), I remember feeling mildly incredulous that such a subject could exist. Women had done laundry. What was there to study?

People have been writing and recording history for over five thousand years, during which time the odd woman picked up a pen. A few more women started publishing two or three hundred years ago, and at moments they proliferated enough to overrun parts of the market. But really, it's been for only the past forty years that a generation of female scholars has begun to rewrite American history to include the stories of women. How then can people claim that feminism is passé, has achieved its aims, or is irrelevant?

I hear such dismissive comments partly as efforts to ward off anxieties about what will happen to children (and men) if mothers are free to live fuller lives. The idea of autonomous women with full citizenship remains frightening. Writing in 1762, Jean-Jacques Rousseau (whose mother died when he was born) captures some of the perennial anxiety and anger when he declares that "She to whom nature has entrusted the care of the children must hold herself responsible for them to their father." He adds that if she is "faithless," her crime is "not infidelity but treason." A few pages later Rousseau puts forth his ideal: "When the Greek women married, they disappeared from public life; within the four walls of their home they devoted themselves to the care of their household and family. This is the mode of life prescribed for women alike by nature and reason."[3]

The woman behind the wall represents a common compromise: stay cloistered and receive some protection. Our generation in the United States is living in one of the rare moments of Western history when doors have opened, and equality between the sexes is in view. Will the experiment progress? It's unclear, too soon to tell if this apparent trend is just one more instance of privileged exception. Often when a society has allowed a bit of movement, it seems that forces gather to reconfine mothers, or encourage them to seclude themselves. Each historical situation, examined carefully, yields particular reasons that mothers have had little direct social power. But if we could line up every society, squares of farmland, and view them from the air, we'd find repeated patterns in the plowing. Examine the contours, and one powerful, recurrent theme is the mother's fear of child loss.

Listening intently to people for many years has also taught me that stories are the mind's, perhaps even the soul's, DNA—the genetic strands, the basic building blocks, of psychic and communal life, the replicating carriers of feeling. This book is filled with mothers' stories. Some are from the distant past, others are contemporary; still others are borrowed by me from works of art, literature, historical documents, or old advice books about mothering. In the chapters that follow, I want to tell new tales and retell old ones in fresh ways—to demonstrate the vast ramifications for mothers of their consuming preoccupation with keeping children safe, and to shed light on the impact of maternal vulnerability upon women's unequal status.

Twenty-five hundred years ago, Euripides described motherhood as "possessing a potent spell." I believe his phrase captures something true about maternal experience. Indeed, I think Euripides noticed how mothers' attachment to children is often so fierce it takes us over and affects all other aspects of our lives. So too, while from the outside mothers' admonitions and behaviors sometimes are difficult to comprehend, and even look irrational, when you understand the centrality of their urgency to keep beloved children alive, and the particular ways it heightens their own vulnerability in families, work, and social contexts, suddenly, like a puzzle that you must stare at hard to comprehend, the scrambled picture makes good sense.

PART I

THE
POTENT
SPELL

Twice Vulnerable

CHILD LOVE makes mothers vulnerable, raises all stakes, and defines much about how we live—and have lived—in the world. Once attached, mothers fear the terrible grief of child loss and change behavior in small and large ways to accommodate that fear. "That awe-inspiring feeling of vulnerability, that awareness of potential loss," one woman called it. "It was one of the most immediate and biggest surprises of motherhood for me, and it just doesn't go away."[1]

Every mother recognizes this expanded sensitivity and vigilance, the fact that once she has a child her feeling life rearranges itself to protect him. Yet its omnipresence obscures its importance not only as a central part of children's survival, but as one underconsidered determinant of women's history. I think this transition has been deemed so obvious as to be unworthy of attention. But I suggest that its apparent inconsequence is an illusion—a *trompe l'oeil* that misleads us and, perversely, distracts us from comprehending its significance to women worldwide, today and in the past.

When a mother attaches to her children, her love encircles them like a web of filaments that reach across physical separateness and link her feelings—her very nerve endings—to their safety and well-being. She thinks, gathers impressions, makes decisions, and acts for a small colony rather than simply for herself. She feels for two, or three, or ten.

She scrutinizes each street anew, confers fresh consequence upon every aspect of her environment. Often she suppresses her own sensation as she tries to comprehend or anticipate her child's. A mother told me about carefully packing just the right warm sweaters for her six-month-old daughter's first trip to the shore on a cold spring weekend. Intent on caring for the child, she forgot to pack a sweater for herself. "I had honestly told myself, as I was packing, that I would be warm, since I had packed her extra-warm hooded sweater."[2] Conversely, my younger son now teases me, "A sweater is what you put on when your mother is cold."

Mothers are contradictions: we are individuals, and yet we also function as the nerve-linked command centers of interdependent groups. As a result, our psychological lives are complex: we continually entertain calls from diverse constituencies—some outside ourselves, some within. We experience our children's needs, our own, our spouse's or partner's, and those of an array of kin, as many lights flashing on a single switchboard. In the back of a mother's mind, often in the front, is a running awareness of her children's situations, their health, urgencies, emotions, current schedules, and the engineering required of her to care for them.

Each mother knows her variation—some more, some less intense—of this mental state. But what about its broader impact? Watch a pregnant woman with a couple of young kids in tow—one in a stroller, the other holding her hand—cross a street. Groups—particularly those containing helpless and immobile small members—are relatively hobbled, difficult to herd and defend. Supplying them with food and provisions, moving them quickly, or fending off enemies can be tough. Once a woman becomes a mother, her mobility—whether psychological, physical, or relational—is exponentially diminished. At the center of her concern is protecting her offspring. And while love, and a good partner, may sustain her, the mission is guided by a steady—sometimes quiescent and distant, sometimes immediate—gut fear of child loss. She remembers the terror she felt the first time her infant was even slightly threatened; she does not want it to wake.

Indeed, having our own well-being so closely knit by love to our children's exposes mothers to losses that we know can devastate us. According to my dictionary, the word *vulnerable* means "capable of being wounded," "open to attack or damage," and "assailable." Harm my child, and you have harmed me. Each child I give birth to may increase the chance that one will survive; yet each additional attachment also increases the number of fronts on which I feel assailable.

"My mother would take a bullet for me," a man tells me in passing. "Of course I would put myself between my children and death," a woman remarks at a dinner party. We know that most mothers—no matter how "bad" they are said to be—feel they will sacrifice even their lives on their children's behalf. Part of the reason is love. Part is love's corollary: each mother knows it would be difficult, if not unbearable, to choose otherwise. How could we live with ourselves if we believed we had not given all to save a child? The misery would be quicksand.

Ask a mother to tell you the worst thing that could happen to *her*, as I have over the years in my work as a psychotherapist, and often she will shift the focus as she answers. It is *her children's* harm or death she most dreads and sees as the largest potential source of pain on her horizon. Does she fear dying? Yes, she has a lot she wants to do; and then in the next breath she adds: If she dies, who will help her husband or partner or kin care for the children? Her death becomes framed as *their* loss of protector.

Although the grief of miscarriage or failed in vitro procedures or stillbirth or an interrupted adoption is more common than we would wish, and although African American boys face heightened risk of death from violence, and gay and lesbian children from suicide in response to social stigma, most contemporary American mothers no longer have children who die in their own lifetimes. But this reality does not alter subjective perception. The world is fraught and terribly complicated. A mother senses that death can sneak up and grab a child, that she must stay alert, that everything rests on her. Writing about her own sons in *Of Woman Born*, Adrienne Rich formulated an eloquent corollary, "*I love them. But it's in the enormity and inevitability of this love that the suffering lies.*"[3]

Within love lies loss, and not simply from death. For the many contemporary women who have not actually had a child die or suffered a miscarriage or infertility, there are the inevitable quieter feelings of loss as children mature. Of course sadness is balanced by excitement and satisfaction, and sometimes by profound relief, but that acknowledgment shortchanges the sorrow. For parenting brings a continual emotional imperative that the mother accept and bear the child's step-by-step departure. It has often seemed to me that my children's development required not just that they grow, but that at each juncture I agree to let go of one child and accept another.

Suppose your daughter wants to have the same book read three times at bedtime. At first it's fun. Weeks later, chafing, a little bored, you wish she would mature a bit and accept a nighttime separation requiring less protracted ritual. Yet, when on an evening, communing with a new stuffed animal, she is suddenly dismissive, you feel sadness and longing along with surprise and relief. However much you may have encouraged the autonomy, the manner and choice of moment finally is not yours. Mothers must repeatedly adjust.

I have always particularly loved the physical aspects of parenting: the holding and hugging, the offering of comfort through touch. As my sons have moved through adolescence, I have had to contain my impulses. I can slip them a quick kiss or squeeze, a touch on the shoulder, but more than that often intrudes. I try to accept the boundary, yet I miss knowing about their bodies. So too, while I relish their grown opinions, I miss the unself-conscious, confiding child talk they leave behind as they become more self-contained, friend-focused men.

Then there are the fantasy losses, the child you created in your mind who never materialized. A friend observed that it was finally dawning on her husband that their twelve-year-old son might not grow up to play major league baseball. And how is it that the two classical musicians I dreamed of raising crash out "punk" and "metal" tunes on guitar, electric bass, and drums? I love their energy, the daily surprise of real people. But now and then I think about chimeric boys playing the oboe or French horn.

A full accounting of feelings must also include the children you did not or could not have. The first, second, third, fourth, the missing son or daughter. The one after where you stopped. I have an imaginary third son who vaguely flits through my mind sometimes. He's younger, and holds my longing for small-child practices that have disappeared. I can still read to him and carry him. Mostly, he is simply one more turn of the kaleidoscope, another different, original person. And there's a daughter . . .

My sons would be the first to tell you that mothers' protective actions are not inevitably gentle, or for that matter even sensible. They have accurately attached the word *harsh* to some of my tirades and eruptions. *Unfortunate* could apply to my more peculiar safety decisions. I remember one of the boys as a toddler trying to paddle around in the water, so corked with safety floats that he could barely move his arms. (Now, when he jumps off the granite ledges at the quarry where we swim, I prefer not to look.) I am saying simply that once a woman has a baby to whom she is attached, her sense of well-being rarely again rests exclusively within herself. While this feeling is an aspect of any love, it is particularly intense, perhaps uniquely so, with children because the young are helpless and dependent, and attachment to them brings a hugely heightened sense of responsibility.

This press of responsibility colors many exchanges. Waiting for lunch to arrive one day at a restaurant, my husband, sons, and I find ourselves laughing hard. One of the boys has just described a skinny friend's diet that—by choice—consists of frappes, mozzarella sticks, french fries, and dog kibble. Part of the humor comes from the ingredients, part from its context—my endless nagging about nutrition. Following the latest health-letter wisdom, I preach wholesome food. My idea of obscene is a two-liter soda bottle. Lest this stance sound pure (or successful), I compromise constantly, and cadge candy from the boys. We muddle along at about a C-plus level.

But behind my lecturing is a sense of dismay that by not making sure my sons eat well, I am failing them as a mother. I think it is primal. At my worst moments, I can see them, middle-aged, visiting doctors who grimly shake their heads, "Yes, hmmm, you seem to have lacked adequate calcium when your bones were growing most quickly. Where was your mother at mealtimes? Didn't she pay attention to your diet?" (That my husband shares the cooking and grocery shopping, and at one point in our family life seemed to believe that all the food groups could be represented by different kinds of bagels, never enters into these unpleasant reveries. The doctor distinctly says "mother.")

As part of my nutritional crusade I taped onto the refrigerator a newspaper clipping listing foods deemed likely to help people avoid cancer. Soon after, my older son irreverently scrawled "But Who Cares?" in small letters along its edge. One of my faults as a mother is ruffling at tiny provocations. So, predictably, I lectured him about the family friends with cancer and the horrors of his chosen diet, and ended my riff with a self-righteous "I care." Poor kid.

Since notions about the relationship of nutrition and health are ever-changing, he will likely live to see the advice modified many times. But it wasn't really food we were arguing. Thinking about it later, I realized I felt slighted in my dedication to keeping him safe. I experienced his message like spray paint defacing the effort and vigilance that (together with luck of many kinds) had succeeded so completely that he *could* be glib. Our almost grown son has not spent a night—aside from his birth—in a hospital and has visited an emergency room only once, with a cut finger. Like a surprising number of the middle-class, cloistered children of his generation he has almost no experience of life-threatening illness or peer death. How could he understand the urgency that undergirded my efforts?

Much is gratifying about protecting children, wonderfully so. What mother—no matter how long since her kids have grown—cannot recall the engulfing delight of rocking a toddler in her lap after his nap, inhaling and returning his affection, his snuggling trust, kissing the top of his head, tying his sneakers, letting him surface slowly from sleep? There is deep satisfaction in caring for others; nurturing sustains the giver. But there is also unending, consuming psychic labor involved in protecting a child, which gets minimized or overlooked. Talking with mothers, I was struck by how many became shy recalling the upset they felt when a child seemed endangered. I think women sometimes collude and keep silent because they feel ashamed of the intensity of their fears and focus. Revealing such uncontained feeling is embarrassing, even risky. Masking the vulnerability may make a mother feel slightly safer.

As you've read along so far, you've indulged me in a large and obvious omission: fathers. What about fathers? Aren't they also made vulnerable by love? Of course. I know as a daughter, wife, friend, and psychotherapist, that men love their children tenderly, that sometimes they are the more loving or kinder parent in a family, that at times they step in to protect children from maternal cruelty or violence. They can worry themselves sick over children. And fathers suffer deeply, sometimes profoundly, over child loss. I have heard stories of families in which mothers finally recover from the death of a child when fathers do not.

Nevertheless, there are differences between the sexes—including how men and women have mostly divided life's labors up to now—that affect what we might call the overall vulnerability quotient of each. The huge loss of mobility, emotional, physical, and economic, that mothers accept once they have children is one significant difference. Another is that men are generally physically stronger than women, enabling them to protect and often to dominate women. Men's greater size and muscle mass, together with the fact that women can be made pregnant by force, sustain—as many feminist writers and evolutionary psychologists have described in other contexts—a bedrock asymmetry. No matter how gentle one's own menfolk, many women are aware of an undefined but overarching threat.

As it happens, I hold with those who believe that a man who carries a baby, gently offers it warmed bottles, puts in days and nights rocking, cooing, wiping, one who takes on the satisfaction, duties, and anxieties of attentive vigilance, of minutely knowing the child, can be as successful a primary parent as a mother. But men have tended not to take that role. This disparity may rest partly on the simple fact that bottlefeeding using animal milk (later infant formula) has been safe for only about a century and a half, since pasteurization.[4] Obviously it also rests broadly upon polarized notions of gender, heavy sanctions of shaming upon individual men who deviate from conventional paths, and practical divisions of labor. Sometimes women push men away from parenting work because they believe themselves to be more attuned to the young, and because they feel territorial, pleased to have a domain to call their own. How large a part biology plays in the whole matter is a good question.

Only time and research will tell us whether a particular hormonal recipe has made mothers significantly more easily alarmable, more quickly attached, more readily focused on a small child's safety, than fathers.

Perhaps our responses are simply conditioned by centuries of mother-work and social attitudes, by our more constant proximity, by the continual piling on of responsibility. In an article about fathering, Richard Weissbourd reports on an informal survey asking parents their children's shoe sizes: "90 percent of mothers answered correctly, and 10 percent of fathers did."[5] How much of the gap in awareness comes simply from an agreed upon or assumed division of labor, how much from innate differences that then get institutionalized and rigidified is unclear.

However caused, this asymmetry has also contributed to the different sum of vulnerability for each sex. For millennia, a baby's survival rested most immediately upon its having an effective initial bond with its mother. The mother may not have felt love awaken immediately, but once she or the child's father decided that the child should live, she had to care enough to sit still and feed the creature days, months, or years before its father had to care at all.

And since often more hours of women's lives, and more of our minds, have been taken up with the intimate feelings and details of child-rearing, since we see ourselves and are seen by others as primarily responsible for the infant's well-being, since we have often carried the babies in our wombs and nursed them, or given of ourselves first when adopted children arrived, child death is often more present for us, more readily contemplated, rests more virulently in the back of our minds, even if the actual long-term pain it creates in each parent cannot and must not be measured one against the other.

Robert Frost's poem "Home Burial" describes an agonizing exchange between the parents of a recently dead child and captures the horror of attempting to compare degrees of caring. Because the husband carries his grief differently from his wife, seems unconsciously to symbolize it for himself by thinking about the fragility of even "the best birch fence," she feels abandoned and alone, doesn't believe he is truly bereaved. She has watched him dig their son's grave and feels estranged by the very fact that he could swing the shovel hard.

Coming into the house from outside, he sees her distress and approaches her, tries to engage her. She won't have it. Becoming upset, frantic at feeling shut out, he implores her, "Can't a man speak of his own child he's lost?" She replies, "Not you!" and adds, "I don't know rightly whether any man can."[6]

Reading the poem, you shrink with the husband from the injustice of his wife's coldness, her harsh inability to see how he pours his sorrow into physical labor. Yet, at the same time, you feel her raw agony, her sense of suffocation. He wants the love between them to compensate for her loss, and seems unable to contain his impatience at her withdrawal. Feeling rejected, he criticizes her. "I do think, though, you overdo it a little . . . To take your mother-loss of a first child so inconsolably—in the face of love." She experiences his words as "sneering" and insensitive. Within the atmosphere shaped by the poem, you imagine her tactile memory of intimate care provided, of worry and responsibility carried. The void with which she contends seems large, horrible.[7]

In spite of the husband's pleading, the wife moves toward the door. He is overwhelmed by pain and rage, and the poem ends with his making a deflated threat, yet one we recognize as damaging simply for evoking a possibility of trumping the standoff through physical violence. "I'll follow and bring you back by force. I *will!* "[8]

Frost brilliantly captures the awful moment, the two people suffering, so miserable that their only release seems to be in an explosive, dreadful exchange that destroys them as sources of comfort for each other. The husband feels helpless and closed out. The wife feels utterly alone. Both feel uncomprehended.

Neither men nor women hold a corner on kindness or on cruelty; yet mothers feel twice vulnerable—to the mix of protective love and potential violent dominance in men, and to the looming fear of loss brought on by their own visceral and immediate attachment to children. This book explores some consequences of these feelings, the way they tangle and knot in our lives today and across time, the way they contribute to how mothers have lived and still live in the world.

2

Night Walks

WHAT MOTHERS KNOW about mothering is often wildly different from the ways the experience is described from the outside. Somehow this incongruity, while easy to mention at the sandbox or in the grocery line, is difficult to translate into confident insight and effective social policies. No matter how often we point to it, the mother's unequal status has not been adequately linked with the way the effort to protect children organizes her response to the everyday world.

However much the world changes, mothers struggle to safeguard children. However much social circumstances evolve, maternal fears invade like insistent strays. Each mother encounters afresh the love coupled with the impossible expectations, the inadequate societal resources, the fatigue, the transforming vulnerability, and the preoccupied vigilance. "I am joyous," a new mother writes me in a hastily scribbled note, "and loony with worry."[1]

A mother I know, a doctor with four young daughters, tells me that she comforts herself with Roseanne Barr's observation, "If my kids are still alive at the end of the day, I've been a good mother." And while Barr's comment makes me laugh, it also captures perfectly a central, repeatedly overlooked truth: the essential work of mothering is trying to keep children alive. Too often, we judge mothers on how they manage details, while obscuring the effort and skilled labor involved in delivering basic survival care.

Though child mortality has fallen in America, contemporary mothers know exactly where the possibility of grief lies. (In spite of our unrivaled national wealth, the United States currently ranks twenty-first among countries worldwide in maternal mortality, and twenty-seventh in infant mortality.)[2] I had an eye-opening experience as I started speaking with mothers—informally and then in interviews—about their concerns. I'd ask an interviewee about her sense of her own vulnerability, and at first might draw a blank stare. Then, a moment or so later, she would say, "Oh, *that* . . . Oh, *of course.*" When I asked women if they ever worried about their children "getting into harm's way," they answered, with spontaneous heightened emphasis, *"All the time"* or *"Constantly!"*

My informants offered stories, small and large, which captured their responses to child danger and the way daily events sometimes trigger deep fear. Although the intensity of their reactions when children were distressed often made them blush in the telling, they remembered the situations vividly months and years later.

One mother, Amy, recalled temporarily being unable to find her eight-year-old daughter in a large Burger King play area at a highway rest stop. "I was terrified. I was really terrified. And I couldn't find her . . . At that point all I wanted to do was say, '*Nobody is to leave* until I search it all!'" She and her husband looked everywhere, through the play area, among the lines of people waiting to buy food; they scanned each table, entered the bathrooms, and scoured the parking lot, but no luck. Had someone driven off with her? Fifteen minutes later, the frantic parents found the little girl, who had gone out a side door and become disoriented.[3]

Another mother wrote to me describing a day seven years ago when her then two-year-old daughter spiked a temperature that "shot up past 105." Her husband was away on business. "My hands shook as I read the thermometer, and I felt terrified . . . I spent all night bringing her fever down, with warm baths and Tylenol, and frantic searches through Dr. Spock and every other book we had. I called the pediatrician early in the night, but I don't think he really believed that the fever was that high, so I felt miserably alone." A few days later the child seemed better, and the family left on a long-planned vacation; then the illness resurfaced. An emergency room doctor gave her a large dose of the wrong drug. Years later the mom reflected, "I guess I've never forgiven myself for letting that man treat her. And I believe I came close to losing her."[4]

Her experience reminded me of how once, on a Mediterranean island in a severe storm that had closed the tiny airport and shut down ferry service, our older son took to his bed with a stiff neck, fatigue, and a fever—right after I'd read a newspaper article about a meningitis outbreak in the city we had just left. Grim scenarios vied for mind space. I felt panicky, and guilty for having brought a sick boy to an island. What if? Out of hearing range of the sickroom, I whispered my fears to my husband, and then found a working telephone. A doctor three thousand miles away talked me down. Such kindness from someone I'd never met. A partner to my own physician, he listened, sympathized, reviewed symptoms, described options, and explained why my son would likely be fine. And he was. When we got home, I wrote a gushing thank-you note. Few feelings rival the heart thaw of fear melting.

Becoming a mother, one finds oneself living in a mental state that moves between quiet vigilance and high alert—even the luckiest among us, even in our ahistorical sheltered safety. The maternal mind is a sheepdog herding a flock in the rain—nudging, circling, barking, nipping heels, keeping an eye out for predators, and panting with effort that may or may not accomplish its aim. We sense that somewhere, maybe close or maybe not, wolves threaten. We labor to keep them away.

A woman with a son in his twenties shyly offered this story: She and her husband had recently purchased a small boat. Her son and a friend decided to take it out in the local bay. Knowing that he was a novice, and that the tides could create dangerous currents, the mother started fretting almost before the duo motored away. All evening, superficially immersed in other tasks, she calculated and recalculated how much gasoline the boat carried, how long the boys had been gone, and how likely they were to make it back safely. The hour grew late. Her fear intensified. Her husband went to bed. Unable to sleep, the woman found a flashlight, pulled on a sweater, followed the long, uneven path down through the dew-soaked grass to the dock, and stood in the darkness waving the small beacon to guide her grown boy home. "You feel lonely," she reflected. "Foolish. You think you are the only mother who ever worried so much."[5]

But such night walks are the stuff of mothering. And even as women often feel embarrassed by the overpowering force of their feeling, children's lives depend upon it. Women so fear danger to their children — fear putting them at risk by making mistakes or bad decisions — that these concerns, bundled with love, become the axis on which the firmament of mothering turns. If the boat does not come safely back, how will a mother manage her grief, her sense that, somehow, she was responsible?

In recent years, women writers have published hundreds of books about mothering — fiction and nonfiction, academic, personal, psychological, biological, theoretical, political. I've read and been informed and moved by voices as diverse as Toni Morrison, Adrienne Rich, Sara Ruddick, Jean Baker Miller, Barbara Ehrenreich, Sarah Hrdy, and Anne Lamott — to name only a few. But I'm not sure — for all their liberating thought and effort — that we've grasped a central inference from what they've laid before us: there is an enlarged sense of *vulnerability*, personal and social, created by becoming a mother — and accepting the intimate mission of keeping a dependent being alive.

Anne Lamott illustrates perfectly the new-mother state I'm describing when she offers a humorous account of her own fears. She recalls driving home from the hospital with her infant son, Sam. "The first time we hit a pothole, I thought, Well, that's that, his neck just snapped; we broke him. He's a quadriplegic now."[6] All moms know the feeling, and quickly learn to scan for potholes of every sort. But I don't think collectively we have made the leap to the bigger story: how thoroughly we dedicate ourselves to keeping the neck intact, and how doing so affects every other dimension of our social, political, personal, and economic lives — and our shared history. Arguably the best way to improve a child's lot may be to improve his mother's. Ann Crittenden has forcefully demonstrated the economics of this point in *The Price of Motherhood* (2001). Yet we have been extraordinarily slow, in the United States and worldwide, to address the problem of equality for mothers.

In fact, large disparities of power, education, access to health care, and wealth continue to exist between the sexes. Why, as the social critic bell hooks notes in *Where We Stand: Class Matters* (2000), are women —roughly half the population—still performing two-thirds of the world's work, but earning "about one-tenth of the world's income"? A 2000 United Nations Population Fund Report states that, worldwide, "at least one in three women have been beaten, raped, coerced into sex or abused in some way—usually by someone they know." Another current United Nations report concludes that while women are the "backbone" of the world's food production, most "of their back-breaking work is unpaid or grossly underpaid." In *Development As Freedom* (1999), the Nobel Prize–winning economist Amartya Sen documents how women in much of the world today are disproportionately denied basic resources like health care and education, and how girl infants in South Asia are regularly killed or allowed to die.[7]

What maintains this chronic inequality? Scholars studying these problems have focused on women's lack of political agency, economic power, and education, but an even more fundamental piece of the answer is the heightened vulnerability created by mothers' attachment to their children, and the diverse restraints and narrowed focus it demands. I suspect that mothers all over the world concentrate so hard on the immediate tasks of keeping at least some of their children alive, and helping them prosper to the degree their environment allows, that they often feel reluctant to debate the larger terms for fear of jeopardizing those resources that are present.

Understanding the depth of a mother's feelings about child loss is central to comprehending how women who are mothers live in the world. I suggest that consciously and, particularly, preconsciously, many women anticipate and fear, often with very good reason, that should they challenge their social role, should they defy the explicit or implicit rules of their environment, they might unwittingly damage their children.

Being (as a group) physically smaller and often more immediately attached to and tied down by young and helpless children, mothers live in an overlooked asymmetry of vulnerability, which has come to affect every aspect of our experience. Some mothers fear that self-assertion or rebellion might lead to their own death or injury, thus rendering them unable to nurture or protect. Or that harm might come to pass because their obvious child love offers such a well-marked target for retaliation.

This is not to say that only women suffer, or that mothers are victims, but rather to suggest how deeply and quickly mothers respond to perceived dangers; it is an indirect or vectored threat that particularly subdues. Worse than your own suffering is your child's. And while mothers will fight hard when a child is immediately endangered — and some will take on all comers — the more common unconscious and reflexive impulse, often the more sensible strategy, is to change course slightly and attempt to avoid the risk.

I remember as an eight-year-old girl in Oregon standing in the cold, clear pool that gathered at the base of a small waterfall, my tin picnic cup in hand, attempting to catch minnows. The tiny fish swam in schools. However suddenly I moved, they just as quickly perceived the motion or its shadow and changed course to elude me. That I distracted them from feeding or avoiding more significant predators was lost on them as they focused on evading the immediate disruption. Because of their reflex, I could have exhausted them by sustaining unimportant threats.

Survival instincts are powerful and overarching. They often move people to avoid challenging the status quo. Perceiving the shadow on the water, the first impulse is to alter course. And mothers often try to increase child safety by accepting the given terms. "Why didn't you speak up?" I asked a mother who disliked something that happened to her child in school. "I didn't want them to retaliate against him," she replied. Reasonable or not, this feeling is widespread. Our protective dodges may offer an illusion of safety as often as they provide the real thing. Yet they create purpose and priorities. In the moment, we feel that we are acting to make our children safer.

Of course, mothers sometimes confront authorities. To picture us simply as compliant is patronizing and not my aim. Think about the mothers in Argentina who risked their safety, and that of their living children, by publicly protesting the fascist government's murder of their sons and daughters. Or the Irish mothers who organized a mass movement against their country's violence. Think of the huge risks taken by

African American mothers who opposed racism during the civil rights movement and every day before and since. Many women would say that they can act on behalf of their children in ways that they can never act for themselves. Indeed people often make analogies between human mothers protecting their young, and ferocious mother bears, or lionesses, or tigresses, protecting theirs.

How can I claim that maternal vulnerability is an important historic and contemporary force if deep down every mother has a fierce animal within her? Because there's a catch: the image of ferocity, certainly acceptable maternal ferocity, is more complex than it first appears. Looking closely at a story will make the point clearer. A near perfect example of the mother as "tigress" can be found in an article from *Parenting* (reprinted in *Reader's Digest*, January 2002), which recounts how a mother wouldn't take no for an answer when her pediatrician dismissed her six-month-old son's brain seizures as "nothing." Her "mother's instinct" took over. "Something in me snapped. Usually I am shy and soft-spoken; I blush easily and have been known to stammer. But at that moment I stood up and said, 'I'm not leaving here until you call a neurologist. I want Zach to be seen today.' I started to weep."[8] Note that the story makes a point of showing how correctly "feminine" this mother is, shy, not given to asserting herself, polite, definitely not a troublemaker. However, the magazine relates approvingly, she becomes fierce when her baby is immediately threatened. Then and only then.

In other words, such maternal actions stand out, become the stuff of inspirational articles, exactly because they are considered exceptional. And while every mother may find herself, in a rare moment, roaring at full volume to protect her child, the posture is much less common than the hundreds of everyday decisions we make to keep children safe by accommodating, going along, appeasing, or making the best of what we're handed.

Suppose for a moment that a mother's fierceness makes her want to compete harder in the work world, labor long hours, advance in her job, even unionize her shop, and protect her children by eventually earning enough money to save for their college tuitions, arguably one of the most effective ways of aiding offspring. Would *Reader's Digest* feature such a story? "Mother's Instinct Says 'No' to Constraints Impose Low Wages, 'Yes' to Union Drive." Possibly, but it seems unlikely. A mother fighting for a sick baby, while important, tends to be palatable because it is in sync with idealized notions of maternal devotion. No boats get rocked. While it is deemed okay for a loving mom to act "out of character" or behave aggressively to save her baby, she may not be so broadly applauded if she wakes the same instincts in a more controversial area.

In truth, the "tigress" cliché is no friend to real mothers. It presents the exceptional moment as evidence that mothers are adequately safe in the world as it is, that their greater vulnerability does not carry significant consequences, that their inequality is not a problem. Don't worry, the construct claims, your maternal instincts will flare and guard your baby as necessary. Indeed, this sentimentalized fierceness becomes an illusion obscuring a much more significant, opposite truth: that the mother's fears of child loss and the derivative fears of harming children or caring for them inadequately have been continually manipulated, overtly and subtly, even aroused gratuitously, to pressure, control, and subdue women for a very long time — possibly millennia.

Currently, a hot-button American issue is whether it is a good thing for mothers to work outside the home, particularly to pursue demanding careers. (I think women and men should be supported to stay home or work outside the home in all manner of arrangements, according to how they assess the best interests of their families.) But that controversy exists within a larger context, as I learned in the course of researching this book. From past eras to present-day public voices — experts and authorities of many timbres — have repeatedly put pressure on mothers to keep their children safe by renouncing assertive or autonomous behaviors, however disproportionate the cost to each mother. Sensing the implications of elevated maternal vulnerability, many advice givers in America have for centuries generated powerful discourses pressuring mothers to behave submissively, and threatening that they will cause child death or harm if they don't.

A best-selling contemporary parenting guide, for example, tells mothers that if they do not stay home full-time, they may damage their child's ability to make attachments, and so diminish his intelligence and emotional stability. In a question-and-answer format, the popular text asks if studies support full-time mothering. Yes, the author answers, but not those headlined "in working women's magazines."[9] In other words, the narrative implies, mothers are being fed dangerous lies by biased feminist magazines that may lead them to think they can safely spend time away from their babies when they cannot. (Whose instincts will recognize the need to see a neurologist *right now* if mom is at work? Fathers and partners are distinctly absent or grossly overshadowed in these tales.) The current cultural leitmotif insists that parental absence is worrisome, and that remedying that societal problem is the mother's responsibility alone; her work outside the home is uniquely bad for children's development; though, as we will see, evidence for such claims is hard to find.

The message that contemporary moms must be continually vigilant and highly attentive gets conveyed in many ways. Pick up any child care magazine, examine it afresh, and you will realize that it is a veritable compendium of child dangers. Whatever their declared intention, the magazines artfully heighten maternal anxiety by alarming readers about all the ways children can be harmed, and thus all the ways that any maternal inattention is risky. Opening to one page, I found "Earlier Screening for Genetic Diseases: Should You Buy Your Own Test?" On the next, "The New Pogos: Danger on a Stick?" Underneath that warning, an inset: "Poison Control, Wherever You Are." Later: "Was Mom Right? The Real Scoop on Child Health Warnings." In a second magazine, the cover advertises "Toy Safety Special." The inside text includes "Cystic Fybrosis Facts," then "Is Your Home Toxic?" then "Danger: Packing Materials," and the inset "Carbon Monoxide Nearly Killed My Toddler." For nursing moms, there is the worrisome "What's in Your Breast Milk?"[10] The meta-message: Dangers abound. Stay nearby. You can't be too vigilant.

When not focused on alerting mothers to endless threats, the magazines push their notions of love. One features "75 Little Ways to Make Your Kids Feel Loved." ("Volunteer to chaperone the class field trip."

"Give her the last bite of your chocolate ice-cream cone." "Get along with your spouse.") Another weighs in with "Your Baby: Best Ways to Bond."[11] The underlying themes: Love more perfectly. Give more of yourself. There's no doubt these magazines distribute useful information, and they can be heartwarming and fun. I found myself repeatedly drawn in. (Okay, how many layers of clothing do *you* think are right for an infant?) Yet, overall they convey a distorted message to mothers: Around every corner lurks a monster. Children are always at risk. Your constant involvement and attentiveness, your ever-improved love, make all the difference. It's on you.

Although the magazines are entitled *Parenting* and *Parents,* I'd be surprised if their readership is less than 99 percent female. Whatever the exact numbers, the basic mother demographic is significant to the message. The magazines do cultural work. While they deliver information, advice, and even comfort, they also, more covertly, perhaps unconsciously, raise anxiety and define intense devotion combined with child-focused behaviors to pound home the fallacy that total maternal dedication and twenty-four/seven vigilance are the primary variables of successful child-rearing.

In none of the magazine pieces is the larger political, economic, or social contexts mentioned, much less analyzed. This skewed focus is easily visible in the article "What's in Your Breast Milk?," a question perfect for spiking any new mom's worry meter. "Many medicines and drinks—even certain foods—can affect your baby if you're nursing. Here's how to make sure you both stay safe and healthy."[12] The text usefully counsels that nursing mothers use caution when or if consuming various medications, alcohol, nicotine, and foods like broccoli and garlic. Certainly, night five of our first son's life would have been a lot happier for all of us, we might even have slept a little, had someone warned me about broccoli (it makes breast milk harder for some babies to digest). Yet, significantly and rather remarkably, the piece never once mentions the large, serious dangers for breast-milk purity of environmental pollutants, radioactivity, antibiotic and hormone contamination from meats, runoff, or pesticide residues. Instead of recipes and grocery coupons, why not clip-out letters to send to elected representatives, lobbying them for breast-milk-safe environments?

The child's whole well-being is made too singularly dependent on mom's behavior. On one page, love is coaxed forward; on the next, dangers are hyped. The combination works perfectly to enhance the mother's concern and burden of responsibility, to make each mother feel that she needs to give more, give better, or risk harming her baby. In the simplest sense, everyone has been a child, only some become mothers; manifest in the magazines is how the adult child's longings to have had a more perfectly devoted mother carry the day!

One mother I interviewed, an accomplished professional woman, told me how guilty she felt as one of the few women in her child's grade who worked full-time at a demanding job. The teachers disapproved of her commitment to work and made comments to her about her schedule and her absence at school events. Though the boy was thriving, they implied that she was failing him. Each time she visited the classroom, they seemed unable to recognize her and insisted on being reintroduced. She felt embarrassed and annoyed, but she didn't say anything. Larger prejudices about how mothers should behave, continually reinforced, whether by psychologists, teachers, parenting mavens, or magazine pieces, gather into an impressive mass. Rather like the winter's thawing, threatening accumulation of snow and ice upon a porch roof, their collective weight makes each mother, babe in arms, inclined to tiptoe as she climbs the steps.

Advice from experts doesn't simply offer information; it tacitly claims to speak for an invisible but informed consensus of authorities who know more about a child than its mother. Such voices become forceful messengers of the culture (and cultures past) which make their way into our sensibilities whether or not we invite them. They gain some of their power from our wish to do right by children and our fear of acting in ways that will harm them. But, oddly, the authorities' admonitions have often harshly and incorrectly punished mothers by suggesting that their children's suffering or death is a consequence of their behavior—usually any behavior deemed to be ambitious, sexual, or independent.

As far back as ancient Greece, writers understood well the terrible pain suffered by a mother whose child dies, and her fears anticipating such an event. Several plays by Euripides show how providing safety to children becomes connected with female obedience and subordination. And as early as the seventeenth century, English and American ministers, doctors, social scientists, and psychologists, often well-meaning people who set out to sell advice and improve the lot of children, in fact spent far too much time threatening mothers. For instance, in a sermon the Puritan minister Increase Mather gave in 1714, he blamed a mother's "unruly passion"—her strong feelings of love for her son—for the boy's death by smallpox. Defy us, public authority figures and professionals repeatedly tell mothers in a host of different ways, and your children will die, or get sick, or suffer awful psychological consequences.

Time has revealed the inaccuracy—even harm—of a significant portion of the advice given by past experts. Many old recommended medical treatments, for example, were abysmal if not deadly. And that is understandable: each day brings new knowledge. Harder to comprehend is why the writer's "errors" so often wrongly lay the blame for children's suffering or failure to thrive upon mothers' autonomous behavior. Why, for instance, did Richard Kissam, M.D., write in *The Nurse's Manual, and Young Mother's Guide* (1834), "If the mind of the mother be withdrawn from her child, to other pleasures, her milk will be less nutritious and less in quantity"?[13] Milk loses its basic life-sustaining characteristics if a nursing mother lets herself think private, pleasurable thoughts? The notion was terrible science, but a powerful way to make mothers feel guilty and ashamed when their attention inevitably wandered—especially when so many infants did die from unsavory medical practices, like physicians who neglected to wash their hands between patients.

Once child mortality fell in the United States at the end of the nineteenth century, advice books refocused on the diverse ways mothers can cause psychological harm.[14] As we will see, the shift was instantaneous. It is a great good thing that psychology has recognized children as deeply impressionable, sensitive creatures, with complex feelings and inner lives. Yet, if somehow we could film the twentieth century's evolving psychological ideas, with their undue emphasis upon maternal harm, and then play them back one after the other, we'd often think we were watching science fiction or cartoons. Why have these stories of maternal damage gotten so much screen time? Though often addressed, the question cannot be fully answered until we see how psychological attitudes are consistent with those of earlier expert ministers and doctors, and consistent, too, with ancient collective myths and unconscious fears.

In *For Her Own Good* (1978), Barbara Ehrenreich and Deirdre English brilliantly demonstrated, starting in the nineteenth century, how advice to mothers shifted constantly in the United States, irrationally driven by whatever popular ideology was in vogue. I want to explore how, starting in Colonial America, a deep grammar of threat, stable beneath ever-changing "facts," continually links and relinks child safety to maternal "acceptance" of a constricted, submissive "feminine" behavior, to a mother's deference to authority and her willingness to stay close to home. But before turning to seventeenth- and eighteenth-century American texts, in the next several chapters I want to create their larger context, to look more closely at loss and at historical, mythic, and archetypal ideas about mothers. You cannot give full dignity or due to a woman who walks out at midnight to stand with a flashlight on a cold dock scanning the sea for her son until you understand more about mothers' larger psychological and historical circumstances.

3

"My Son Who Died"

MANY YEARS AGO, my husband and I were visiting friends in France who took us to the small village home of a woman who cooked in her open stone fireplace. She and her husband then served us at their kitchen table. We ate bread soup, pâté, tomatoes stuffed with sausage, home-cured ham, duck confit, goat's cheese, white asparagus, and on and on.

After hours of eating and drinking ("you are surviving the blows?" the French sometimes inquire on such occasions), we paid and made ready to leave. Hoping to take home a bottle of the local brandy, we asked if Madame had any to sell. She did not. Unusual frosts had ruined the plum crop for the past couple of years. Instead, she directed us to a neighbor who distilled the drink from pears. As we walked toward the nearby farm, our friends recognized it as belonging to a couple who, years earlier, had kept a flock of rare white turkeys. We knocked on the door, and a reticent woman answered. We mentioned the white turkeys. The woman invited us in. We explained our wish to buy *eau-de-vie*, and she nodded.

Then, seemingly out of nowhere, she asked, "Have you heard about my son who died?" We stood quietly in her dark, old kitchen with its heavy, worn rectangular wood table, stone floor, and copper half-moon sink fed by a small, hand-filled cistern, and listened as she told about her boy who seven years earlier had set out down the hill from their house on a motorized *bicyclette* one rainy day, lost control on the wet leaves that covered the road, and died when his head struck a rock. I do not understand spoken French well, but I understood the story because she enunciated clearly to make sure we followed her, and because her carefully phrased anguish defied linguistic barriers.

When she had finished, we stood together in the makeshift intimacy that sharp grief creates, shook our heads, and looked for words with which to meet her sorrow. She went to the cellar and retrieved a bottle of pear brandy, accepted our money, and said good-bye. We left subdued. Perhaps she was suggesting that buying homemade brandy is an intimate act. Maybe she was incredulous that we could know about her flock of turkeys and not her boy. Mostly she needed to talk. Later, I thought about the Ancient Mariner, urgently, almost compulsively, stopping strangers on the street, seeking what? Comfort, relief, human contact, absolution by repeating his tale of death? A broken record, people of my generation say. With certain traumas, the melody does not progress because the needle cannot cross the divide. And then he, and then he, and then . . .

If a child is harmed or dies, how does a mother manage? What does she experience? Where can she find comfort? And within what frame of meaning does the event settle? Throughout history, the majority of mothers have lost children, so mothering cannot really be understood without understanding the fear and the impact of child loss. However various the reactions, grief has been common if not constant. When we think about bereavement, we often visualize it in its most immediate and perhaps dramatic form. We see sobs, terror, faces sinking into hands. Less visible is the aftermath, all that transpires when the mourners have gone home, daily life demands attention, and yet the pain and doubt continue and the comfort one seeks comes only intermittently, sometimes from foreigners at the door.

We can become frightened when people we love grieve. We know they have left us because at this moment the departed person matters more. Even now, I am frequently struck by many people's intolerance of grief. (I have met people who have lived half their lives before they lost someone they loved; they suffer over their emptiness but also from their inexperience in dealing with it.) Contemporary American mourners who cannot hide their suffering quickly become pariahs. Men and women are left alone with terrible loss. They blame themselves for feeling it. They try not to and go numb in the process, or get angry, or ill, or drink, or gamble, or shop or work too much. Many become depressed.

Psychotherapists must often begin by persuading patients that their need to mourn is not crazy or weak. Near strangers telephone me when someone beloved has died to ask if it is normal for their pain to linger past three weeks. Three weeks? With some losses you've barely begun; and the duration depends on how much you loved that person, how your body and psyche metabolize feeling, how many other people you have lost, how your culture of origin approaches mourning, and so on. What about many months or several years? And for the important losses, the deep loves—the toddler who, before the cholera, or measles, or polio epidemic suddenly took her, had a smile like none you'd ever seen—what about, intermittently and in more muted ways, forever?

No matter how varied the circumstances, loss has been an omnipresent part of mothering across time; and any discussion of mothers needs to start with some exploration of how the two twist into one skein. For it seems that the first obligation mothering places upon a woman is the demand not just that she attempt to keep the child alive, but that she accept the fact of living closely with death. Men express awe about women enduring the pain of giving birth, a phenomenon that James Joyce, in *Ulysses,* distills into "Woman's woe with wonder pondering."[1] But perhaps we've allowed the flashbulb quality, the hopeful suffering of contractions and delivery, to blind us to a larger reality. A woman agrees to death when she becomes a mother, not simply in the uncertainty of pregnancy and childbirth, nor in the symbolic sense that by participating in the creation of the next generation she confirms her own mortality, but because of the risk of loss she assumes.

Nowadays, among those of us who have a choice in the matter, it is the depth of joy and love that desired children bring that first frames the experience. We talk more readily about those feelings. And they are huge. Less easily named is how, once a woman has imagined a child as hers—whether *in utero,* at birth, or upon adoption—she knows she can henceforward instantly be made bereft to the unfathomable and ultimately unalterable center of her being. Two lenses, one of helpless love, the other of irreparable loss, align to bring into focus the mother's psychological experience.

I remember once meeting an older woman whose son had died years before. I don't recall what allowed our discussion to become frank, but she talked openly about her experience. "It took at least twelve years," she allowed, "before I could reenter the world and take pleasure in any significant way." Her timetable may not be every woman's, and imposing a duration for grief is as harmful as denying its frequent tenacity. But her experience underscores a larger cultural inclination to minimize the problem or prematurely to smooth it over. Only by recognizing the enormous power of child loss, and thus the terror of anticipating it, can we understand the essence of mothering, maternal responsibility, and particularly of a mother's sense of ongoing vulnerability.

If many in recent American generations have been spared the death of an infant or child, we are, historically speaking, exceptional. Our good fortune is extraordinary. Yet, in its own way, the relative safety, and the permission to make an emotional investment in a single child that it sanctions, also stoke the fear. Furthermore, the mother's vigilant concern is reflexive and does not rest on statistics; it is a preventive mechanism, an alarm triggered whenever a child is threatened.

Maternal grief is made more vexing by the mother's feeling that if a child dies, she has failed in her role as protector. Valerie, the mother in Conor McPherson's contemporary Irish play *The Weir,* arrives too late to witness or prevent her daughter's death at a swimming meet. We learn her story as she recounts it months later to strangers in a village bar. Like some cork float loosed from a fishing net in a storm, the death has carried her out of her own life, into this new one. The child's accident, though told briefly, is the play's emotional center.

Valerie planned to attend the swim meet. "But I got . . . I was late, out of work, and I was only going to be in time to meet her afterwards, but em, when I got there . . . There was an ambulance." Valerie attempts to tell herself and the audience just *why* she was not with her child when her child died, and to rationalize *how* she shifted her intention from watching the child swim, to greeting her afterward.[2]

That she is detained by work seems central and inevitable in a contemporary story about mothers. Valerie might have narrated the event differently had she been with another child at the doctor; and differently again had she been drinking in a bar. McPherson's text captures and draws power from cultural conflict. A mother who is at her job instead of with her child is a touchy matter: at the same time, external obligation provides partial dispensation. Work-is-sort-of-something-some-mothers-have-to-do. But maybe not quite. Did she really have to? Maybe no job is as important as watching your child. And what if you were late because you were more excited by work than by a swim meet?

This ambiguity asks and leaves unanswered the central question in Valerie's mind. Did her daughter die because she was a neglectful mother? Her sentences hesitate and wobble like the social and personal uncertainty that they attempt to encompass. If, for instance, Valerie stayed longer at work because the boss "made her," the death is less her fault. If she lingered by preference, defying her maternal obligation, then she is more culpable. McPherson senses mothers' essential fear that an everyday choice might have devastating consequences.

Describing how the death distanced her husband, Daniel, Valerie reveals more confusion about her own behavior: "I don't know if he actually, blamed me, there was nothing I could do. But he became very busy in his work." McPherson conveys Valerie's guilt, and her uncertainty about how much the feeling of blame originates inside her, how much actually comes from Daniel.[3]

Compounding the difficulty between the parents is Valerie's belief that the dead daughter has telephoned her. Awakened by a phone ringing, she is certain she briefly heard the child's voice on the other end of the line. Her experience creates more distance. "Daniel felt that I . . . needed to face up to Niamh being gone. But I just thought he should face up to what happened to me. He was insisting I get some treatment, and then . . . everything would be okay. But you know, what can help that, if she's out there? She still . . . she still needs me."[4]

Valerie moves from Dublin to a small rural village. Loyalty to the dead girl appears to surpass other feelings, and abandoning the people who knew her provides a means of paying on her guilt and contemplating her daughter with fewer distractions. Alone, she can listen for otherworldly messages. Has she ended the marriage, has he? We don't know. We sense that bad feelings have hammered the banks of rational thought, eroding union and love. Such damage is hard to contain not only because grief is a flood tide, but because it can be insidious, seeping into and rotting places where it cannot be directly observed.

"He was insisting I get some treatment, and then . . . everything would be okay," Valerie says. In this phrasing, counseling becomes quick and mechanical, like dyeing one's hair or swallowing aspirin for a headache. However lovingly Daniel may have intended it, however wise his perception of her need (which is perhaps also a displacement of his own), Valerie construes the suggestion as a dismissal of her pain. She implies that her husband wants her feelings fixed for his own sake. As the audience, we have no idea of the justice of her assessment, only its consequences.

Valerie's stuttering, hesitant efforts to describe her circumstance also point up a social rule: painful feelings are to be understated. You can express them in the privacy of therapy, in some intimacies, in prayer, or perhaps in a staccato burst to bar mates. But if you get too loud, strident, or messy about them in public, if you make other people uncomfortable, you become an outlier. Perhaps her dead daughter's phone call is Valerie's mind bending to compromise between the social rules of pain management and the intensity of what she feels.

Rules about behavior are everywhere, and all of us—even the rowdiest—obey them with a regularity that should surprise us. We do so to survive, to fit in, and to reduce encounters with shame. I remember that when I arrived at the hospital maternity ward to give birth, a friendly nurse mentioned, almost as an aside, how tiresome it was when certain immigrant women screamed in response to their contractions. I immediately caught the coded query: Are you one of them or us? And the accompanying instruction: a good patient, thus a (white? middle-class?) woman of acceptable character, perhaps a woman who would make a good mother, does not scream or otherwise reveal the extent of her pain during childbirth. I'm not suggesting that screaming is preferable to more constrained responses, even if at moments it seems like the obvious choice. Yet I'm intrigued not just by the evocation of cultural difference to induce shame, but by the ways rules of behavior are composed. If you are a maternity nurse, yelling jangles your nerves, makes you feel helpless. Caring for agitated patients on every shift probably constitutes an occupational hazard.

So codes develop. But who knows whom they serve. Perhaps the nurse spoke partly from compassion, believing we endure pain a little better when we focus on relaxing or controlling our response. But, then again, maybe we are only embarrassed into silence for the benefit of others. Strong feeling tends to create discomfort in bystanders. Child loss is frightening, and discussing the details of its impact is taboo. This is Valerie's suspicion. No matter what his intent, she experiences her husband's suggestion as an attempt to separate her further from her dead daughter to whose memory she clings. Forced to choose, she will trade him to keep an illusion of her.

Mary Shelley must have been feeling a similar wish in 1820 when she wrote *Maurice,* her idyllic children's story (complete with noble parents, a cruel stepfather, and a virtuous son) of a long-missing boy reunited with his family. At the time Shelley wrote the story, three of the four children born to her and her husband, the poet Percy Bysshe Shelley, were no longer alive. In fact, William, who lived the longest, until three, had died suddenly during the preceding year. Little wonder she dreamed about children returning.

In *Maurice,* the father narrates. "Soon after our marriage we had a little boy of whom we were dotingly fond. All our joy was in watching this little creature, who was as beautiful and good as it was possible to be." The husband and wife loved to take long country walks. One summer day, leaving the toddler with his nurse, they set out. "When we returned we were dreadfully frightened to find the nurse asleep among some hay and no child near her." They search everywhere but without success. Years pass. The father continues, "For my part I have never given up hope that I shall one day find him again . . . So every year I spend two months in Devonshire going over the whole county looking for him. I dress myself meanly that I may enter the cottages with greater freedom and make enquiries of the country people in a familiar manner; I walk about from village to village, and never pass a solitary cottage without looking at the children, and asking questions concerning them." The repeated telling of the tale and endless searching are rewarded. The psychological wishes of the narrator, first that the nurse, not the parents, are responsible, and second, that repetition and words will undo loss, are gratified. The book climaxes as Maurice, the lost boy, throws himself into his stranger father's arms and sobs. "I am your son!"5

To feel utterly bereft is unbearable. This knowledge is implicit in reunion fantasies. And it is further confirmed by how hard our psyches work to avoid such feelings. People hallucinate when the mind can find no other route to relief. If all else fails, you will hear your dead daughter's voice briefly on the telephone, or write a story that allows your husband and dead son to fall into each other's arms. Such imaginings appear to be a default position, a safeguard of the mind—or grace.

The Weir contains talk of ghosts, and ghosts might be best understood as a disguised embodiment of residual feelings that linger when people leave or die. This leads us to a central point. Unless she tells you, you cannot know what a mother feels. You cannot know what her child meant to her, or to what degree she resolves her loss. The child in the psyche is separate from the child in the world. While one mother begins to notice her attachment to an infant when it has been alive a month, another may have started to love it the day it was conceived. Their grief may be different. Because child love combines the imaginative with the visceral, the biological with the fantastic, no tool exists to calibrate it with other women's feelings; there is no objective measure of its quantity.

Historically, a near universal response to loss has been prayer and religious supplication. But the religious landscape has become more varied in recent centuries, and more frequently interrupted by the secular. Valerie wonders about ghosts, but makes little mention of God. If her daughter is calling from heaven, the site is unnamed. Her situation is contemporary. Separated from community and church—with its dog-mas and rituals for grief—uncomforted by other living children, the arrival of more infants, the proximity of similarly suffering women, or communal imperatives, she manages as best she can. She is strikingly freer and more isolated than similarly aggrieved women in the past. This transition, the shift from a life collectively framed to experience defined more individually and secularly is critical to understanding many contemporary mothers' overall psychological situations, and their children's as well. But, for the moment, let us use Valerie's predicament as an archway to the past.

4

Giotto's Tears

IN THE EARLY FIFTEENTH CENTURY, Isabelle Romée, the mother of Joan of Arc, walked from her home in Domrémy several hundred miles to Le Puy to kneel before the statue of Mary and pray for her daughter's safety.[1] The story of Joan—the girl who rallied the Dauphin's courage and saved France from the invading English before she was burned for heresy—caught my imagination years ago. But now, mother to mother, I identify with Isabelle. I would like to travel back in time and watch her as she departs from her home. What expression is on her face? What does she wear? What does she carry?

What would it feel like to become her for a while, but not quite—to enter her sensibility completely, understand her language, yet also to be an observer on the side? In my fantasy, Isabelle sets out from her village to make a pilgrimage because she is beside herself imagining her daughter's peril. She has lived long enough to know that a country girl cannot advise a prince, command an army, and claim to possess direct knowledge of God without making powerful enemies and sooner or later endangering herself. Isabelle walks to Le Puy because it has become unbearable to await death's messenger at home. Overwhelmed by foreboding, restless, she needs to *do* something to protect her child.

Though owned by the village church since at least the eleventh century, the carved figure of mother and child to whom Isabelle made her supplication was probably much older. Hannah Green in *Little Saint* describes how, when an eighteenth-century scholar carefully unwrapped its clothing and examined it, the baby was covered with Greek crosses. Its head was painted black, suggesting that the piece may have originated in ancient Egypt, a representation of Isis and her son, Horus. How it came to Le Puy is not known. We do know that it was torn from the church there and burned by soldiers during the French Revolution.[2]

New religions often build their churches upon older foundations—both spiritually and materially. Visiting a baroque Catholic church in Naples, I looked down through a glass window in the middle of a stone floor to see Roman and Greek temple ruins that had been excavated below. When the scholar in Le Puy examined the statue of Mary and her baby, he found that she, too, had had earlier incarnations. But the essential form, the mother with the child held close against her chest, remained intact even as across centuries it rested upon diverse altars, serving many faiths and meanings, absorbing maternal fears spoken in varied tongues.

The layers of identity that made up the statue mark a space where three of my own interests come together with my experiences of mothering to shape this book: my work as a psychotherapist, my desire to gain perspective on the contemporary world by reading history and literature, and my pleasure in art. This confluence—made material in the story of a polychrome carving—also encourages two questions: What in each mother's experience leans toward the universal, what toward the particular? And how can earlier eras shed light upon the present?

Scholars would warn us to use history carefully, not to take stories out of context, to telescope places and eras, or hastily project current prejudices or states of mind back onto the past. Good historians hate generalizations. And their injunctions are deeply useful. Yet an opposing truth also carries weight. "In order to judge of the inside of others," Lord Chesterfield wrote to his son in the eighteenth century, "study your own, for [people] in general are very much alike."[3] Working as a psychotherapist daily reminds me that each person is unique, that to do my work I have to *not* know—to listen in order to learn. At the same time, basic emotions—love, grief, joy, fear, anger, separation anxiety, abandonment anxiety, sorrow, and depression are universal, even as their expressions, their aims, their intensity and the meanings people give to them are particular. Somehow we have to hold both these competing verities.

I claim that the mother's fear of child loss is common, perhaps close to omnipresent—once mothers attach to infants. It is certainly widely present, however varied the quantities and manifestations in different women. Whatever the risks of overgeneralizing it, a much higher price has already been paid by women for having its importance underappreciated. Far too much of what has been written about both mothers and child-rearing has failed to credit or comprehend the ramifications of maternal apprehension. Indeed, accounts of mothering that exclude this consideration are deeply flawed; at the very least, they tax mothers with failure and manipulate their fears of doing harm, while overlooking or obscuring the worth of their huge effort.

The consequences for mothers' work are ubiquitous, and some seem broadly to transcend place and moment. For example, it has been argued that for thousands of years the mother's need to stay near young children in order to nurse and protect them defined what could and could not become women's work. In *Women's Work: The First 20,000 Years* (1994), Elizabeth Wayland Barber suggests that women traditionally spun yarn, wove cloth, and cooked food because such labors fit better with child-rearing. She makes her point vividly: "Contrast the idea of swinging a pick in a dark, cramped, and dusty mine shaft with a baby on one's back or being interrupted by a child's crisis while trying to pour molten metal into a set of molds." Barber cites criteria, published by Judith Brown in 1970, for predicting which tasks societies were likely to assign to mothers: a woman's work could not require her to "range very far from home," or "place the child in potential danger," or demand "rapt concentration." Indeed, as every mother knows, it has had to be "easily interruptible."[4] (I recall hearing once about some moms in a play group with young children who contemplated awarding a prize any time one of them could remember the beginning of a sentence when, after countless interruptions, it finally reached its end.)

Certainly, there is infinite variation in how women have spent—and now spend—their lives. If the historical record were complete enough we could likely find many exceptions to Brown's premise, and at least one mother's name attached to every trade—from soldier of fortune to sea captain. What's more, many women have relished the world as they found it, have been able to take pleasure and create meaning whatever their legal or social circumstances. (A friend once told me an old Polish story that captures this point sweetly and with irony: Two women were imprisoned for a long time and became good friends in the course of sharing a rather miserable cell. After some years, they were freed. Once outside, instead of departing, they stood beside the prison gate and continued laughing and talking together until—the sun setting—an irritated guard finally shooed them away.)

At the same time, in the vast majority of societies for which we have records, most women have been politically, economically, and socially dominated by men, and excluded from many areas of activity, be they political or commercial. And this reality has occasioned significant hardship. The power disparities are real. Raise the subject, and someone remembers hearing about a woman who did something extraordinary, or a tribe somewhere led by women, where life was . . . Perhaps. There is variation in how much freedom, value, and autonomy women have had in different cultures, classes, races, times, and locales—and every relationship has found its own informal power balance. But overall, as a group, mothers have been oppressed and rendered unequal—frequently to the point of near or actual enslavement.

So too, however much some would like to believe in a benign prehistoric paradise when women shared power equally with men or even ruled, it seems not to have existed. In *The Myth of Matriarchal Prehistory* (2000), Cynthia Eller states succinctly, "The myth of matriarchal prehistory is an impressive—and to some, a beautiful and enticing—house of cards." Summing up her careful review of the evidence, she acknowledges that the myth is possibly true, but very unlikely. In fact, she writes, there is "nothing in the archaeological record that is at odds with an image of prehistoric life as nasty, brutish, short, and male-dominated." Additionally, she points out that in many societies, "Women may have powerful roles, but their power does not undermine or seriously challenge an overall system of male dominance."[5]

If Eller is correct, if women's inequality predates recorded history, an obvious question is "Why?" What has sustained this dominance for so long? A too little examined answer is the power of women's attachment to children, and the simple reality that the diminished mobility, heightened dependence, and thus the increased maternal vulnerability that accompanies pregnancy, childbirth, and child-rearing might well have made submitting to men the most ready way to protect children.

One hears how maternal attachment was weaker in the past and is still diminished in some places and circumstances. Starting in the 1960s with the work of Philippe Aries, a group of scholars—Lawrence Stone and Edward Shorter are often mentioned—argued that childhood in western Europe before the eighteenth century was quite different from what we know today, and that in the "premodern family" parents cared less about the well-being of individual children. They claimed that mothers felt little love, or at least waited until the child was through the first years, and thus less likely to die, before they signed on with the full complement, the level now sometimes kindled by the ultrasound image of the fetus at eight weeks.

From the 1980s on, other historians, Steven Ozment and Hugh Cunningham among them, have challenged these notions and argued that western European families in previous centuries had much in common with our own—at least where basic emotions were involved. Because family history is a relatively new area of interest, archives of letters and diaries, objects of material culture, heretofore dismissed for not shedding light on large public events, offer fresh material. As scholars have begun to explore these more diverse and often private sources, evidence increasingly suggests that strong, loving attachments between parents and children were common in many places and times.

Two short passages in Hugh Cunningham's *Children and Childhood in Western Society Since 1500* are illustrative. Summarizing recent scholarship on the Middle Ages, an era for which historians have tended to minimize attachment, Cunningham writes that although small, the "body of evidence on actual child-rearing indicates a concern for even very young children, and provides examples of close and loving relationships, especially between mothers and children." Later he notes, "A seventeenth-century Dutch print shows the gruesome figure of Death dragging off a crib with a swaddled baby inside while the mother sleeps; it must have been a picture to haunt the dreams of parents. The consensus of recent opinion is that the emotional withdrawal from young babies in conditions of high mortality . . . finds no support from the primary evidence."[6]

Summing up this argument, Robert Baldock, a history editor at Yale University Press told the *New York Times,* "The modern family is not a radically different construct. Despite technological changes, lives in the past were very similar to our own in terms of emotions, relationships and ambitions. We may have a broader horizon, but we are not necessarily more sophisticated or more spiritually developed than people who lived 600 years ago."[7]

Recently, when art restorers cleaned Giotto's (1266–1337) *Escape from Egypt,* a series of frescoes in a chapel in Padua, an angry critic of the project groused, "Who cares that they found tears . . ." Well, I do. Indeed, the tears that the restorers uncovered beneath centuries of salt and grime visibly streaked down the faces of three mothers whose children had just been murdered by Herod's soldiers.[8] Whatever the technical controversy, the mother's grief offers a confirmation of Baldock's point, and mine.

Scholarship in future years will continue to unearth accounts of mothers with widely differing behaviors and feelings about their young. However, I would be surprised if it discovers large populations, aside from those temporarily experiencing upheaval or extreme duress, in which mothers were without apprehension about children's safety or tearless when they died.

Of course it is possible that one of Giotto's mothers wept for her infant, another for her own loss of the glory and gold her son's adult renown might have brought her, while the third cried out because the soldier had hurt her arm. Yet chances are that Giotto was referring more simply to the heart-crushing pain of traumatic, wretched loss. Nevertheless, the argument of this book, the way mother love often brings with it a subduing fear, requires no purity, simply a basic attachment.

Writing in her diary in Philadelphia in 1783, Nancy Shippen described a fear-filled morning. Her daughter was sick, and Shippen was terrified that the toddler might die. "I was waked this morning at five o'clock with the cries of my baby. It seemed to be at a distance. I jumped up—frightened half to death . . . and found it almost in fits with pain. I screamed as loud as the child—to see her in such agonies. Papa was obliged to take me out of the room or I should have fainted. I never in all my life felt as I did then." At the end of the day she added, "It is near twelve o'clock—every creature in the house sleeps but me—I have no inclination. I will watch my dear baby all night—I feel pleasure in doing her this service."[9]

In becoming a mother one becomes a hostage to fortune. Bluffs, postures of indifference, fall away at the birth of a baby the way a makeshift play fort, boards propped against a tree, collapses in the gust of a storm. Once a desired infant is born, you wish only that she outlive you. Maternal responsibility accepts many frames, the gold-leafed or the tin, but I believe this one is the mother's own. You don't toil to keep your son or daughter alive for country or kin. You do it because the alternative, the child's misery or the threat, however remote, of her death is unbearable. Yet throughout history, most mothers have had to live through the death of a child—or sometimes many children.

Women likely did use many tricks to outrun the rogue monster loss that relentlessly pursued them. Different women in different centuries, cultures, and social classes probably tried everything for a little relief: emotional distance, wet nurses, multiple pregnancies, detachment, chastity, abandonment, birth control potions, depression, deep prayer, nunneries, brothels, opium or wine, even infanticide.

In *Mother Nature* (1999), the sociobiologist Sarah Blaffer Hrdy claims that human mothers, unlike other primates, select which infants to love and which to kill or abandon. Her assertion is interesting. There is research, notably in the anthropologist Nancy Scheper-Hughes's *Death Without Weeping* (1992), about very poor mothers in contemporary Brazil, which suggests that in certain profoundly disrupted situations, mothers can become indifferent to children's well-being.

We know that at moments that are psychically or physically dire, for instance if the mother is suffering a postpartum or psychotic depression, even the most attached can become murderous while remaining deluded about her own destructive practices: "I have stopped feeding this child because it makes him feel better." Furthermore, some mothers feel little fondness for their children. And attachment and cruelty can coexist rather more readily than we would hope. One famous account of the resulting suffering is Christina Crawford's *Mommie Dearest* (1978), which describes the severe, often alcohol-induced, abuse the writer secretly endured at the hands of her adoptive mother, the actress Joan Crawford. Mothers, like all humans, are a mixed bag: on occasion meaner than snakes. The problem is how to hold such knowledge in fair balance, give it its due but not allow it to minimize or obscure the reality of many, perhaps most, mothers' helpless love.

History texts are only beginning to offer even fragmentary portraits of the bereft mother's grief. Few observers have attended to its significance. This silence testifies not only to widespread female illiteracy, a shortage of paper, and the biases of male scholars, but probably also to the way religious practices, prayer, and conversation with friends silently absorbed much maternal feeling. Overall, mothers' experiences of love and loss have been taken for granted within their contemporary worlds, such that "inevitable" became blurred with "inconsequential" in the books.

The resulting long silence has created an odd kind of terra incognita—a place at once proximate yet unmapped and unexplored. Information slips through in stories, letters, diaries, and art, which, in spite of the massive historic absence of the mother's perspective, refer continually to the pain of loss. I suspect this sorrow was a social commonplace, a tulle veil so readily worn by women that the world they saw through it became the normal world, and their faces, slightly obscured, patterned with the shadows of its texture, became the common face.

Early Western art made millennia ago recognized mother's feelings; Greek drama played upon mothers' fears about child loss to heighten audience emotion. "This is too much grief, and more than anyone could bear," Andromache cries, learning that her young son is to be killed, in Euripides' *The Trojan Women,* written in the fifth century B.C.E. Then, addressing her child, she adds, "O darling child I loved too well for happiness, your enemies will kill you and leave your mother forlorn." Describing the unnatural effects of the plague in *Oedipus Rex,* Sophocles' chorus observes, "The plague burns on, it is pitiless, though pallid children laden with death lie unwept in the stony ways." In more normal times, the text suggests, each child death occasions tears. In the *Odyssey,* Odysseus's mother, Anticleia, dies for love of him during his long absence.[10]

In real life, grief is often disturbing to witnesses, who usually want quickly to get on with things. The Romans, according to Seneca, found crying widows discomforting and made laws to limit sorrow's duration. ("And so our ancestors, seeking to compromise with the stubbornness of a woman's grief by a public ordinance, granted the space of ten months as the limit of mourning for a husband.")[11] Women's anguish may well have been seen as something to contain rather than amplify. Better to declare females frail and uncontrolled than to contemplate the pain behind their expressions.

I am not saying that women simply experienced children as love and loss. Women have killed, abandoned, tortured, exploited, and neglected children, and, to all appearances, have felt primarily either rage or indifference. Most loving mothers feel plenty of anger and hate. But I focus on mother love and the resulting fear of loss because our view of women in the past will remain lopsided until these feelings are given their due.

We know, for example, that many children were abandoned in the course of Western history. But we don't know what their mothers experienced. If a woman abandoned a baby because she already had three hungry children and doubted she could feed a fourth, what can we assume about her feelings? Much depends on her psychological experience, which throughout history has usually gone *completely* unrecorded. Did she hold and suckle the infant before she laid it on the church step, or in one of the revolving cradles some European churches found themselves building so parents could deposit infants anonymously? Did she have fantasies about her baby's future? Or was she simply so worn and burdened, so urgent to be free of the creature, that bundling it carefully before she turned and fled was the best she could do? Afterward, did she carry a memory of the baby that, year by year, became an older child? Or did amnesia overtake her, hiding her from herself as she enacted the sorry event three or four more times. Did she increasingly contemplate a reunion in heaven? I posit that although one mistake has been to sweeten mothering into treacle, another just as serious (and related) error has been to flatten the story, to ignore mothers' sorrow, to misread numbness, or depression, or relief over surviving herself.

In Euripides' *Ion,* the mother Creusa, confessing to a trusted slave how she exposed her infant son, recalls her lonely, heart-wrenching grief: "If you had seen the child stretch out his hands!" Years later, she can describe exactly the contents of the wicker cradle in which she abandoned him. The slave expresses surprise that she committed the act herself. In turn, Creusa explains how, raped by Apollo, she felt she had to hide her shame and her pregnancy from her mother. What would her mother's response have been? Her father's? The play doesn't tell us. Nor do we know how Euripides came to invent her words.[12]

Yet Creusa's poignant recollection of the moment is eerily familiar. Contemporary women have told me similar stories about giving children up for adoption, or saying good-bye to stillborn infants. However many years have passed, they can recount the moment in detail. And, of course, in a world where marriage has so often been *the* option for young women, many babies have been abandoned, as Creusa's was, by girls attempting to preserve their futures, even their lives, and to avoid the alternatives for the "spoiled" female: slavery or prostitution.

There may be a protective mantle that sometimes shelters women in harsh circumstances so that a death coexists with relief, or is muted by focusing on the other children, or is simply overwhelmed by a larger numbness. Certainly many religions offer comfort for such suffering (even as they may support social practices of female subordination that increase it). But they also absorb it without record, and in the absence of mothers' texts, particularly those in which women might have felt safe to speak openly, deeply, and intimately, it would be as much of a travesty to assume wide indifference as to imagine uniform benign affection.

John Boswell's history of child abandonment, *The Kindness of Strangers* (1988), suggests that most decisions about the fate of infants and children (he starts with the Romans) were made—or at least adjudicated and recorded—by men. Rarely was a woman's voice heard on the subject, certainly not in a way that explored her feelings. Describing the typical Roman tale of abandonment in myth and literature, Boswell writes, "a male figure orders the abandonment, to the regret of the mother." Later, summarizing a case by Quintilian, he states "a husband setting out on a trip orders his wife to expose any child born to her while he is gone, regardless of gender."[13]

Examining the nineteenth-century "epidemic" of infant abandonment in Italy, largely set in motion by policies of the Catholic church, David Kertzer suggests in *Sacrificed for Honor* (1993) that while unmarried women were legally forced to give up infants, a number of married women did so voluntarily, and sometimes demonstrably not out of dire economic duress. Some seem to have believed that they were nobly giving children to God, making them little angels and improving upon their mortal lot. But what were these mothers feeling? Had they on some level collectively agreed to imagine babies as easily expendable creatures? Or did they suffer secretly? While historians can track the extraordinary numbers of infants left in public places (approximately 100,000 a year in Europe in the mid-nineteenth century), we have no full testimony of the women's motives. And in a society as highly patriarchal as most have been, we also have no idea of their real circumstance, choice, or volition.[14]

Since most women throughout history have had little social power, it is reasonable to suppose that where abandonment and infanticide are concerned, women were—at least sometimes, maybe often—forced to give up children they grieved for, and their losses were mostly unacknowledged or at least underacknowledged. Other times, the social power of men may have compelled them to accept painful responsibility for choices that relieved their wives as well. Women could diminish some of their own guilt by blaming men and embracing powerlessness. We know little about men's feelings on these occasions; we know simply that they had the legal authority. In the particular case of Italy, as Kertzer makes clear, they created the horrendous abandonment laws under which the women lived, laws that, for instance, imprisoned women for out-of-wedlock pregnancy and forcibly separated them from their own infants, who usually died as a result, while compelling them to serve as wet nurses to other women's babies, who also frequently died.[15]

Equally important is the reality that women were sometimes bearing children ambivalently if not totally against their own wishes. They had "unprotected" sex whether or not they wanted to, and they often got pregnant. (Boswell has pointed out that abandoned children not infrequently became prostitutes, and that they were deemed useful to wealthier men in ancient Rome who sought to avoid impregnating their own wives. This wish to limit unwanted children, as much as pedophilic fantasies, may explain some of the attraction of using young boys and girls for sex. At the same time, men who visited prostitutes were continually warned that they risked having sex with their own abandoned children!)[16]

Furthermore, to say that sexual desire—even within marriage—was fraught for women is to understate women's predicament. Sexual desire led to pregnancy (varied strategies of birth control notwithstanding), to possible death in childbirth, to the birth of another infant difficult to support, to the child's risk of death. And since women were usually defined as property, suppressing their own desire did not always change their situation. The miracle is that there were loving marriages, and times and places of contentment. So too, it seems that often—given a land not at war, a decent shelter, bearable kin or partners, and enough grain to survive the winter—many women and men very much wanted at least some of their children and delighted in them.

No doubt feelings of love varied by moment, household, and child. Even if we assume that famine, severe poverty (or, occasionally, huge wealth), overwhelming fertility, and varied social events could disrupt families, making some mothers very selective about their attachments, it was inevitable that most women lost children they loved. Deep maternal attachment, and the attendant risk of loss, is widely manifest across Western history. Walk through a museum, visit any Christian church, and you will see pictures and sculptures of the Virgin Mary, a woman impregnated without her own knowledge or before-the-fact consent, whose beloved son dies before her. Little wonder she was and is the object of such passionate devotion. Her story has been everywoman's.[17]

Some of my own concern about recognizing mothers' feelings comes from the years I spent as a psychotherapist in a clinic in a housing project, with people whom the larger society had condemned in countless ways. Poor, welfare recipients, often addicted to drugs or alcohol, abused, sometimes abusive, utterly marginalized, these women were models of maternal failure or indifference, or so the public stereotype would have it. But the truth was otherwise. Many labored against impossible odds to promote their children's well-being, even if they did not always go about it in ways outsiders would choose.

I still recall one extraordinarily moving session of a mothers' group I led at least twenty years ago, in which a woman, then in her thirties, spontaneously talked about her unintended teenage pregnancy, and how she was hidden away in a home for unwed mothers and forced to give up her newborn for adoption. She spoke hesitantly as she described the ongoing feelings of loss and was startled when other group members nodded. Several poignantly told how they kept track of their own lost children's ages, imagined hair color and features, silently marked birthdays, and examined young strangers with particular care.[18]

Given a safe place to say what they felt and thought, the mothers I came to know would tell stories of suffering and grief, of sacrifice and concern for children in the face of utter personal hopelessness, of crushing feelings of responsibility, inadequacy, and shame. Their accounts were not only close to unbearable to hear, but they taught me indelibly that no subject is fully comprehensible unless people are given opportunity to speak freely and at length. These women were not saints or martyrs; they were multidimensional, filled with complex feelings and thoughts, not to mention caught in much harsher social binds than the distorted and impoverished public record showed.

Without presuming that we can understand the full spectrum of any mother's feelings, or the meaning she makes of them unless she tells us, there is plenty of evidence to suggest that deep love and attachment has been a common maternal experience across time.

5

Semele Remembered

ONE OF THE OLDEST Greek stories tells of Demeter, goddess of the harvest and of fertility. Demeter's only daughter was Persephone, whom she loved dearly. One day, wandering outside in the sun collecting flowers, the beautiful Persephone strayed too far from her young friends. Hades, god of the underworld, seized her and raped her, then charioted her away to his dark home deep within the earth.

Demeter searched everywhere for Persephone but could not find her. Bereft, she withheld spring, and the frozen world languished. In her *Mythology*, Edith Hamilton recounts, "The year was most dreadful and cruel for mankind over all the earth. Nothing grew; no seed sprang up; in vain the oxen drew the plowshare through the furrows." Zeus, Persephone's father, tried to temper Demeter's wrath and sorrow. He pleaded, urging her to let Hades keep their daughter, but she would not yield. Finally, realizing that he had no choice, Zeus ordered the god of the underworld to return Persephone. Reunited, mother and daughter fell into each other's arms "and held fast there." All day they spoke about what had happened to each of them while they had been apart. But their joy would be tempered. Because Persephone had eaten a pomegranate seed while in his realm, Hades maintained a hold over her. Every year, she would have to leave her mother and return to him for four months. Hamilton observes, "Demeter, goddess of the harvest wealth, was still more the divine sorrowing mother who saw her daughter die each year."[1]

Imagine the relief that fair weather and longer days offered the worshippers of Demeter. Families tried in autumn to store food to last until the sun returned and the first crops could mature the following spring. Having fertile seed to plant was critical. That this ancient story, about the very essence of survival, should be told through the metaphor of a mother's intense grief over child loss speaks to the timeless centrality and large psychic hold of the maternal experience.

Whenever I read a Greek myth or drama or the epics of Homer, their accessibility surprises me. While we know little about what the stories meant to their audiences, basic emotions feel familiar—like Demeter's sorrow and stubborn wrath. This question of familiarity is similar to one which Freud raised about Sophocles' *Oedipus Cycle*. Why is it, Freud wondered, that seeing or reading the ancient play of Oedipus still affects us emotionally when many other more recent tragedies of destiny do not?

Freud's answer was deceptively simple. Oedipus's story moves us, he said, "because it might have been ours."[2] Freud believed that the tale, of a young man who unknowingly murders his father and marries his mother, closely paralleled an unconscious wish and fear that is common in children's psychological development. The faithfulness with which the superficially removed plot traces unconscious feeling frees viewers' emotions.

Whether or not the Oedipus complex is as universal as Freud thought, it is clear that each of us comes of age with abiding unconscious sentiments that can be stirred by particular stories, rather the way the strings of a wind chime vibrate in a breeze angled to catch them. When we identify with a literary character, and witness his fate for making a choice that we might have made, we are deeply moved. We stand on the precipice, we feel the terror of taking one more step, but we do not. He does. And we unconsciously understand exactly why he did. The drama's emotional veracity temporarily confuses us: whose foot just moved?

Freud implied that some stories are more perfectly aligned than others with widely held, unconscious feelings. Certainly, whenever we sit dry-eyed watching a movie that causes a seat neighbor to sob, it reminds us that we are affected variously, by particular experiences of desire, love, and loss that have formed our psyches, and the way the storyteller's theme parallels and resonates with them. And we can be startled by our own reactions. Some feelings rest hidden and still as trout in streams; then, set in motion by aims difficult to discern quickly, they flash through surfaces. "Gee," patients will say to me, "I cried through this movie last weekend, and I have no idea why." As we talk, they quietly, often tearfully, recognize their own related, previously unconscious, feelings and closely held memories.

The idea that a character's destiny moves us because it might have been ours also underscores the way some stories hit hard because of the dread we carry. We fear loss, harm, violation, and death. We fear our own passionate mistakes, and our inclination to repeat them.

But stories also win us through enchantment and gratification of fantasy. Demeter is able to save her daughter because she is a powerful goddess who can make winter permanent and destroy humankind. If not exactly equal to Zeus, she is certainly strong enough to resist him. Indeed, she outwits him by recognizing and enacting a gender role reversal. Demeter threatens Zeus's earthly "children" with starvation. She renders him as vulnerable as any mother, and he yields. We also appreciate the Persephone story because Demeter possesses the very qualities that mothers so often have lacked—adequate resources and strength to protect their children, particularly daughters—and because the myth first awakens and then relieves the anxiety of child loss. One function of goddess worship, Cynthia Eller points out, has been to compensate for the devalued or enslaved status of real women.[3]

If Greek myths speak about wishes embodied by gods, the early Greek dramas focus more on humans tangling with gods. Of the classic plays, those written by Euripides almost 2500 years ago contain, as Aristotle observed, the first examples in the Greek theater of characters who carry on ordinary conversations, including loving exchanges between mothers and children. The plays often feature women who are outspoken about their servile state. We know little about Euripides' life. As a result, its mysteries, particularly the question of how he came by his empathy for his female characters, are much debated.[4] Unique among his contemporaries, he frequently portrays the cause-and-effect connection between women's relative powerlessness in the Athenian world and their suffering. Even his most violent, disturbed mothers speak movingly about their predicaments. Euripides' stories about the condition he referred to as a "potent spell" help frame our understanding of mothering tensions in later eras.

Mothers in Euripides' plays express fears of child loss and grief over dead children. Additionally, his dramas highlight those maternal behaviors said to keep children safe, and those that endanger them. I'm not sure anyone has portrayed more clearly the basic dilemmas for mothers who must raise their children in a male-dominated world.

Contemplating Greek art, one wonders at moments if its whole mission wasn't to lay the human unconscious bare, to let us glimpse it bathing, to reveal it so completely in stories, dramas, vases, mosaics, statues, that every single human motive, every impulse, feeling, and fear, would be displayed. Look here, each work seems to say. *Here* are the inner workings of the psyche, *here* are the curves of the human, unveiled before you.

Exploiting this bounty, I want to use two of Euripides' dramas loosely in the quasi-archetypal way Freud used Oedipus, to explore conscious and unconscious levels of feeling about mothering and mothers, and particularly about mothers' vulnerability and fears of child loss. However changed the circumstances, the experiences of the women Euripides created inform our contemporary dread that their looming tragedies might be ours.

In ancient Athens, women had little freedom and few legal rights. Like women in parts of today's world, they were essentially their husbands' property, viewed as inferior and closely controlled. A good Athenian wife rarely left her home. Though Euripides often locates his tragedies at the place where the arrangement fails, child safety is broadly equated with female submission to men, and to male rules and law. Mothers who hope to keep their children safe must obey their husbands, fathers, and other male kin.

While the extreme patriarchy of Athenian society is not legally sanctioned today in the United States, it offers a point of departure; in truth, its premises and laws underlie our contemporary world much the way the last century's highways determine today's traffic patterns. For many contemporary mothers, pressure to comply with expert opinion and cultural constructs like devoted motherhood seem to have partly replaced direct acquiescence to one's own menfolk. Yet, like our Athenian predecessors, if we seek power we are often accused in overt and more insidious ways of damaging children. The implication is that we have abandoned our proper role in the home. Furthermore, old assumptions underlie a covert question continually faced by today's women: Are children really safer and better off when mothers forsake equality and autonomy?

Virtue for womankind, as a chorus in *Iphigenia in Aulis* defines it, is "love in quietness." Euripides' plays suggest the terms of a basic safety contract between the sexes: if a wife is virtuous—obedient, dutiful, sexually loyal, and homebound—a husband is obligated to protect her and their children. When Clytemnestra, summoned by her husband, Agamemnon, arrives in Aulis, she greets him, and says, "Obedient to your command, we are here." Later, he orders her, "Obey," and she answers, "I am accustomed to it."[5]

Clytemnestra has reason to tread cautiously. She recalls for Agamemnon how he made her his wife against her will by murdering her first husband. Then he "dashed my living babe upon the earth, brutally tearing him from my breasts." Because he was the stronger man, she became his; her child that was not Agamemnon's lacked male protection and was killed. Even so, she reminds him, "I became reconciled to you and to your house." Defining virtuous womanhood, she adds, "I, as your wife, have been blameless, modest in passion, and in honor seeking to increase your house so that your coming-in had gladness and your going-out joy." She has borne him four children: a son and three daughters.[6]

The sexual violence that Clytemnestra describes might be more aptly attributed to gorillas (though our primate kin might bristle at the claim). She hopes obedience and submission will keep her and her children safe. It is an uneasy gamble, and, as it turns out, a mistake.

Agamemnon, after much agonizing, has decided to kill their daughter, Iphigenia, as a sacrifice to the gods so that the Greek ships, long becalmed, can sail to battle for Helen in Troy. Realizing that Clytemnestra would never agree to the girl's death, Agamemnon has lied and lured the pair to Aulis by claiming that he has arranged a wedding between Iphigenia and Achilles.

"Your child and mine—do you intend to kill her?" Clytemnestra asks her husband, starkly, stunned, as she grasps his plan. Once she comprehends his intentions, she is overcome by grief. "Now, I cannot hold them back, these streams of tears. I am lost, utterly." How, she implores him, can he sacrifice their "best beloved"?[7]

Her sense of betrayal comes from her belief that submission and sexual fidelity *should* protect her offspring. She has accepted her husband's harsh terms, yet *still* her child is taken. Particularly unjust, Clytemnestra points out, is that the Trojan War was caused by Helen's infidelity to her husband, Menelaus—not her own to Agamemnon. Shouldn't *their* child be sacrificed? "Kill *his* daughter for her mother's sake. For look, my girl is torn from me, from me who has been faithful to my marriage."[8]

The chorus says, "Oh, what a power is motherhood, possessing a potent spell. All women alike fight fiercely for a child." The implication is that mother love is so strong that it reaches beyond the human into some other realm of feeling; its intensity has a life of its own, which overtakes women and creates an almost incomprehensible state of mind. They will, at times of life and death, sometimes talk back to men! Perceiving the extent of her sorrow, even Iphigenia attempts to reconcile her mother to her own death. She begs Clytemnestra not to weep for her or mourn her. "What are you saying, child," Clytemnestra responds incredulously, "when I have lost you forever?"[9]

The threat of violence keeps the "protection system" in place. Athenian society deemed that a mother's only route to child safety was through a husband's guardianship.[10] Yet Agamemnon kills people at war *and* at home. How safe is anyone in his family? With nowhere to go, Clytemnestra's inclination (typical among trapped battered women even centuries later) is to work to please her violent husband in the hopes that through virtuous action she will appease him, and prevent him from attacking again. Euripides displays the arrangement while revealing his skepticism about its terms.

Is there no other way for a woman to protect herself? Without supportive laws or independent economic opportunity, apparently not. Of course, women can resort to violence, and some of Euripides' mothers, including Medea, Agave, Hecuba, and later Clytemnestra, eventually do murder. But to what end? Even though the provocations Euripides describes are profound, all the women are subsequently seen as monsters unfit for human contact. Male violence can be heroic or base; female fury is always grotesque.

Nor can women and children survive in the Athenian world living apart from men. Repeatedly in the plays, if a woman has children but no husband, the children are placed in grave danger. In the play *Hecuba*, Priam's widow, a Trojan, is faced with the death of her last two children (out of the fifty she bore!). Hecuba appeals to Odysseus, whose life she once saved, to step in and spare her daughter Polynexa from being sacrificed on Achilles' tomb by the victorious Athenians. But since Hecuba is now husbandless, and thus without status in the male, public world, Odysseus sees no point in extending himself. Rather, when she resists, he threatens her, "You understand your position? You must not attempt to hold your daughter here by force, nor, I might add, presume to match your strength with mine."[11]

Men are stronger. Women with children need male protection, without which other men can rape or kill them or their children. (Clytemnestra justifies briefly leaving her younger daughters only because "In maiden chambers they are safe and well guarded.")[12] To "earn" safety, females must cloister themselves, avoid men who are not family, accept control from men who are, and by so doing attempt to evoke restraint or tenderness. Violence or its threat, often against children, reminds mothers that they are weaker and without rights. If they retaliate violently, they are killed or exiled.

Real women in ancient Greece may not have been trapped in this exitless circle; yet it describes the underlying predicament of patriarchy: how women's lack of equality made them overly reliant on the goodness of their individual guardians. To the degree that men control public life, the law, and economic resources, children are most immediately kept safe if their mothers submit to those who have legal dominion over them. If women want to preserve themselves and their children in situations in which they have few independent rights, their best hope is to behave virtuously; even as such obedience often provides skimpy cover. The dilemma is summed up by Creusa, the mother in Euripides' play *Ion*, when she observes, "Unhappy women! Where shall we appeal for justice when the injustice of power is our destruction?"[13]

To understand the larger consequences for mothers and children— psychological and actual—of women defying these protection rules, one good place to look is Euripides' last, and arguably greatest play, *Bacchae*. I claim its relevance even though no mother appears on stage until the final act. What's more, when Agave does appear, she carries the bloody head of her only son, Pentheus, whom she has just murdered. So, you might demand, as my older son humorously does in other contexts, as when I mention that his room is a mess, "Your point?" Indeed, this most horrendous of all maternal acts tells us a lot about the way violence plays upon mothers' fears of child loss. Furthermore, the fact that women are peripheral to the drama mirrors their lesser status in Athenian culture, and our larger dilemma of excavating the lost maternal experience that helps us understand the present. *Bacchae* is filled to overflowing with psychological ur-stories about dilemmas of mothering, maternal feeling, and maternal protection, which reappear everywhere today.

Although the character's names are foreign, the basic themes of illegitimacy, rivalry, humiliation, rage, child loss, and mother loss are familiar, the stuff of current soap opera. If you lose your way, think *Sopranos*.[14]

Bacchae relates the story of Pentheus, a young and arrogant king in the city of Thebes, who derides his cousin, the god Dionysus, and denies his divine status. As punishment for the disrespect, Dionysus cruelly lures Pentheus into an elaborate trap, and has him murdered by Agave.

In order to appreciate the intense hatred between the cousins, understanding the back story is crucial: Agave had a sister named Semele.

Some years earlier, Zeus made love to Semele, who became pregnant with Dionysus. Learning of Semele's pregnancy, and thus, once again, of her husband's infidelity, Zeus's jealous wife, Hera, murdered Semele. The fetal Dionysus miraculously survived, carried to term in a womb Zeus created in his own thigh.

Pentheus, Agave, and their side of the family have enraged Dionysus by claiming that when she died, Semele wasn't really carrying Zeus's baby at all. They say some other man made Semele pregnant, and that Semele's father forced her to lie, to protect the family honor by alleging divine sperm. According to their story, Semele's false claim made Zeus angry, so he killed her and her baby with a lightning bolt. They say there is no god Dionysus; rather, the human infant died unborn.

Little wonder the disagreement is fierce; if Dionysus is Zeus's son, he is more powerful than Pentheus. If he wasn't fathered by a god, Dionysus is either dead or a social outcast. In ancient Greece premarital sex ruined a daughter and dishonored her family; it disqualified her for another marriage, and destroyed her social standing and that of any offspring; had she lived, Semele might even have been sold into slavery. In *Bacchae,* Dionysus, indeed Zeus's son, takes murderous revenge against his kin's shaming insults.

Dionysus's method of vengeance is eerie and terrible. Casting a kind of spell, he convinces Pentheus to dress up in woman's clothes so the young king can spy on the sacred Bacchic rituals in which many women, including his mother, are participating. Then Dionysus deludes Agave so that when she spots Pentheus hiding in a tree, she sees him not as her child, but as a mountain lion. She is transformed from protective mother to deadly hunter. Led into madness by the god, Agave tears Pentheus limb from limb and returns from the mountains to Thebes, proudly holding her boy's bloody head high for all to see.

"I am Dionysus, son of Zeus. My mother was Semele, Cadmus's daughter." The god's pronouncement of paternity and maternity opens the play. A boy whose mother died before giving birth to him has grown to manhood. There are conflicting versions of his family past, and he wishes to set the record straight.[15]

To picture Dionysus, imagine a young, mostly naked man-god wearing only a fawn's skin. He is bearded and wild-looking, yet slightly feminine and soft; an ivy crown rests upon long, dark hair that sometimes has snakes writhing in it. Dionysus is the god of wine and of tragedy, patron of the wild Bacchic rites. Visiting Thebes in *Bacchae,* he disguises himself as a mortal.[16] Unfortunately, instead of welcoming him, his cousin Pentheus derides him and attempts to jail him. Since Dionysus *is* a god, the king's abusive behavior leads to his own death at his mother's hands.

The horrid brilliance of the mother-as-murderer is that it enables Dionysus to demolish two enemies at once: Agave destroys the person she loves most, and her own humanity, while killing the god's rival for him. Euripides dramatizes a forbidden and terrifying extreme of maternal behavior, the protective tigress run amuck. Agave's action rivets because it is hideous, but not beyond the range of what children unconsciously dread about mothers. Like every bad witch that Walt Disney ever animated, Agave becomes an embodiment of maternal protection lost.

While the vulnerability of a full-grown man to his mother may be more psychological than physical, the alarm audiences feel watching Agave stems from the universal reality of an infant's or child's dependence on maternal restraint. Mother is bigger, stronger; she could kill me, but she doesn't. Why not? The question is profound, and consequently often unstated, misinterpreted, or taken for granted.

Indeed, the disparity and contradiction between mothers' power over young children and their own relative powerlessness within their societies is confusing. Who is harmed, who is harming? Some mothers seriously injure, even kill, children. All mothers—the bearers not only of life, but of mortality's bad news—deliver a sense of limitation, of the sacrifices required to live communally. And these realities can be confused with more personal damage.

Bacchae reflects our collective subliminal awareness that sometimes the protective balance tips. The haunting psychic question, the mystery that unconsciously confronts every child, is when and how? Dionysus can make it happen. But what or who else? Must men control women to preserve themselves and their offspring?

Some claim that patriarchal law fundamentally arranged itself around men's unconscious worries and inflated child fantasies about the frightening potential of unfettered mothers. Adrienne Rich quotes Simone de Beauvoir: "It was as Mother that woman was fearsome; it is in maternity that she must be transfigured and enslaved."[17]

Fantasies of the killer-mother who might spring at any time likely provided the ancient Greeks, and many others before and since, with a convenient rationale for stringent repression, as well as a tableau of projected male guilt for enslaving women. But they also indirectly acknowledged how the mother's intimate contact with infants and children is, at moments, beyond anyone else's control, no matter how draconian the laws. Children have survived most immediately through the self-restraint and love of mothers. Perversely, Agave honors this truth. When, at the end of his long life some 2400 years ago, Euripides wanted to dramatize the outer reaches of sensational, taboo-breaking behavior, he fantasized a mother killing her only son. At the same time, *Bacchae* suggests that only a very powerful, punishing state of madness inflicted by a god can overcome the protective potent spell.

I earlier suggested four borders within which a mother typically acts. *First* is her wish to keep beloved children alive. *Second* are the threats of loss, some devastating, some mundane, to which the wish continually responds. *Third* is the way the sense of vulnerability becomes a central—though often silent—presence in mothering, and translates primarily into reflexes of accommodation or submission. *Fourth* is the fearsome possibility that through some mistake, insubordination, or bad choice of her own, a mother can bring about the loss or harm she most dreads.

Euripides explores these conditions of mothering in *Bacchae,* albeit indirectly. Both mothers are destroyed for violating rules of women's behavior. And they lose their mortal children. Although Semele does not appear in the play, the ambiguity of how she became a mother is a point on which the tragedy turns. Dionysus's identity rests on her virtue. If she behaved "well," which would have meant giving her virginity to Zeus as he demanded, and her life as the price for Hera's wrath, then her son is a god. If she behaved shamefully, as Pentheus claims, then her son is dead or at best mad, and her forbidden sexual behavior has destroyed the child. Neither version allows Semele to live—nor her child to have a mortal life. Because she did not take the acceptable path for a woman—virgin marriage, motherhood, submission, and fidelity—she has sacrificed her life and his. Or, as Pentheus says (like a child spitting out a nasty playground rumor), "The truth about Dionysus is that he's dead, burnt to a cinder by lightning along with his mother, because she said Zeus lay with her."[18]

In *Bacchae,* Dionysus's authenticity, his very existence, rests on whether Semele was obedient to the most powerful male in the field—in her case, Zeus. That her son lives or dies by her compliance—defined as virtue—again suggests a vectored threat. Semele's only chance to save her child is, by one story, to obey her father and lie *about* Zeus, or, by the other, to accept death from Hera for lying *with* Zeus. The good—or life-promoting—mother, by this account, obeys men completely.

A recent magazine piece describes a married fourteen-year-old girl in India, raped by her father-in-law, whose own father insists she kill herself—or he will kill her. She has destroyed the family. Her story would fit naturally into a Euripides play. Women in many parts of the world are still ruined by, if not killed for, out-of-wedlock sex and pregnancies whether they choose them or not. With remarkable consistency across thousands of years, many daughters, however loved, have been considered primarily of value as unspoiled property for marriage.[19]

The ambiguity about Dionysus's status is heightened by the mystery of his birth. Women *can* give birth alone. Before the modern wonder of DNA testing, only the mother knew for sure that she bore a particular child, and which man fathered it. This threat of female power is paid tribute in *Bacchae* by the fact that Zeus usurps the mother's prerogative. Zeus mysteriously transfers the fetal Dionysus from the dying Semele to a rigged-up womb in his thigh and then presides over the birth himself. Compensating for the unconscious anxieties of the men who imagined him, Zeus becomes the conceiving father, the life-giving mother, and the exclusive knowledgeable witness, to the birth of his son.

Paternity is a question Greek men worried about constantly. How much their fears were well founded, how much a projection created by their own promiscuity and double standard, is hard to say. But the issue is everywhere, as the classicist Sheila Murnaghan has observed. Oedipus's first glimmer of his tragic fate arrives when a drunken man, "maundering in his cups / Cries out that I am not my father's son!" Or, as Telemachus says about Odysseus to Athena early in the *Odyssey,* "My mother tells me I am his son, but I don't know."[20]

Dionysus wants to believe his mother is good. He tries to restore her dignity, as well as his own. "I must vindicate my mother Semele by manifesting myself before the human race as the divine son whom she bore to immortal Zeus."[21] Even though Dionysus speaks from on high with distancing certainty, you feel the poignancy of his words. Imagine a bereft child growing up with no mother, but with two stories about her, one that makes her larger than life, a god's beloved, and the other that makes her shameful explicitly in the matter of *his* conception.

What's more, these conflicting tales may be all he has of her outside of, say, a single gold barrette. How hard he has to work to preserve the possibility of a mother he might have loved, or who might have loved him. Euripides has implied well the starkness of the child's choice. In this sense, Dionysian acts of vindication represent a common psychic process. Children respond protectively: they try, often unconsciously, to undo the debit of shame and damage incurred by their parents, and at the same time to keep for themselves a usable representation of a protective caretaker.

But Dionysus's plight is more profound still, and the woozy, uncanny insanity of the play emanates from the way he re-inflicts his own suffering and confusion upon the community that has harmed him. Maternal absence is at the heart of his predicament. Dionysus has lacked a loving mother to provide a primary intimacy: to worry about him, raise him, temper his extreme feelings, civilize him, or simply keep him company. Setting aside his status as a god, the subjective experience of imagining himself a god derives from the need to renounce the unbearable feelings of parental loss and worthlessness. Like a small, lonely child comforting himself by pretending to be a superhero, Dionysus creates a psychic fantasy to counter his bereftness.

In this sense, Dionysus, the patron god of theater, demonstrates how creativity comes out of loss, out of attempts to fill an absence; how a prototypal creative act in childhood is learning to mother oneself while awaiting one's mother's return. For Dionysus, the creativity is manifest in the Bacchic rituals when he makes music, dance, wine, milk, and honey pour forth. His murderous rage erupts each time he rediscovers that nothing he does will restore his mother, or undo his own psychic deprivation.

Indeed, the absence of mothering has left Dionysus psychologically uncivilized. He is unstable in the deepest sense of the word. And it is by imposing his nightmare on his abandoning family and their city that he destroys them. Two stories meet here and roil the psychic waters. In what might be called the basic narrative of patriarchy, Dionysus's mother's absence represents the price the ancient Greeks paid for civic order: men must dominate, female disobedience must be punished. Yet more quietly, we hear other overtones: her absence represents the damaging societal repression of the strong-enough mother. There is no independently powerful Demeter who can fight back, no counterpoint, and the narrative reveals the cultural instability created by placing too much power in the hands of one gender. The unreconcilable tension between these two views reveals the core unconscious question of *Bacchae*: "What happened to my mother?"

Dionysus is famous in Greek mythology for championing the Bacchic rituals. And they are central to *Bacchae*. These wild rites created an ecstasy of flute music, wine, and frenzied dance, which was meant to free people temporarily from the crushing weight of both personal identity and earthly sorrows. "Life, as we find it, is too hard for us," Freud once wrote, "it brings us too many disappointments and impossible tasks."[22]

Female followers of Dionysus were called Maenads, and scholars have pointed out how their token liberation may have served as a safety valve for Greek women, an image of freedom and an oasis to summon when the constricting rules governing their real lives pressed in too hard. Psychologically, we might understand the Bacchic rituals as part of Dionysus's fantasy recreation of his missing mother. Women participants, the chorus observes, can relax and behave like happy and protected daughters, "And, like a foal with its mother at pasture, runs and leaps for joy every daughter of Bacchus." Who protected Semele? Dionysus offers other mothers what his own was not allowed to have or give to him: sanctuary, delicious foods, joy, playful freedom.[23]

Bacchae poses basic questions: Can mothers behave responsibly on their own, can they be allowed freedom of movement, or will they do right by men, children, and "civilization" only if men control them? Then again, why do we need them at all?

So too, the play reminds us of the ways men feel justified defending against the possible damage of maternal power: If a woman chooses, she can kill her fetus. She can deny the child accurate knowledge of his father. She can mix sperm. She can refuse to circumscribe her behavior enough to promote her offspring's safety or her own. The drama gains a haunting vibrato from the barely suppressed fear, the constant vigilance between the sexes.

Pentheus mocks Dionysus's manliness, refers to him as an "effeminate foreigner."[24] In return, Dionysus sends Pentheus to his death. But Dionysus first tricks him into dressing like a woman and humiliating himself by parading along the streets of Thebes in women's clothes. When Dionysus helps Pentheus put on the feminine dress, the scene's extreme mothering gentleness against the backdrop of such deadly intent makes it particularly poignant and cruel.

> DIONYSUS: Come, then; I am the one who should look after you. . . . There; lift your head.
> PENTHEUS: You dress me, please; I have put myself in your hands now.
> DIONYSUS: Your girdle has come loose; and now your dress does not hang as it should, in even pleats down to the ankle.[25]

The tenderness is maternal. Dionysus dresses Pentheus carefully, as a loving mother might assist her child, as Clytemnestra might have dressed Iphigenia for her wedding to Achilles. Doing so, Dionysus becomes the mother he never met, fills in her absence by enacting gestures she might have made toward a child had she lived. Dionysus's long curly hair suggests femaleness, as it did to ancient audiences. By creating a ghostly presence, he also evokes the enormity of his loss, and in the gesture recapitulates the rage he feels about her suffering and his own. He avenges her by conjuring her absent love and using it to deceive and destroy her disloyal family.

Agave does not appear onstage until the play is almost over. Before we see her, we hear an account of how she has killed her son. Because Pentheus is disguised, and because they both are deceived by Dionysus, his mother looks at him without recognizing him. (If one person on earth would know you, wouldn't it be your mother? Yet would Semele recognize Dionysus after all this time? And then again, does any mother who has nursed a tiny helpless infant son ever completely recognize him as a grown man?) Agave's lapse testifies to the fact that something extraordinary has occurred.

A messenger recounts Pentheus's despair when he realized that his mother is about to kill him—how he tore off his headband, cried to her, and touched her cheek, trying to make her see him. "It is I your son Pentheus, whom you bore to Echion. Mother, have mercy; I have sinned, but I am still your own son. Do not take my life!"[26]

But Agave, foaming at the mouth, is too mad to listen. "[N]ot in her right mind, but possessed by Bacchus . . . she paid no heed to him. She grasped his right arm . . . set her foot against his ribs, and tore his arm off by the shoulder."[27]

Agave kills her child and exults in the act. We witness her innocent excitement when, coming onstage for the first time, she holds up Pentheus's bloody head for us to see. "I caught him without a trap, A lion-cub, young and wild."[28] She strokes his head tenderly as she speaks. Her hand, seemingly the only part of her to escape Dionysus's spell, poignantly caresses her child's hair, even as her words announce her deception.

It falls to Agave's father, the patriarch Cadmus, to bring her back from the madness Dionysus has imposed. He demands that she look at what she holds in her hands. "Come," he admonishes her, "to look is no great task." She screams. The spell is broken.

AGAVE: What am I looking at? What is this in my hands?
CADMUS: Does it appear to you to be a lion's head?
AGAVE: No! I hold Pentheus' head in my accursed hand.[29]

Dionysus punishes Agave for her disloyalty to Semele and to himself. He transforms her from female to male in her pursuits, from protective mother to murderous hunter. ("I have left weaving at the loom for greater things, for hunting wild beasts with my bare hands.")[30] The implication is that when any Theban mother leaves "weaving at the loom," she not only jeopardizes her own position and the safety of her children, she gives up the unspoken privilege of experiencing herself as correctly feminine, deserving of male protection, as protective of her child, and not a killer.

In other words, according to this classic notion, one which we will see reemerging repeatedly across time to the present moment, the archetypal patriarchal myth is that women who behave like men, who defy male rules of gender, who resist the trade of inequality for protection, will break the spell, lose both their earned protection and their own protectiveness, and destroy their children.

However damaging and oppressive this story, that it and Greek society placed the burden of decision for a child's life or death on men may also have engendered some comfort and relief in women—as well as grief and suffering. When infants had to be abandoned, and child death was always near, maybe women felt overwhelmed by pain, guilt, and responsibility. Maybe they felt unconsciously murderous, and feared that having more power would only make them feel more terrible. Perhaps female equality had to await the lowering of child mortality, and the consequent diminution of the mother's own unconscious confusion about her part in causing her children's deaths. Or perhaps female oppression, enforced by violence, was just that.

Bacchae shivers with feelings about how deeply mothers' behavior and maternal death affect children. Mothers, as well as giving physical care, provide a shielding love that gradually helps children create psychic order and emotional modulation. We see only bits of such nurturing in the play, and know it mostly through its absence. In a sense, the madness of *Bacchae* is the psychic world without mother love made manifest. Dionysus struggles to become and create his own mother, but the task is impossible, the outcome tragic.

As observed earlier, Agave's behavior is also every child's fear of the unspeakable possibilities of maternal power gone off the rail. What is fantasy, what real danger, remains fraught, hopelessly tangled, because so much fear and desire meet in this psychic question. How much of this view of Agave-as-monster is a myth created by children's own rage projected out, or unconscious male guilt at treating so badly people they also depended upon and sometimes loved, a projection by men onto women of all that they fear about themselves? Women are emotional, irrational, lustful, and violent. They are easily hoodwinked by gods and other males. Therefore we are wise to keep them under close surveillance, confine them within the home, arrange things so they have few options but to care for us and our offspring.

The social denial of female equality and thus the lack of experience with women as equals also leaves room for amplified fantasies about possible female aggression. The image of the uncontrollably angry mother becomes unduly magnified. Men fear and despise her, and see her as justification for their controlling impulses. Women renounce the traces of her they find in themselves. Children perceive her as life-threatening. The collective aversion is intense, and it reinforces mothers' efforts to suppress themselves.

But *Bacchae* also contains a recognition of the human beast of both genders, the fear of an irreducible ferocity from which people may not be able to free themselves, a psychic Minotaur or Harpy that sleeps and wakes in each person. How best to manage it? To see it exclusively in men? In women? To imprison mothers, or favor a sentimental view of them which claims false innocence?

The poet Robert Hayden refers to "love's austere and lonely offices" — the endless effort required to fulfill parental duties. The pediatrician and psychoanalyst D. W. Winnicott describes how useful and sustaining is the singing of songs like "Rock-a-Bye Baby" for creating a symbolic and thus safe venting of maternal aggression. Hostile thoughts expressed as melody allow mothers to keep rocking. "Sentimentality," Winnicott writes, "is useless for parents, as it contains a denial of hate."[31] Winnicott's point is that intense destructive feelings *denied to oneself* (what one tells a child is another matter) almost always become emotional distortions that harm. Only when acknowledged—if not with full consciousness, at least with symbolic expression—"down will come baby, cradle and all"—can they safely be discharged.

Bacchae is elemental; it is tragic. If an elegy is a song expressing sorrow or lamentation, we might call *Bacchae*'s series of variations on a theme the "elegies of patriarchy." The play overtly laments female badness and the need for repression; yet the hidden, unintended, but critical lamentations of *Bacchae* are about the suppression of maternal power and its harsh consequences. The songs are mournful because the singers believe the sacrifices described are necessary, even inevitable. (Female hegemony, equally undesirable, would produce its own lamentations.)

Bacchae offers a full rendering of a mother's essential life dilemma: how the imperative to preserve the child radically circumscribes her own choices, and how if she chooses wrong, the child may die. The sons suffer death, one literally, the other figuratively, for their mothers' transgressions: they also suffer for women's powerlessness, which they confuse with the capacity for active harm.

A mother living in a patriarchal society operates within a narrow margin. The consequences are harsh should she rebel. She is an often helpless agent of her child's survival. She is sometimes a monster. Often the monster's mask is placed upon her face by others. The gesture is intended to keep her in her place, but it also recognizes an aspect of her being. These conditions, her inevitable limitations together with the fragility of her children's lives, the nearness of death, and the loss through psychological departure, have for centuries been her grief.

Finally, the even more basic lamentations are ones of mortal limitation. Dionysus struggles with maternal absence, with all the ways that there is not—has never been, will never be—enough perfect mother love to fill each child's needs and desires. This hunger is the child's lament.

As we turn in Part II to examining specific advice books for mothers from the much more recent American and British past, admonitions in the texts will make a different kind of sense when you read them within the context of the archetypal gender tensions and power struggles illuminated by these ancient stories.

THE

NATURE

OF

ADVICE

6

John Flavel's *Token for Mourners*

IN 1674, John Flavel, an evangelical Puritan minister and prolific popular writer, published a book in England that would also sell many copies in America over the next century and a half. *A Token for Mourners* is a short volume of mourning advice addressed to a mother who had lost her only son. The book is intended to guide her in her grief, and its subtitle is instructive: "The advice of Christ to a distressed mother, bewailing the death of her Dear and Only son; wherein the Boundaries of Sorrow are duly fixed, excesses restrained, the common pleas answered, and divers rules for the support of God's afflicted ones prescribed." While the title names only the mother's loss, inside Flavel acknowledges Mr. J.C. as well as Mrs. E.C. One suspects that the minister understood both his era and the business of marketing; however much fathers suffer, it is better to approach their feelings indirectly.[1]

I came upon this book listed in a library's holdings, and initially dismissed it as a distraction. But the title kept appearing on lists of advice books for mothers. Gradually I became more curious and read it. I wondered who else had read it. Research, Internet queries, and conferences with generous reference librarians yielded a brief biography of John Flavel but little contextual information. So it was rather a surprise gradually to discover the popularity of *A Token for Mourners* in seventeenth-, eighteenth-, and nineteenth-century America. The fragile, brown-edged copy I read in a rare book library was printed in 1813 in Vermont.

In a world as glutted by publication and print as ours, it is hard to imagine the very different past. For instance, during the first half of the eighteenth century in England, it has been estimated that an average of ninety-three new books and tracts were published *yearly.* Remarkably, the American colonies produced about seventy-nine new books and pamphlets a year during the same period. In 1707, *A Token for Mourners* was one of the tiny number, its first American edition published by Timothy Green, a printer and bookseller in Boston. Already, it had been printed at least three times in seventeenth-century England. And copies exist from at least five American reprintings in the course of the eighteenth century, and another four in the early nineteenth.[2]

Timothy Green kept good company in Boston. The minister Cotton Mather officiated at his wedding, and both Cotton and his equally famous father, Increase Mather, bought books at his shop. They likely bought *A Token for Mourners.* Certainly they had cause for such a purchase: Four of Increase and Mariah Mather's ten children died before their father did. Eight of the thrice-married Cotton Mather's fifteen children died, three of measles in a single five-day period.[3]

Boston was from its inception a town of books and booksellers. Many of the Puritans arrived with libraries. Along with other necessities like hogs and pots, from the first they imported books. Records of what they ordered are mostly lost, but an occasional ledger remains. We know, for example, that in 1683, John Usher, a Boston bookseller, imported twenty copies of *A Token for Mourners,* and two years later imported fifteen more. James and Ben Franklin's newspaper, the *New England Courant,* mentions in 1722 that they kept Flavel's writings in their shop as part of an informal lending library. And a rare sales slip from the era shows that the Puritan judge Samuel Sewall in 1728 purchased two copies of *A Token for Mourners* from a Boston bookseller. Of the Sewalls' fourteen children, seven had died before the age of two.[4]

A Token for Mourners sold steadily for many years and seems to have become something of a popular classic. It is listed along with the likes of *Robinson Crusoe* and *Don Quixote* on a 1763 advertisement of sixty-nine chapbooks for sale by the Philadelphia book importer and printer Andrew Steuart. Chapbooks were "cheap" books or pamphlets printed on bad paper, in that era imported from England and widely distributed by itinerant traders who carried them inland from the port cities to rural farms and villages. They were read until they crumbled, and for many titles no copies survive. William Gilmore's close study of reading habits in late-eighteenth and early-nineteenth-century Vermont also cites Flavel as one of the most popular authors and lists *Token* as a book present in many households. The evidence suggests that *A Token for Mourners* sold well in America for a century and a half, which implies that it was embraced and found useful by several generations of readers.[5]

With paper expensive and in short supply, and writing considered a male prerogative, we can long for but not find many intimate first-person accounts of Colonial female experience in the seventeenth and early eighteenth centuries. The only explicit evidence of a woman reading *Token* that I know of is a 1725 inscription in a Boston copy stating that it belonged to one Mary Huntington. Nevertheless, a female readership seems likely for several reasons: mothers were the book's named audience; pious women were encouraged to read devotional books; mothers suffered frequent child loss; and literacy for women was considered important as a means of teaching the Bible to children. While many did not write—sewing being the preferred skill to teach Colonial girls well into the eighteenth century—a majority of white New England women read. (The Puritan poet Anne Bradstreet announced her exception to this "no writing" rule and the anxiety it caused: "I am obnoxious to each carping tongue / who says my hand a needle better fits.")[6]

A Token for Mourners is a serious book of advice, meant for a devout audience. At the same time, in its search for a popular market it anticipates the lay guides for mothers that proliferate in later centuries. A few books like *Token,* together with sermons, the Bible, religious poems, almanacs, and conduct books, were the texts that the literate European American women read for guidance.

John Flavel, the author of *Token,* was no stranger to traumatic loss. His parents had been imprisoned overnight by religious enemies at the height of the Great Plague in 1665 by captors who knew that Newgate Prison was abysmally infested. They died a few days later. Death came prematurely to many in London, but it must have been particularly terrible for Flavel to understand that enemies had purposefully placed his parents in harm's way. What's more, the minister buried three wives (one with a newborn infant) in the course of his sixty-four-year life; a fourth outlived him.[7]

John Flavel, who was, like his father, often in the thick of holy strife, felt an intense relationship to God. He prayed constantly and seemed to believe that his devotion entitled him to safe passage. Once, imminently threatened by shipwreck in the midst of a wild tempest, he addressed God, reminding him rather pointedly that if he (Flavel) perished, "the name of God would be blasphemed." A minute later, the wind mysteriously changed, and the passengers were saved.[8]

According to Flavel's biography, this sea voyage was preceded by a dream in which a father "lashes" with a "little whip" a baby fussing in a cradle. Flavel takes the dream to mean that God will soon discipline him—thus predicting the storm. Flavel's God often takes a free and heavy hand with a whip, a device everywhere mentioned in the advice he offers grieving parents.

Whips were a common item, whipping a common punishment in seventeenth-century New England, and the historian Mary Beth Norton describes countless acts for which a "severe" whipping is the prescribed punishment: for example, young lovers engaging in premarital sex; or disorderly behavior in childhood, like stealing apples; or husbands not controlling wives adequately; or servants who run away. The "rod," as the historian Philip Greven has richly documented, was also considered indispensable in a parent's quest to save a child from eternal damnation. From the Puritan point of view, whips were useful tools for enforcing a system of social order that featured hierarchical relationships and obedience.[9]

Psychologically, whipping also likely encouraged mental dissociation as a means of coping with pain, a phenomenon that may have contributed to a heightened spiritual intensity. In *A Token for Mourners*—and in the communities in which the book was read—whipping becomes a correlative for the psyche's experience of loss. Psychic pain is to be endured like a beating. By inflicting a certain number of lashes and then stopping, the Puritans enacted a crude drama of emotional survival.

The Puritans, who could be tender and loving as well as harsh, must have wondered if a single person would live through his first year in America. Early on, in July 1630, right after they arrived in Massachusetts Bay, the new settlers started dying of dysentery and scurvy. Fearful of attack, they had pitched their shelters too close together on a spit of land in Charlestown and became infected by their own waste. They were tired, disoriented, frightened, and malnourished. The scurvy did not abate "until the arrival in February [1631] of a ship from England carrying a quantity of lemon juice."[10]

What was it like to be an ill mother with an ill child, praying for lemon juice? Infants with scurvy bleed under the skin and often scream when touched. How could you hold and comfort one? Or manage your own sickness and fear at the same time? And what did you feel (if your baby was still alive) when finally, having dragged yourself through the worst of the first winter, a boat carrying lemon juice tacked into view across the half-frozen harbor? In these small asides, noted briefly in narratives of church leadership and laws, one glimpses the mothers' stories.

We may never recover the full range of mothers' experiences in early Puritan New England. Even as women historians in recent years have done remarkable work, there is simply an absence of first-person female sources. Without such accounts, it's difficult to speak about women's states of mind, their worries. Furthermore, people are often reticent to reveal much about their intimate fears.

Perhaps most significantly, it is hard to determine from the outside what is accepted as a given—or *donnée*—in a centuries-old environment. Is loss endured or dismissed more readily because its danger has been dulled by familiarity, or is what is not accepted simply silenced or disavowed? Many contemporary Americans are probably too afraid of flying in airplanes and inadequately worried about sunbathing. Fear doesn't necessarily correlate with risk, and much of how we perceive danger relates both to our own fantasies, and to how our culture focuses attention and spins its narratives.

Many early New England women possessed great courage, vitality, and ingenuity. "Elite" white women, especially as they aged or were widowed, often came to enjoy autonomy and informal social power. No doubt those who survived took pleasure in their prospering families. There were ways in which the new land increased possibility for European women. Nevertheless, where child love was concerned, their situation was fraught. All but the luckiest lost at least one child. Young children were imperiled by infections, epidemics, accidents, bad medicine; their constitutions were chronically weakened by worms and other parasites. And women were aware of their risk in childbirth, and frightened. Many mothers worried that they might die and abandon helpless youngsters.[11]

Furthermore, the Puritan doctrine that dominated the early New England women's lives pointedly attributed their children's death and suffering to the mothers' sins. Mothers had cause to live in a state of high anxiety. Their children could die instantly, their religion demanded that they examine their souls to see if the death was due to some sin of theirs, and they could not know if the dead child would go to heaven or hell.[12]

How does *A Token for Mourners* suggest a mother manage the death of a child? The book's answer is intense, and at moments off-putting in the extremity of its attempt to mold feelings according to dogma. At the same time, the advice confirms how hard the psyche must work to manage the pain, and reminds us how some people in the past were encouraged to cope.

To endure the death of a child, Flavel counsels, "Labor to bring your hearts to a meek submission to the rod of your Father." Death is God's doing. He whips you to remind you that he is God. To feel better, accept the pain as a manifestation of his power, and focus your faith in him.[13]

Flavel begins his treatise by advising that mourners not "be too hasty to get off the yoke which God hath put upon your neck." He counsels, "Oh desire not to be delivered from your sorrows one moment before God's time for your deliverance be fully come alive." By making concrete the discomfort as a yoke from God, Flavel acknowledges the emotional labor and time involved and offers a rationale for tolerating it. Taking matters further, Flavel suggests that a mourner tell herself, "It is good for me that I have been afflicted." The minister urges readers to look for unseen causes, to examine their own impieties.[14]

Perhaps most remarkably, he implies the mother's fault may be to have loved a child too much and thus to have made God jealous. "If the jealousy of the Lord hath removed that which drew away too much of your heart from him . . . O then deliver up all to him." He adds, "I wish that all the love and delight you bestowed on your little one may now be placed, to your greater advantage, upon Jesus Christ." Furthermore, it is good to "die daily to all visible enjoyments," to prepare for your own death.[15]

Just when you think that Flavel is tempered, he becomes severe. Maybe you were enjoying life so much, he writes, you needed to be "whipped" by having a child die. "Did not thy fond, secure, carnal temper, need such a scourge, to awaken, quicken and purge thee?" He suggests that the mother wonder what she has or has not done spiritually to deserve the loss: "What sinful neglect doth it come to humble me for?" But, at the same time, the minister urges her not to show resentment or anger for fear of provoking worse retribution. "And really, friend, such a carriage of this under the rod, is no small provocation to the lord to go on in judgment." Instead, she should be grateful. "Well, then, whatever God takes, be still thankful for what he leaves."[16]

At the same time, Flavel is aware that grief can make mothers lose their desire to live, and warns repeatedly of the peril of unrestrained sadness. He deems it bad "to faint under the rod." He would have mourners at once endure the blows and yet avoid "the extravagances of our sorrows." For if one goes too far, one participates in "such a mourning for the dead as is found among heathen, who sorrow without measure" and hold no hope of resurrection.[17]

Sometimes, poignantly, Flavel reveals the enormous suffering he attempts to manage: "Oh friends! How many graves have you and I seen opened for our dear relations. How oft hath death come up into your windows and summoned the delight of your eyes?" At the beginning of the book, he tells readers that his son has recently died. Viewing children as parental copies, and sons as the more valuable, he writes, "To bury a child, any child must rend the heart of a tender parent; for what are children but the parent multiplied? . . . But to lay a son in the grave, a son who continues the name and supports the family; this was ever accounted a very great affliction."[18]

Yet Flavel counsels against evoking specific memories of a child, and in doing so lets us glimpse the extent of some parents' suffering. "I have known many who will sit and talk of the features, actions and sayings, of their children, for four hours together, and weep of the rehearsal of them, and that for many months after they are gone; so keeping the wound continually open, and excoriating their own hearts, without any benefit at all by them: A lock of hair, or some such trifles, must be kept for their purpose, to renew their sorrow daily, by looking on it." The minister also warns against what-ifs. "O if this had been done, or that omitted; had it not been for such miscarriages, and oversights, my dear husband, wife or child, had been alive at this day! No, no, the Lord's time has fully come . . . Let that satisfy you. Had the ablest physicians in the world been there, or had they that were there prescribed another course, as it is now, so it would have been when they had done all." Flavel attempts to discourage mourners from contemplating worldly failings (like summoning the doctor too late), and to focus on the religious one of forgetting a primary loyalty to God. "If God be your god, you have really lost nothing by the removal of any creature-comfort."[19]

And what is the reward? For those who follow his advice, Flavel promises reunion. His fantasies are evocative and precisely rendered. When the Resurrection comes, he writes, you will be reunited with lost loved ones. Their actual bodies will be restored so that you can recognize them. You shall be able to "single them out among the great multitude, and say, this was my father, mother, husband, wife, or child; this was the person for whom I wept, and made supplication." What is more, "they shall be unspeakably more desirable, sweet and excellent, then ever they were in the world . . . You shall have an everlasting enjoyment of them in heaven, never to part again."[20]

What a promise, and what comfort, especially for communities so familiar with early death. It is moving to think about people now dead whom one has loved, to suppose oneself reuniting with them. Imagine the crowd of faces. You feel first the anxiety of looking, the fear of not finding, then the relief and pleasure of recognition, finally the collective witness to the fact of having found.

The hours-old neonate distinguishes his mother's smell from that of other nearby women. Could this instinct be an early source of the same wish? I will find you on whom my survival depends. At moments of intense grief mourners think they have glimpsed the dead loved person in a crowd. Walking in a cemetery, spring—dogwood, periwinkle, pansies—thinking hard about a recently deceased friend, I look up and briefly, far in the distance, see him, familiar in posture, leaning against a parked car on the crest of a small hill. He is surveying the scene. Did he know I was coming? Then he is gone, absorbed within the body of a stranger.

That the rediscovered person will have been improved by his stay in heaven may be Flavel's nod to ambivalence. There are many people with whom you might reunite joyfully, only to remember those traits that oppressed, irritated, or drove you mad. One inspired illustration of such mixed feelings comes at the end of Bernard Shaw's *Saint Joan*. Her persecutors are gathered around her in the afterlife, fawning, and apologizing for killing her. All kneel and praise her. Recognizing their remorse as at best ambivalent, Joan panics them by offering to return. "And now tell me: shall I rise from the dead, and come back to you a living woman?" The men scatter. They don't want her alive, as she knows. They simply want to free themselves from the awkwardness of having murdered her.[21]

Similarly, Flavel frees his followers from the worry that mixed feelings might reawaken when people reunite with dead kin, and simultaneously, by doing so, more fully consigns his readership to the obligation of faith. (The mind's quiet excuse—I will not obey because I'm not sure I want to be reunited—is removed.)

Since God's rules for Puritans were mostly interpreted and written by men, women often functioned on a psychological level as props, moved around to represent emotions and behaviors disavowed by the storytell-

unself-consciously blame child loss on a mother's loving behavior, her "unruly passion." Mather, like Flavel, felt entitled to blame child death on mothers when they failed to submit completely to the rules of the church.

As the historian Daniel Boorstin has pointed out, the Puritan sermon was "a public affirmation that the listeners share a common discourse and a common body of values."[24] However dour Increase Mather was, it is unlikely that his interpretation of the reasons for the mother's fate would have shocked his congregation, in which, by this era, regular women worshippers outnumbered men. Furthermore, the minister believed that he was hectoring women for their own good, reminding them of their primary obedience and protecting them from eternal damnation. At the same time, Mather's sermon offers another vivid example of indirect threat. When mothers do not follow the rules, their children suffer and die.

On one level, Mather's severity was natural, in that Puritan society was premised on hierarchies of authority. Demands for obedience and severe punishments for disobedience, inconceivable to many of us now (though still preserved in some countries, communities, and religious sects), were taken for granted. Servants were to obey masters, wives husbands, children parents, and everyone God. One illustration of the grievous punishments for defiance is a 1648 Bay Colony law that inflicted the death penalty "on rebellious children—sons and daughters over sixteen who cursed or struck either of their parents." It is unclear if it was ever invoked, but having such a law on the books is remarkable enough.[25]

Nor did men escape unscathed. Puritan diaries contain examples of children suffering God's harm from their father's failings. When Cotton Mather's daughter was seriously burned in a household accident, he took it as a sign of his own sinfulness. "Alas for *my sin* the just God throwes *my child* into the *Fire*." And Judge Samuel Sewall apparently felt so guilty for "condemning the guiltless" in the Salem witch trials that when his infant daughter died soon after, he took it as a sign of God's displeasure with his bad verdict. Yet it seems that men apportioned the guilt for children's harm or death, blaming women when they defied certain rules: for instance, when they were too attached to children, or too outspoken. Additionally, the historian Elizabeth Reis suggests that Puritan women, recognizing their devalued status, were more inclined to condemn themselves as bad, while men saw their own sins as more specific and remediable.[26]

Seventy-five years before Mather preached, the dissenter Anne Hutchinson was exiled to Rhode Island in 1638 for socially dangerous religious views. Arriving in Massachusetts from England in 1634, she had made the mistake of affiliating with a group that disagreed with Governor John Winthrop about the relationship of church and state, and the control of the pulpit. She was also learned, smart, and unrepentant; when called before the authorities, she refused to condemn Winthrop's opponents.[27]

Soon after her banishment, Hutchinson had a menopausal pregnancy in which the fetus died and surrounding tissue formed a hydatidiform mole (a diagnosis unknown at the time and hypothesized retrospectively). The mole was eventually expelled "with great difficulty." When news of the event traveled back to Boston, this "monstrous birth" was taken as proof of providential justice. God transformed Hutchinson's fetus to punish her defiance. In a rather ghoulish antecedent, Governor Winthrop dug up another baby stillborn to Mary Dyer, a follower of Hutchinson's, when he heard rumors of its "monstrous" shape. Apparently more than a little agitated and obsessed, Winthrop was eager to confirm that God shared his objections to the women's beliefs and had punished them accordingly, mirroring their ideological monstrosity with malformed human beings. That Hutchinson's womb produced a monster both revealed her as satanic, and manifested God's punishment of her for defying woman's silent role. A judge at Hutchinson's trial (for defamation and sedition) declared, "You have stept out of your place, you have rather bine a Husband than a wife, and a preacher than a Hearer: and a Magistrate than a subject."[28]

Anne Hutchinson, together with five of her children, was slaughtered by New Netherland Indians in 1643, five years after her exile. When word got back to them, the Puritan leaders took the event as additional evidence of their righteousness and her evil. The Puritan Thomas Welde wrote, "as she has vented mishapen opinions, so she must bring forth deformed monsters." Hutchinson had given birth to fifteen children, three of whom died before she left England. During her trial several of her sons were held to have been in error for allowing their love of their mother to come before their love of God.[29]

Even the more compliant Puritan poet Anne Bradstreet struggled with how to manage obedience, faith, and child loss after three of her grandchildren died, the third, Simon, in 1669. "No sooner came, but gone, and fall'n asleep, / Acquaintance short, yet parting caused us weep," her elegy begins. And although she attempts to confirm the good of the Almighty, anger, fear and doubt leak into her syntax. "With dreadful awe before Him let's be mute, / Such was His will, but why, let's not dispute, / With humble hearts and mouths put in the dust, / Let's say He's merciful as well as just." Let us say it; let us try to hold onto our faith, let us stifle the desire to protest, and increase our safety through muted compliance, she seems to suggest, in spite of, perhaps, our own deepest feelings.[30]

Further light is shed on early New England women's anxiety about infant loss by a piece of buried history recently excavated by Mary Beth Norton. In 1649, Alice Tilly, a beloved fifty-five-year-old Boston midwife, according to the petitioners, "the ablest midwife in the land," was jailed. Though the court record has been lost, her crime—besides possessing "excessiue pride" and "an ouer-much selfe conceitedness" (traits the Puritans probably ascribed quickly to women)—was some alleged act or acts of malpractice that resulted in the death of infants and mothers under her care: "the miscarrying of many wimen and children under hir hand."[31]

Her imprisonment profoundly upset the women of Boston and neighboring Dorchester. The colony was not yet twenty years old. Alice Tilly was the midwife most likely to deliver mothers and their babies safely. The women valued her abilities and did not want to face childbirth without her. They were afraid that the court would punish her with death. (In their first petition, the women inquired nervously "whether mrs tillys life is not now quesioned.") Still, the women had no permission to voice themselves publicly and were frightened of opposing authority. Their decision, in context, was quite extraordinary. That they organized six petitions, and thus participated in what Norton describes as "American women's first collective political action," speaks to the depth of their anxiety over childbirth and child loss.[32]

The shadow of Anne Hutchinson hangs over this event. She had been known to her contemporaries as an able healer, educated in the uses of medicinal herbs; adept, too, at delivering babies. Her exile and murder must have frightened women. Whatever the political and religious disagreement, the subtext of her defeat suggested that even an upper-class and relatively powerful woman like Hutchinson was no match for the authorities. Among the petition signers for Tilly, Norton points out, were a number who earlier had been Hutchinson's supporters.[33]

One imagines the Boston women feared that if they did not speak up—however harsh the consequences—their midwives would be taken from them, and they and their babies would be consigned to die. Although they imagined themselves to be in God's hands, women felt that safe delivery of their babies more immediately depended on good midwifery. Since midwives were the only Colonial women with any recognized social power, they probably were at least unconsciously looked upon as protective "mothers" by the other women. The petitions also manifest how a midwife's ability to bring children safely into the world awakened feelings of gratitude, loyalty, and attachment. Trying at the same time to avoid the wrath of the court, or a fate like Hutchinson's, the Boston women pitched their pleas with great humility.

Reading the awkwardly worded, oddly spelled documents, one sees how the petitioners also carefully attempted to protect Mrs. Tilly. They knew the court disliked challenges, so they struck a tone that was deferential, at moments obsequious: "wee yor humbl petitioners doe no desyr to put in to interrupt the Corts proceedeing as God shal giude them: yet humbly Craveing that the Cort would be pleased to beare wth the weakenes of yor pore petioners in this one request, (Namely) that thee Cort would be pleased that the sayde mistris Tylly may be authorized to proceede in hir office . . . and yor petitioners shal be thereby ffurther oblidged to pray for yor worships." If you humor us weak women and let our midwife work, they suggested, we won't ask anything else of you, and we will owe you even more devotion and prayer.[34]

What comes through from the old documents is a deep pathos about the women's own child loss experiences, fears, and wishes. In her deposition on behalf of Tilly, Lydia Williams recounts how she felt a child alive emerging through her birth canal and yet born dead. "I myself have had a child allive iust cominge at the birth, & yeat dead borne." She credits Tilly with "the savinge of my life."[35]

In the fourth petition, the women describe their fear of giving birth without Tilly. They are "affrayd to putt our selves into the hands of any besides our midwife tht wee haue had experience of." And then they implore the court, "Now the lord Guid your worships tht you may heare the cryes of mothers, and of children yet unborne tht soe yor worships may bee moued thereby to Grant unto us yor Humble petitioners the liberty of our midwife."[36]

The fifth and sixth petitions, in which the women continued to try to increase Tilly's freedom, angered the General Court, whose members apparently felt their authority undermined and "urged the petitioners to halt their efforts on the midwife's behalf."[37] Nevertheless, the petitioning had succeeded in softening the sentence. While she was not freed, Alice Tilly was allowed to leave jail to deliver babies.

For women of the era to pursue public action speaks to their extraordinary degree of worry. Had they not been made miserable by fears of infant (and maternal) mortality, it seems unlikely they would have taken such a risk. Not only, as their tone amply manifests, were they well aware of the danger of alienating their husbands, ministers, and legislators (who must also have been inclined to a certain sympathy as they doubtless wanted their wives and infants to live), but they also seem to have feared that making such a request, however humbly, could invite retribution. They were in a bind, consigning themselves to "monstrous births" if their behavior was interpreted as defiant, and to increased risk if they kept silent and gave up their competent midwife.

Yet another sword hung over Puritan mothers' heads, and must have upped anxiety over child loss. According to their theology, infants who died, lacking the experience of grace and thus not among the elect, could not go to heaven, and so had to spend eternity in hell. In 1662, a dozen years after the Tilly affair, a Massachusetts Bay resident, Michael Wigglesworth, wrote a poem, "Day of Doom," which discussed the inevitability of infant damnation. It was a runaway bestseller, printed so many times that one in twenty New Englanders eventually owned a copy of the pamphlet. Wigglesworth enthralled his readers with his gruesome portrait of Judgment Day and detailed the torments of the damned, who "gnash their teeth for terrour; They cry, they roar for anguish sore, and gnaw their tongues for horrour."[38]

The best Wigglesworth can do for infants is to locate their eternal damnation within "the easiest room in Hell." But he does promise parents that once Judgment Day comes Christ will alter their feelings so that *they* will feel nothing for their dead damned children. *They* will love *only* their saved offspring. "The tender Mother will own no other of all her numerous brood, / But such as stand at Christ's right hand." The need to posit this liberation, of course, is just more evidence that mothers who lost infants still loved and missed them deeply.[39]

At least a small measure of Wigglesworth's impact can be seen in the funeral poem that the poet Edward Taylor wrote for his wife, Elizabeth, who died in 1689 at age thirty-nine after the couple had already lost five children: "Five Babes thou tookst from me before this Stroake." To demonstrate his wife's piety he mentions her continual reading of Wigglesworth. "The Doomsday Verses much perfum'de her Breath, / Much in her thoughts, and yet she fear'd not Death." Married at twenty-four, dead by thirty-nine, having borne eight babies, it is not hard to imagine that continual pregnancy, birth, and loss wearied Elizabeth of this world, and made her hope to reencounter her lost children in the next.[40]

The Puritan young were not sheltered from ideas about their fate—quite the opposite. Ever the upbraider, Increase Mather, in a sermon in 1678, warned children, "If you dy and be not first new creatures, better you had never been born: you will be left without excuse before the Lord . . . Your godly Parents will testifie against you before the Son of God." In a 1711 sermon, Mather portrays a parent gladly helping Christ pass "a Sentence of Eternal Death upon his own unsaved dead child."

David Stannard, who discusses these sermons in his essay "Death and the Puritan Child," describes how Jonathan Edwards told a group of children, "I know you will die in little time some sooner than others. Tis not likely you will all live to grow up." Not surprisingly, Stannard notes, Puritan diaries are filled with references to terrorized children dreading death and an eternity in hell. Samuel Sewall's daughter Elizabeth, traumatized by a Cotton Mather sermon, "again and again 'burst out into an amazing cry . . . [because] she was afraid she should goe to Hell.' "[41]

James Janeway's very popular text *A Token for Children* (1671), published first in England and then in the Colonies, is a collection of religious biographies of thirteen "exemplary children who died young." The stories were "written specifically to provoke sadness and fear within the hearts and minds of young readers." And should any child miss this intention, Janeway appended an afterward that was even more explicit. He asks his young readers: "Did you never hear of a little child that died? and, if other children die, why may not you be sick and die!" and "Are you willing to go to hell, to be burned with the devil and his angels! . . . O! hell is a terrible place: God's anger is worse than your father's anger; and are you willing to anger God?" Janeway's excoriation makes it hard to remember that his intention was to protect.[42]

In several tales, the very pious children have come to their fervid prayer after seeing siblings die. Death has frightened them, and their fear is taken as an opportunity to encourage devotion. Janeway describes how John Sudlow, who died at twelve, worried about eternity when his little brother died. "When he saw him without breath, and not able to speak or stir, and, when carried out of doors, and put into a grave, he was greatly concerned." Seeing his brother dead, John asked whether he must die too, and "when about four years old, he desired to know what he must do that he might live in another world."[43]

Janeway's good children are sometimes presented as wiser than their mothers. In fact, several chasten their mothers for feeling and manifesting too much grief. The dying teenager Tabatha Alden, like Iphigenia two thousand years earlier, implores, "Dear mother, you have done so much for me, you must promise me one thing before I die, and that is that you will not sorrow over-much for me. I speak this to you because I am afraid of your great affliction." The child seeks to protect her mother from pain, and also from the retribution that might be invited by intense mourning.[44]

How much were Puritan mothers comforted, how much tormented, by the thought that resisting a child's death might assure it, and that a second child's death might be punishment for an earlier protest, a brief and secret doubt, or irreverent feelings? The Puritan culture placed mothers in a difficult psychological situation. They nursed their own babies and loved them fondly; yet to "save" them, they had to give them up to death without protest. I would imagine that the combination of tender affection, death, self-doubt, self-blame, and blame by others drove some women close to mad.[45]

I picture women who, during the leeward time of tasks, when labor was required but not concentration, occupied their minds with prayer and religious thought. A worry or hope would surface, a physical pain; a prayer would form. Would next week bring more smallpox, next winter more hunger? Would the previous night's sex mean pregnancy? Would their neighbor's hog eat the corn crop? Would the infant survive its fever? By asking what they had done to incur God's anger, the Puritan women organized anxiety and processed traumas small and large through the activity of belief. No matter how bad things were, praying harder and purging oneself of sin more rigorously might relieve them.

Flavel, Mather, and Wigglesworth also remind us that giving over one's mind to another whom one perceives as more powerful—whether parent, leader, husband, or God—has been a common human tendency. Such a practice can create stability through hierarchy, maintain group order, modulate feeling, focus anxiety, and provide a kind of clarity. The ministers offered mothers comfort for child loss in return for submission. If you do as I say, God says, you will not feel completely bereft or singularly responsible or unbearably alone.

Is God a humanoid male with a whip who punishes intense child love? For the Puritans, this God rewarded obedient mothers with the possibility of reuniting with lost saved children in heaven, and punished defiant ones with the death of unborn and living children and with eternal damnation.

Almost like the Puritans' notion of Satan, this dynamic—subduing women by repeatedly connecting their self-assertion or rebellious impulses with their fear of child loss—has seemed compelling, nearly reasonable, in each context in which it arises. In the next chapter, we will look at the nature of the increasingly secular advice given to mothers, mostly by doctors, in the late eighteenth and early nineteenth century.

7

William Buchan's *Advice to Mothers*

MANY OF THE EXPECTATIONS mothers experience today and much of the advice that supports current "standards" of mothering have their genesis in late-eighteenth and early-nineteenth-century America and England. The era that produced the first real factories also manufactured the prototype of the modern "good" mother. Her specs and ours have much in common, and understanding her helps us understand ourselves.

This mother has proved remarkably durable, a sturdy mannequin defining correct proportions; an ideal figure, redraped with each new decade's garments, but structurally intact. Her staying power might be attributed to the variety of ideas and fantasies laminated to create her. She includes bits of the quasi-medical, philosophical, and scientific, together with economic, ideological, and religious pieces. Her primary characteristics include a self-effacing urgency to be correctly devoted to her children and the acceptance of too much responsibility for their fate.

Beyond bearing and nursing infants, a seventeenth-century Colonial mother's duty was to feed, clothe, and help teach skills like spinning and reading. Fathers—as the sovereigns of the home—were deemed responsible for religious education and directing their children's lives. Children assisted parents with household tasks, and were often sent away—from midchildhood on—to learn a trade or refine their domestic skills.

At home or apprenticed out as servants, older children helped raise younger ones—with mothers, grandmothers, and sometimes fathers making their appearance between household and field labors, at meals, bedtime, the sickbed, moments of crisis, to settle conflicts, or to supervise tasks. While it's clear that Puritan mothers loved their children and vice versa, women were so busy struggling to perform daily household labors, and bearing and nursing infants, that it is hard to imagine any one child consistently receiving much time in a mother's day. Laurel Thatcher Ulrich's *Good Wives* documents this point well.

By the early nineteenth century in the United States, family size was beginning to shrink. (New England led; the rest of the nation followed gradually.) Children were coming to be seen more as creatures who developed as they grew, and who needed nurture to thrive. Mothers were becoming defined as the people who provided that attention. Catherine Scholten writes, "After 1750 the advice literature increasingly told mothers to demonstrate concern for their children by feeding them carefully. For the first time, authorities claimed that the survival and, more interestingly, the happiness of child and parents depended on the strength of the maternal bond."[1]

Experts helped articulate this new motherhood. And, thanks to cheaper paper, books became more common. Throughout the Colonial era, paper, made from rags, had been in short supply and expensive. In 1828 an entrepreneur in Pennsylvania manufactured paper from straw, a discovery which spread quickly to other mills and, when combined with better printing techniques, increasing literacy, and an expanding population, paved the way for a proliferation of advice books. Doctors captured some of this new market.[2]

In James Janeway's *Token for Children,* a father asks his sick child if he should summon a physician, and the child dissuades him. "By no means," answers little Susannah Bicks, "for I am now beyond the help of doctors." Rather, she explains, she is in the hands of the "heavenly physician." Later, her dying younger brother, Jacob, insists that he "will have the doctor no more; the lord will help me." Janeway implies that fearful parents try too hard to keep their children in this world. John Harvey, a dying five-year-old, sternly admonishes his mother, sobbing over her own brother's death and doubtless fearing her son's, that everyone must die. "I pray, mother, do not weep so much." One can easily imagine an ill and frightened child struggling to maintain his faith against his mother's tears, yet, as Janeway tells the story, the sad woman is merely foolish in her fear, and weaker than her son.[3]

Since the medicine of the era often recommended inducing diarrhea, vomiting, blistering skin, and other painful treatments, it's little wonder that children did not want the physician called. Perhaps the more observant among them recognized that such caustic interventions were mostly useless as well. To turn away from medical care in the seventeenth century arguably spared as much suffering as it inflicted.

Nevertheless, by the late seventeenth century in England physicians were beginning to become the earthly and increasingly secular rivals of ministers. When Janeway's heaven-bound children suggest the physician stay home and let the minister take over, one whiffs not only some mix of common sense, faith, and fatalism, but also professional rivalry. The shift of social power in England and America, where first doctors and educators and then psychologists demanded from ministers a share of the "expert" role, gathered momentum across the eighteenth century before truly bursting out in the nineteenth and twentieth.

In reality, children and families would have to wait until well into the twentieth century for medical science to begin consistently curing illnesses. During the last quarter of the nineteenth, doctors became aware of the existence of germs and the need for antiseptic practices. But, as one medical historian notes, "The alliance between science and clinical medicine remained shaky and ambiguous before the First World War." Research indicates that American maternal and fetal death rates did not improve from their Colonial levels until about 1940. The doctor and writer Lewis Thomas, who sometimes accompanied his own physician father on home visits in the early decades of the twentieth century, makes a similar point. His father taught him that while morphine, digitalis, and insulin had efficacy, almost all of the other medicines he daily prescribed were at best placebos. Most cures came naturally as the disease ran its course—or not at all.[4]

Thirty years ago, thanks to a class in American women's history, I read the abolitionist and suffragette Elizabeth Cady Stanton's memoir, *Eighty Years & More: Reminiscences* 1815–1897. Stanton was a remarkable woman, ahead of her era in many ways, and unusually able to express an independent point of view. She raised seven children, six of whom outlived her. A story she told about mothers and doctors has stayed with me. The Stantons' first infant, Daniel, was born in 1842, apparently with a "bent collar bone." One, and then, because his mother was dissatisfied, a second doctor came to the home and examined the child when he was a few days old. Both insisted on bandaging the collarbone to pressure it into place. Needing to anchor the bandages, the first doctor wound them around the baby's arm, the second around its hand—so tightly that each time the limb turned blue.

Stanton realized that if she left the bandages in place ten days, as she'd been instructed, the infant would lose its arm. So she untied them, studied the angles of the problem, and found a solution that "gave the needed pressure without impeding the circulation anywhere." When, a week or so later, Elizabeth Cady described her efforts to the doctors, they "smiled at each other" and praised her "mother's instinct." She replied, "Thank you, gentlemen, there was no instinct about it. I did some hard thinking before I saw how I could get a pressure on the shoulder without impeding the circulation, as you did."[5]

That Stanton would include the story in her memoir—that I would remember it for so many years—testifies to its novelty, and her rare strength of character. It is most unusual for a new mother to contradict two doctors who have independently agreed on a course to assure the well-being of her newborn. At the same time, Stanton deftly resists the patronizing dismissal of "instinct" as the source of her success. Of course, economics and social class need mention. The Stantons had enough money to hire a nurse (who—poor and foreign—is forced to serve as the foil in the story, refusing to remove the bandage, saying, "No indeed, I shall never interfere with the doctor"). No doubt social status helped Stanton feel she could assert herself. At the same time, her striking ability to stand by her judgment cannot be so easily explained.[6]

Ministers or doctors have been summoned to bedsides, and advice books have sold well across centuries, because the help of others is essential to good mothering. Everyday dilemmas, not to mention moments of intense worry and suffering, will, rightly, cause sensible people to seek treatments, information, opinions, support, and comfort. Yet mothers often pursue advice not only to access knowledge, but because they experience professionals as the official voice of the culture, and their only hope apart from spouses or partners for establishing a sense of shared responsibility for life-and-death decisions. Stanton's experience is part of a larger phenomenon we will explore, wherein medical practitioners helped mold new notions of motherhood that to a large degree emphasized beneficent instinct, sacrifice, and exemplary maternal virtue.

Furthermore, Stanton's doctors illustrate how experts' pronouncements about what children needed offered a hodgepodge of folk knowledge and bias. A brief look at advice about nutrition further illustrates this point. It was during the eighteenth century, according to the advice historian Alice Ryerson, that physicians observed the health virtues of fruit and vegetables. (No one yet knew about vitamins and minerals.) Advice guides started insisting that a child eat what is good for her. Ryerson notes that by the end of that century, "Food had ceased to be a simple pacifier of hunger and had become a medical prescription."[7]

Yet, as John Locke's influential 1693 treatise, *Some Thoughts Concerning Education,* demonstrates, opinionated admonitions about what foods children should and should not consume precede the discovery of nutritional usefulness! Locke forcefully rejects "melons, peaches, most sorts of Plumbs, and all sorts of Grapes" because their juice is "very unwholesome." He favors strawberries, cherries, apples, and pears. Locke, a physician as well as a philosopher and political theorist, sought to define an upbringing that would create virtuous, rational, and manly men. In this context, "unwholesomeness" becomes a *moral* quality of the fruit, akin to decadence.[8]

Seventy years later, when Jean-Jacques Rousseau wrote *Emile* (1762), another very influential book on child-rearing, he specifically disagreed with Locke's assertion that it is unhealthful to immediately give water to a thirsty child. (Locke suggests starting with bread, for he wanted children to drink slowly.) Rousseau's opinion came not from better science, but from attempting to create a model of child-rearing that followed his ideas about the superiority of what was natural. So too, Rousseau did not want children to eat meat because he believed that it would harm character, as the "great meat-eaters are usually fiercer and more cruel than other men." Such guidance, as it initially encountered science and became medicine, piled into an ungainly, difficult-to-sift mound of conventions, inventions, prejudices, and true observations.[9]

It is also worth noting that authoritative writing about child-rearing apparently required little personal experience. John Locke was childless and unmarried. Jean-Jacques Rousseau forced his mistress to place all five of their children in orphanages—where they died before, some time later, he tried to retrieve them. John Abbott, a young American minister who in 1833 published a best-selling guide for mothers, was in his twenties and just married when he started lecturing female congregants on how they should do their work. Though in the late eighteenth and early nineteenth century, the occasional mother, like Mary Palmer Tyler, wrote successful advice guides, most of the authors were men.

By the nineteenth century, mothers had become the primary audience for child-rearing advice. Locke and earlier writers had addressed themselves to fathers. Indeed, until the nineteenth century, fathers were the center of the household and, at least in theory, the final authority on all matters, including questions concerning children, certainly sons. In the first half of the century, fathers disappeared from most advice guides. In *The Mother at Home,* John Abbott moved fathers so far to the edge of his frame that finally, toward the end of the book, he asked, rhetorically, "Is there nothing for fathers to do?" He asserted that of course fathers matter, and "no father can be excusable for releasing himself from a full share of the responsibility." Still, his awkwardly phrased defense is paltry. Men, as they increasingly worked outside the home, turned over to women the emotional task of family guidance; women, eager for something to call their own, and wishing to do right by children, embraced it.[10]

Advice to Mothers on the Subject of their own health, and on the means of promoting the Health, Strength, and Beauty of their Offspring, by William Buchan, M.D., is one famous, popular, example of a genre of book for mothers that came onto the American scene in earnest in the early nineteenth century. It illustrates how a practice developed whereby each bit of new knowledge quickly became defined as an important maternal responsibility out of proportion to what was actually known or within the mother's control.

By 1804, the year William Buchan's book arrived in America, much that was relevant to its reception had changed from Puritan days. Significantly, post-Revolutionary America was developing an ideal of Republican maternal virtue which sanctioned women's education to make mothers better teachers of their children, and children, therefore, better citizens in the new nation. Consequently, between 74 and 91 percent of New England white women could read, the highest percentage in the North Atlantic world outside of Sweden. And those who could afford books increasingly read more broadly.[11]

In the seventeenth and early eighteenth centuries, literate women mostly read the Bible, conduct books, and devotional writers like Flavel and Janeway. For medical suggestions they might have turned to almanacs, the very popular compendiums of seasonal calendars that contained advice on subjects from astrology to gardening and included many pages of remedies for ailments. Kevin Hayes, who catalogued the reading habits of Colonial women, mentions how the occasional volumes on medicine and midwifery that made their way into women's hands were treasured, and often shared widely. Nicholas Culpeper's *Directory for Midwives* (1651) was one such book, and Hayes found that copies of it were carefully handed down from mothers to daughters.[12]

The American Revolution changed women's lives in many ways, two of which are immediately relevant here. Forced during the war to manage without their men, women, according to the historian Mary Beth Norton, became more aware of their own capacities and more politicized. This recognition, together with a revolutionary ideology proclaiming the virtues of equality, helped women examine and alter their view of themselves. Close on the heels of the Revolution, the enthusiasm for creating a new country, together with prosperity, scientific and technological advances, and the continuing impact of European philosophies—like the Enlightenment—provided momentum to the new ideas. Childhood attracted notice. This sea change affected mothers. Hugh Cunningham writes, "The love between parents and children, and in particular between mother and child, long sanctified in Western iconography, now became imbued with a new intensity as it became secular."[13]

In his quirky and quite wonderful book *Reading Becomes a Necessity of Life*, the historian William Gilmore looked—almost house by house—at the reading habits of four hundred families in the Upper Valley of Vermont during the years 1780 to 1835. (Estates were inventoried when people died.) Gilmore found that both literacy rates and available reading materials shot up in the years after the Revolution. Citizens subscribed to newspapers and bought increasing numbers of magazines and books. They read more travel books, fiction, poetry, history, how-to books, science, and advice books. With this increase in reading, they broadened their thinking. "They learned the heritage of the Western cultural tradition, and no one told them not to take it seriously." While sacred books were still favored by many (and Flavel's remained among the most popular), Gilmore points to the decade of 1800 to 1810 as the transition point when secular books began to dominate in the households he examined.[14]

Choosing a government without a monarch exhilarated Americans but also made them anxious. What would keep people safe from their own worst impulses? In the years after the Revolution, an idea emerged: the new Republic would prosper if virtuous mothers helped educate sons to make them good and upright citizens. (Previously, the mother's domain had been daughters.) As part of this new responsibility, women gained social permission to read more broadly. An ignorant mother could not produce an informed son. Daughters were also directed to learn, and the first schools for girls started in this era. Their education would make them worthier parents.

Thus, early in the nineteenth century mothers' roles swelled; they were encouraged to provide more care, education, and moral guidance. Additionally, in the course of perhaps fifty to eighty years—almost overnight—it became a common belief that mothers determined their

children's success in life. This idea—in part an outgrowth of philosophical tracts like Rousseau's *Emile,* as well as economic and social changes
that would gradually lead to men defining themselves more through
work outside the home—coexisted with various energized, often Evangelical, strands of Protestantism that had their own reasons for increasingly glorifying pious mothers. (Church attendance was largely female.
And women probably bought more advice books.)

John Abbott's widely read guide for mothers, *The Mother at Home;
or The Principles of Maternal Duty familiarly Illustrated,* describes how
George Washington's dutiful mother, Mary, "taught her boy the principles of obedience, and moral courage, and virtue." (By contrast, Lord
Byron's mother was selfish and rageful and thus taught him to "give
himself up to the power of every maddening passion.") According to
Washington's biographer James Thomas Flexner, the real Mary was no
saint, and, in fact, had a stormy, difficult relationship with George. She
was devoted to him, but in ways that he found unbearably demanding,
hypercritical, and humiliating. Hardly the stuff of idealization, but advice writers cared little for biographical fact. Describing the popular stories in the new magazines for mothers that appeared in the first half of
the nineteenth century, Catherine Scholten sums up, "A common moral
illuminated all the maternal morality stories: a great man is the product
of his early childhood upbringing, and therefore all his public actions
are explicable by the kind of care his mother gave him."[15]

At the same time, contemporaries worried that allowing freer access to books was risky. Men and women both felt considerable unease
about what could happen if women read the *wrong* books. Might it not
diminish their sense of responsibility? Distract them from their children
and divert them from household tasks? The correct books would en-
force maternal self-sacrifice, restraint, submission, and rationality. The
wrong ones—fiction and romance novels—were likely to stir women's
passions, or make them act immodestly. One of many writers decrying
these dangers, Hannah Webster Foster wrote in 1798 that novels "fill the
imagination with ideas which lead to impure desires . . . and a fondness
for show and dissipation . . . They often pervert the judgment, mislead
the affections, and blind the understanding."[16]

"These attacks on fiction," observes the historian Linda Kerber, "it is clear, were in large part attacks on emotion, on passion and on sexuality."[17] Their concerns are similar to what the Greeks feared in *Bacchae,* the Puritans railed against in their sermons, Rousseau bemoaned, and, as we shall see, doctors condemned when their turn came: unruly passion. There's something to be said for adults moderating their expressions of intense emotion and sexuality, certainly around children. But advice givers repeatedly imply that female passion is singularly harmful and, to protect children, women must be guided and controlled by others. This debate about the dangers of reading also reveals the era's deeper tensions about women. Given freedom to consider, mothers may have found their ideas and desires plausible. If so, what would become of them as dutiful helpmates and breeders?

In the context of advice-giving power migrating from ministers to doctors, it seems fitting that William Buchan, the Scottish author of the best-selling guide *Domestic Medicine,* first published in Edinburgh in 1769, and its later companion, *Advice to Mothers* (published in America in 1804), was sent as a young man to study divinity in Edinburgh but gave it up for medicine. *The Dictionary of National Biography* lists him as an "amateur doctor." Buchan wrote successful, popular texts, printed in many editions and places. (The empress of Russia sent Buchan a gold medal after she read *Domestic Medicine.*) William Buchan was a humane man, a social reformer, against slavery and oppression of the poor. He is frequently cited for his enlightened contributions to public health; for example, he was one of the first doctors to advocate the benefit of bathing more than once a year. When he died at seventy-six in 1805, he was honored with burial in Westminster Abbey. According to the *Dictionary,* Buchan was so "benevolent and compassionate" he could not hold onto wealth. A "tale of woe always drew tears from his eyes and money from his pocket." His popular style and large contemporary impact have been compared to that of Benjamin Spock.[18]

Buchan greatly influenced the American nineteenth-century child-rearing writers who followed him, and whose texts often included unattributed material taken from his. But *Advice to Mothers* is also significant because the doctor helps transform mothers—albeit precariously, ambivalently, and rather dangerously—from simple childbearers to more broadly influential creatures, deities when they are "good," and scorned, harmful failures when they are "bad."

Dr. Buchan announces in the first line of *Advice to Mothers* that much of his professional work has been devoted to preserving the lives of infants. (The child mortality rate had not improved since Colonial days. Observers in America, as well as Buchan in England, believed that as many as half, easily a quarter, of all children died before age twelve.) He secures his readers' attention by telling them the book's focus: "I am sure of being listened to with kind attention by the tender and rational mother, while I am pointing out to her the certain means of preserving her own health, of securing the attachment of the man she holds dear, and of promoting the health, strength and beauty of her offspring."[19]

Buchan then—in language that is a departure from the past—praises mothers fabulously, elevating them and comparing them with God:

> The more I reflect on the situation of a mother, the more I am struck with the extent of her power, and the inestimable value of her services. In the language of love, women are called angels; but this is a weak and a silly compliment; they approach nearer to our ideas of the Deity: they not only create, but sustain their creation, and hold its future destiny in their hands; every man is what his mother has made him, and to her he must be indebted for the greatest blessing in life, a healthy and vigorous constitution.[20]

Once offered, the accolades are quickly placed in jeopardy when the doctor sets about defining the qualities of the mother worth admiring. "[B]y a mother I do not mean the woman who merely brings a child into the world, but her who faithfully discharges the duties of parent." She "feels all her cares amply repaid" by her infant's growth and activity. While it praises, this sentiment also brushes away the real risk of the undertaking, as well as any sense that the mother's contribution of child rearing might incur a larger social debt than one paid back by the satisfaction of a healthy infant.[21]

In this way, Buchan quickly hammers together a closed system. His remark assumes that devoted mothering satisfies women completely, and thus frees the rest of the world to go about its business. No one need attend either to the actual work mothers do or to the possible benefits of including women in the public world. To reinforce his point, the doctor becomes stern when he mentions mothers who *do not* care adequately for their children. "No subsequent endeavours can remedy or correct the evils occasioned by a mother's negligence; and the skill of the physician is exerted in vain to mend what she, through ignorance or inattention may have unfortunately marred."[22]

Buchan justifies his book as a corrective for other wrong-headed books about childhood illness. Because of the pernicious influence of these books, he asserts, scared mothers and nurses are *causing* ill health in children by dosing them with bad medicines. ("The natural effect of such publications is to excite terror, and to prompt mothers and nurses to keep *dosing* poor infants with drugs on every trifling occasion, and to place more reliance on the efficacy of medicine than on their own best endeavours.") He makes mothers' desperation and credulity—their naïve approach to the texts—responsible for illness rather than pointing to the overall absence of knowledge, the ignorance of physicians and apothecaries, of aggressive pathogens, malnutrition, filthy environments, and other difficult social conditions.[23]

Greatly influenced by Rousseau's *Emile* (except apparently its fierce disapproval of doctors), Buchan aligns himself with the idea that health is best defined by following nature. To make his case, he describes mothers who do the opposite and are in need of education. Buchan suggests his book will teach mothers "to prevent diseases that are almost always the consequences of mismanagement."[24]

Doubtless Buchan observed situations in which mothers mismedicated children and poisoned them. Certainly plenty of maternal behavior was ignorant, even atrocious. But at a time when serious childhood illnesses were basically untreatable, their causes not understood, to emphasize those child deaths that resulted from mothers' incompetent dosing seems at best one-sided. He sums up his introduction by saying that because mothers aren't taught well themselves, they make "a variety of fatal mistakes respecting their own health, as well as that of their children." Mothers who turned to Buchan for advice on how to take better care of infants were told that they were causing their children's deaths and must be taught not to by this doctor.[25]

Aspects of William Buchan's philosophy are progressive. His basic prescription is straightforward and sensible: women should "seek for beauty in the temple of health." He counsels temperance, exercise, fresh air, sound nutrition (fruits and vegetables!), cleanliness, good humor, and abstinence from strong liquor. Discussing "Health for Women Before Marriage," he warns would-be mothers against using cosmetics that contain lead or mercury. He spots what is apparently a contemporary form of bulimia and suggests that losing weight by drinking vinegar is a bad idea. ("When swallowed in draught for the purpose of reducing plumpness, it proves highly injurious.")[26]

Buchan's more specific prescriptions rest on his notions of female propriety. Walking is good for a woman's health, as is horseback riding, and dancing if it is not "fatiguing." If she wishes to be sedentary, a woman may play a musical instrument, sing, or read aloud "delightful pieces of poetry." But "Young ladies and mothers should resign the card-table to old maids." Buchan mentions women who like to swim in the ocean while pregnant, but adds, "I think their example too bold, and too dangerous to be recommended to general imitation."[27]

The doctor feels no compunction about laying a mother's death at her own feet if she doesn't do as he says. "Indolence in pregnancy" *causes* "puerperal or child-bed fever, so fatal to delicate mothers." (A pair of twentieth-century historians note that puerperal fever "is probably the classic example of iatrogenic disease—that is, disease caused by medical treatment itself." Doctors spread it from woman to woman, often by not washing their hands. Their opinion provides some measure of the text's reflexive bias.)[28]

And pity the dissipated mother-to-be who seeks beauty other than in health: "her charms will fade; her constitution will be ruined; her husband's love will vanish with her shadowing attractions, and her nuptial bed will be unfruitful, or cursed with a puny race, the hapless victims of a mother's imprudence." Once again, she *alone* will be responsible for harming her child.[29]

Should readers miss the point, Buchan adds another remarkable assertion. He notes that women who wear stays that are laced tight—and thus press hard against their breasts—tend to have daughters without nipples: "it is not improbable that the daughter may bear this mark of a mother's imprudence."[30] While the iffy science is qualified by the double negative, its moral implication is clear: women who flaunt or even enjoy their sexuality will mutilate their daughters, destroying the next generation's wholesome ability to suckle infants.

Buchan wants to help make a better world. Mothers are the center of his hope. And the heart of his ideal is breastfeeding. There's something so correct for him about breastfeeding that it realigns the moral universe, dissolves decadence, and—more specifically—ends maternal and infant death. He returns to this theme many times. (The historian Marylynn Salmon has pointed out that breast milk was accorded almost magical healing powers in early modern England and America. Sick adults would sometimes suck from nursing women.)[31]

Nursing is "a sacred duty." Failing to nurse is "a rebellion against nature" and "dangerous to the mother herself, to say nothing of her child." Buchan adds, "If we take a view of all animated nature, it is shocking to find, that woman should be the only monster capable of withholding the nutritive fluid from her young." Society has alienated her from what he deems natural: "Such a monster, however, does not exist among savage nations." Besides killing her infant, the doctor explains, stacking threats, a woman who does not nurse is likely to harm her own womb and render herself barren.[32]

Buchan's assertions outline a complicated issue. Though overstating his case, he does correctly perceive the immunity-enhancing function of breast milk. Furthermore, in his era there was no good substitute for women's milk. Infants deprived of it, fed unsanitary, non-nutritive substitutes in poorhouses or foundling homes, did die.[33]

Yet Buchan's stance is based as much in morality as in health. To improve the world, mothers must nurse: "But were I called upon to point out any one remedy for the greatest part, not only of the diseases, but of the vices also of society, I would declare it to be the strict attention of mothers to the nursing and rearing of their children."[34] Women's devotion in these areas, he claims, would end child death. It seems that between the lines, he is warning elite British women away from wet nurses. Whatever the medical pros and cons, one cannot help also hearing sexual politics, for women who used wet nurses had a little more freedom of movement. Otherwise, before sterile bottles, breast pumps, and formula, how many hours could a mother part from her baby, no matter what urgency compelled her?

Buchan's ideas reveal the medical basis of the prejudice that will become the later psychological template of maternal responsibility. Human perfectibility rests on devoted mothers. In the nineteenth century Buchan asserts that breast milk will end infant death; later correct, pure mother love (should we call it "breast love"?) will end psychological suffering.

If mothers devoted themselves singularly to breastfeeding, Buchan exhorts:

A stop would be put to the cruel ravages of death in early life. The long catalogue of infantile afflictions would almost become a blank, or contain nothing to excite alarm. Every child, invigorated by his mother's milk, would, like the young HERCULES, have force sufficient to strangle in his cradle any serpents that might assail him.—Occasional illness would be to him only part of a necessary course of discipline, to enure him by times to bear pain with manly fortitude.—In short, health, strength, and beauty, would take the place of puniness, deformity, and disease; society would be renovated: and man, instead of dwindling away, as he now does, by gradual degeneracy, would soon rise to the original perfection of his nature.[35]

Elaborating his notions of human perfectibility, and anticipating (perhaps helping give birth to) the worst of eugenics, Buchan speaks out against imperfect mothers reproducing. "It is little short of intentional murder on the part of a weak, languid, nervous, or deformed woman to approach the marriage bed. Improper passions may urge her to become a wife; but she is wholly unfit to become a mother. She risks her own life,—she disappoints the natural wishes of a husband,—and should she have children, her puny, sickly offspring, as I before observed, will have little cause to thank her for their wretched existence." He sums up the larger evil such a mother imposes on society, and states that no hero can "be moulded or cherished in the womb of debility."[36]

In a fuller discussion of pregnancy, Buchan warns that the "mother's least neglect" will injure the embryo. Though every woman of the era had friends who died in childbirth or lost babies to miscarriage, Buchan dismisses the reasonable worries as female fears ("her terrors are groundless"). He mixes a potentially useful observation—that "pregnancy is not a state of infirmity or danger"—with a punishing one—"the few instances (a woman) may know of miscarriage or of death, were owing to the improper conduct of the women themselves."[37]

Should the mother become fearful, sad, or angry, she will harm herself and her baby. "Though the chilling influence of fear, and the depression of melancholy, are very injurious to the mother's health and the growth of the *foetus* in her womb; yet anger is a still more formidable enemy. It convulses the whole system." And it kills infants. "I have also met with a most shocking instance of a fighting woman, who, in the paroxysm of rage and revenge, brought forth a child, with all its bowels hanging out of its little body."[38]

Reason in pregnant women is apparently fragile. If, the doctor warns, a pregnant woman has a "more disgusting wish" to "partake with a flock of carrion-crows, which she saw feasting on the flesh of a dead horse," don't honor it! In spite of his claim that pregnancy is a naturally healthy state, Buchan is drawn to an image of the pregnant woman's bestial irrationality—even insanity—which in turn justifies her need for supervision and the physician's wisdom.[39]

Buchan observes that alcohol abuse poisons embryos, and sympathetically remarks that a poor woman ("the wretched hireling") is sometimes worked so hard by her employer when she's pregnant that she miscarries. He presciently describes the importance of cleanliness in the birthing room and cautions against excessive and damaging use of instruments (like forceps).[40]

Birth—in seventeenth- and eighteenth-century America and England—was often a communal and female event. Adrian Wilson has described how, when a woman went into labor, her husband traveled around the neighborhood gathering her friends. The women who attended ate and drank together, prepared the room, told stories. They soothed and held the mother-to-be as she gave birth. Depending on the temperament of one's female kin and neighbors, and the quality of the labor, this could have been a wonderful or an awful experience. Buchan sees the negative. He warns against "the noxiousness of the breath and perspiration of several people in a close room." Though supportive of midwives, he otherwise condemns the whole female culture of birthing, "the officious folly, the silly tattle, the inconsiderate language, the fluctuating hopes and fears of so many gossips, must be productive of the very worst effects."[41]

In many ways, Buchan is a progressive champion of social reform. Children—girls as well as boys—need to breathe good air, to run freely, to avoid contagion. Infants shouldn't be given physics to rid them of meconium, or put to sleep with opium, or constantly dosed with laxatives or emetics. His aversion to "dosing" children stems from his experience running a foundling hospital—he appears to have been horrified by what he himself witnessed. Foundling hospitals were started in the fourteenth century in order to respond to child death and infant abandonment. "In legend at any rate the origins of this movement can be traced to the moment when fishermen in Rome brought before Pope Innocent III (1198–1216) the bodies of babies who had been drowned in the Tiber." There were apparently so many that they regularly showed up in nets alongside the fish. Hugh Cunningham notes that many families in many centuries have been able to afford to raise only one or two children. What could they do?[42]

However humanitarian their genesis, in time foundling institutions became overwhelmed by numbers, and de facto functioned to kill abandoned children. How much of the killing was intentional, how much circumstantial, is hard to say. Buchan states that when he took over the foundling hospital in Ackworth, Yorkshire, half the children there died each year. He surmised that their deaths were in large measure from being overdrugged (apparently much to the profit of the local apothecary), and he ordered the practice stopped. The death rate plummeted, he claims, to around one in fifty.[43]

Buchan believes that overall not one in ten children survived in foundling hospitals. The death rates he cites for children assigned to parish (that is, local community) care in England are even worse. Not one in seventy, he believes, made it. He is appalled that poor children are routinely separated from their mothers and placed in such care. Could he be correct when he asserts that the institutions' nurses were specifically hired to murder their charges? "This testimonial of their expertness in murder, was deemed by the overseers, who had tried them, the strongest recommendation to constant employment."[44]

Buchan is an early child advocate. He rails against the deadly work conditions of chimney sweeps and against the hours girls are confined "at the needle in learning fancy works."[45] The nineteenth century is widely held to be the era in Western history when children began to receive more attention and organized protection. Witnessing poor children who languished in poverty, wealthy children who were deposited with wet nurses, and mothers who feared child bed death or child loss, Buchan works to minimize danger and to encourage engagement. He feels that if he can get mothers to relax, administer fewer poisons, and give themselves over to their infants and children, he can improve the life expectancy of the young.

On one level, Buchan's advice is sensible. On another, he oversteps badly, attributing infant and child death far too singularly to mothering, and child safety far too exclusively to maternal action; he even makes mothers into murderers. Using the new medical language, he helps to establish the dangerous practice of focusing children's well-being too narrowly on mothers' behavior. *Advice to Mothers* helped form new notions of mothering in the nineteenth-century United States. Catherine Scholten observes, "The argument that the care of young children is an exacting, time-consuming, and important activity that should be the center of women's lives had emerged clearly in didactic literature by 1830, along with the innovative contention that the mother is socially the most important parent."[46]

Buchan's ideal of the good mother — a creature unthreatening to any status quo — emerges most clearly when he compares mothers to inferior, hired nurses. He writes, "A hired person . . . has not the motives for subduing her passions, restraining her appetites, sacrificing her pleasures and her rest—in short, for practicing the self-devotion and self-control which the office of muse demands." The muse must be prepared cheerfully to give up everything to achieve glory.[47]

Buchan demonstrates the burden that society, by focusing too much of its hope on mothering, imposed on women. Once deemed important, mothers, and maternal misbehavior, can be held responsible without limit. Here is a small example he offers among many: "Let not the fairest part of the creation be offended with me for saying, that, in all cases of dwarfishness and deformity, ninety-nine out of a hundred are owing to the folly, misconduct or neglect of mothers."[48]

Perhaps, Buchan reflects, the state should pay mothers an annual premium for raising healthy children. "The effects of premiums have been proved in a variety of other instances, such as the cultivation of vegetables, the growth of flax . . . and the improvement of the breed of cattle. Is it not a matter of just surprise that no attention of this sort should ever have been paid to the personal or bodily improvement of the human species?"

Anticipating the bias of modern psychology, and revealing familiarity with Locke, he adds, "Everything great or good in future life, must be the effect of early impressions; and by whom are those impressions to be made but by mothers; who are most interested in their consequences?"[49] All the same, he finds, mothers are too emotional, become excessively fond of their children, and therefore turn them into less than robust adults. He makes criticisms that will later get taken up too enthusiastically by psychology. Mothers "do not seem to know the proper medium between cruel neglect or indifference on the one hand, and the fatal excesses of anxiety and fondness on the other. In giving way to the strong impulses of natural affection, they commonly go too far, and do as much mischief to their offspring by misguided tenderness, as by total insensibility."[50]

"A mother," Buchan chillingly asserts, "may blunder on, as most of them do, till she has killed a number of children, before she is capable of rearing one." Why? He believes that education destroys mothers by alienating them from nature, and murders children. A "genteel education" can make women so ignorant "of everything with which a mother ought to be acquainted that the infant itself is as wise in these matters as its parent." He opposes teaching girls painting, drawing, the playing of musical instruments, "which at best will afford them only a momentary gratification," when they would be much better "employed in practical lessons on the duties of wives and mothers . . . ignorance of which will cost them many an aching heart."[51]

Buchan's writings demonstrate how the helplessness of a well-meaning person can be transformed into misguided threats and emphatic instructions. Some of his insights are keen, and clearly the product of careful observation. But because he insists on ascribing too much child morbidity to maternal practice, he is unable to confront central issues: the extent of mothers' suffering, their social oppression, and their real helplessness. Surrounded by untreatable, sometimes inexorable illnesses, and all the contagion-breeding aspects of urban life, their best efforts often could not beat death.

Buchan popularized much that still haunts women today. By comparing mothers to deities, he declares them powerful. *Advice to Mothers* describes a better world populated by heroes, and rests that possibility on correct maternal devotion. This ideal becomes a renewed justification for controlling women's behavior. If she wishes to raise a hero, a mother must be very careful. She must stay home, pay "strict attention." She may not express passion, sexuality, melancholy, or anger. If she succeeds she will end the "degeneration" of the race. If she fails, she will kill her children.

A person placed on a pedestal—no matter how seductive the admiration—will eventually become queasy sensing the 360 degrees of possible missteps. Idealization is a sometime thing. What stability it has is maintained by devaluing everything that detracts from its perfection. For every glorified maternal trait, there must be a devalued counterpart.

The role Buchan and others offered to mothers at the beginning of the nineteenth century was a terribly complicated and ultimately rather deceptive social "gift"—a kind of Trojan horse. By publicly recognizing women's importance to children, experts made possible a new source of self-esteem for mothers. But they also raised expectations exorbitantly, and wantonly expanded the boundaries of responsibility. Furthermore, because the new power rested on idealization, no obligation was felt to back the mother's work with resources or political rights. Deification created a further bind: any goddess who demanded an earthly treasury de facto denied her heavenly place and risked losing the idealization. Yet, if she challenged the attribution, she lost what little the idealization offered her.

Freud wrote that "man has, as it were, become a kind of prosthetic God." We are as crude artificial limbs to an image of God's perfect being. Buchan demonstrates how mothers increasingly carried the liabilities of being but prosthetic goddesses. Traits, wishes, and desires once assigned to heaven gradually made their way back to earth. Furthermore, as infant and child mortality dropped toward the end of the nineteenth century, the notion of a potential superman, created or destroyed by mothering, would infect psychology.[52]

Real mothers, meanwhile, were weighed down by these burnished expectations—even as they embraced them. They became the pedestals on whom rested the great bronze statues of nursing, smiling, docile deities, placidly holding babes in arms.

From Medicine to Psychology

WHILE VASTLY DIFFERENT, *Iphigenia, Bacchae, A Token for Mourners,* and *Advice to Mothers* outline a common predicament—created by the confluence of mother love and threat of loss—that seems to transcend individual eras. A heightened vulnerability descends upon women when they become pregnant, give birth to children, and attempt to keep them safe. Fear of loss—accompanied or not by actual death—is a core part of mothers' emotional experience once they have attached to infants. This sometimes subliminal, sometimes overt apprehension guides decisions, as well as actions. The larger culture repeatedly engages mothers' concerns and anxieties, perhaps with generous intentions, perhaps not, often, it seems, to control women's behavior. A central recurring idea is that the well-being of children depends upon women staying, metaphorically and often literally, obediently within the four walls of the home.

We have seen Agave's punishment linked to her leaving her loom; Anne Hutchinson's miscarriage attributed to her speaking out forcefully in public; Increase Mather tying child death to insubordinate mother love; and William Buchan telling women who sought education that by abandoning the role nature intended for them, they would kill their babies. What are we to make of all these strictures and prohibitions? The speakers likely felt that their assertions flowed naturally from their authority. They wanted to create order, define moral and behavioral codes, make livings for themselves.

Some advice was compassionate and sensible. Nevertheless, kindness came hand in hand with intimidation. In John Flavel's terms, the rod was always waving above women's heads, ready to remind them of their transgressions. The effectiveness of the threats rested on the depth of maternal attachment and fear. If women did not care about keeping their children alive and safe, about doing right by them in a wide variety of ways, then the ideologies linking child safety to female submission, the reinforcing personal coercion, would have been less constant and effective. The writers would have told different stories.

In the course of the nineteenth and early twentieth centuries, medicine and psychology emerged as potent social voices, and sources of maternal guidance and sanction. During this same time period, the threat of death gradually became the quieter yet still menacing partner to a new, loud claim that mother's incorrect love was the primary source of children's imperfection and psychological harm. As child mortality fell[1] and mothers could no longer so readily be held responsible for killing children, the advice literature shifted to accuse mothers of destroying children's potential. While this thesis, as we have seen in John Abbott's *The Mother at Home* (1833), emerged long before as a moral claim—that is, Lord Byron's lazy mother made him decadent—proponents recast it as science and took it up with new fervor at the beginning of the twentieth century: but for maternal failings, each child could be a "superman." Few contemporary observers seemed curious about how comfortably the new fallacy wore the clothes of the old.

I want first to look briefly at this metamorphosis, to see how the professional advice template that Buchan helped to cut joined with the burgeoning power of the medical profession, and with social idealism, to create the form, stance, and philosophical bias that would determine the modern psychological view of mothers.

It is difficult to overstate the grotesque nature of much of what constituted nineteenth-century medical expertise about women and mothers.

When I was beginning to write this book, I serendipitously purchased a famous medical textbook called *Woman: Her Diseases and Remedies,* by Charles Meigs, M.D., an esteemed nineteenth-century American doctor and medical educator. The text, first published in 1850, went through many editions. Mine, the fourth, was printed in 1859. Although the book contains new knowledge and records significant medical advances, it is also a staggering compendium of ignorance, arrogance, and barely repressed sexual sadism, all delivered with upstanding intentions. Announcing his overall assessment of women and setting the tone—and the era's context—for the discussion, Meigs remarks, it is "easy to perceive that her intellectual force is different from that of her master and lord."[2]

Dr. Meigs observes how, as a medical man, he "can recognize the power of woman in the family"—and thus in all society, which he sees as "moulded and controlled by the gentler sex . . . But for the power of that female influence, which one of you would doubt the rapid relapse of society into the violence and chaos of the earliest barbarism?" Meigs also lists what women cannot do: administrate, battle, understand "the course of planets," speak in public, compose great literature, or govern. "She reigns in the heart; her seat and throne are by the hearth-stone. The household altar is her place of worship and service." As many have pointed out, this division helped finesse the devaluing of women's home labor while rationalizing the denial of their right to participate as equals in the public world.[3]

Examples of misguided pontificating are rife. The doctor states categorically that patients with dysmenorrhea (menstrual pain) will be infertile, that physicians do not spread puerperal fever, that women who menstruate before age fourteen or fifteen are likely to die early. He describes casually how to cure an inflamed uterus by dropping leeches through the speculum onto the patient's cervix. "Drop three or four Swedish leeches into the open end of the speculum, and push them down to the bottom with a bit of sponge large enough to keep them from coming out again."[4]

Meigs's techniques may have been the best his era could avail, his mistakes a necessary step in the development of modern medicine. To his credit, the doctor moves problems like miscarriage out of the realm of moral failing. He believes in physical exercise as a basis of good health. He cautions his students against horrendous—yet apparently accepted—practices like the daily cauterizing of a woman's cervix with nitrate of silver, a burning agent; or sending women with uterine difficulties to bed for months. Also, with rare enlightenment, Meigs cites the clitoris as the anatomical center of women's sexual responsiveness, a fact quickly denied by later psychoanalytic "experts."[5]

Good medicine or bad, a major achievement of *Woman* is to develop further the authority of medicine. However ignorant, the doctor perceives more than the patient. Through his specialized knowledge, he knows her in ways she cannot know herself. Thanks to Meigs's text, we can witness at first hand an example of the casual, but stunning, way this new power is used to discredit the patient's subjective experience in the name of superior scientific expertise. Several decades later the same template will characterize Freud's early psychoanalytic cases, like "Dora," in which pompous pronouncements mix with keen insights.

Dr. Meigs visits a woman with an abscessed breast, and asks her if her breast hurts. Here is their exchange, which begins with the doctor's inquiry:

> "Which of the breasts hurts you?—the right or the left one?"
> "My breast doesn't hurt me, doctor."
> "Yes it does."
> "No, doctor!"

He then asks to touch her breast, and does. "Ouch," she exclaims, and adds, "Why, I did not know that I had anything the matter with the breast!"

He answers, "But I did, you see."

> "It is very strange that you should know that I had a pain, when I myself didn't know that I had it."
> "No, it is not at all strange; it is very easy to know that; because it is very easy to perceive in the rate of your pulse, your breathing, your heart; in the tint of your complexion; in your physiognomical

expression; in your gesture and attitude; in the absence of pain in the abdomen; in the state of your intellect, evinced by your answers to my questions, that nothing else could be the matter with you."[6]

Thanks to his new scientific techniques, the doctor is more astute than his patient, about *her* body. He knows what she is feeling before she does, even in her own breast, symbolically the emotional center of her being. Since pain is rather the sine qua non of intimate subjectivity, his abilities are extraordinary and omniscient. It seems he has married the older—and now waning—social power of the minister with the insight of a god.

This exchange anticipates the future in medicine. When science improves and doctors acquire better technology—MRIs, CT scans, blood tests, and electron microscopes—the doctor actually will be able to see more than the patient can. It's fascinating and a little frightening to observe how the claim precedes the tools, and has a life of its own. The same notion, that the psychoanalyst can see what is invisible to the patient about her own mind, becomes a basic assumption of early psychoanalysis.

Sexual predation disguised as medical care, also sometimes a problem in psychotherapy, is manifest in this text. During a trip Dr. Meigs pays to a "magnificent Hospital" in Brussels in 1845, he admires the work of a Dr. Grauiex and proudly recounts Grauiex's treatment of a woman with a bladder infection and painful urination. His report is noteworthy less for the certainty of cure, than for his unself-conscious satisfaction in the beautiful patient's submission: "[W]e arrived at the bedside of a very fine-looking young woman, about 22 years of age . . . I found she had been for a considerable length of time under treatment of a catarrhus vesicae, and that she had made no progress towards a cure. The frequent micturition was painful and annoying."

After examining her, Dr. Grauiex "passed a long seton [needle] from side to side, near the upper edge or limit of the mons veneris, to the great chagrin and vexation of the young girl. *But Dr. Grauiex was master in the case and she was obliged to submit.*" (Italics added.)[7]

The seton needle was several inches long and typically attached to a piece of cotton and linen that was pulled into an infected area and then left for a while to help it drain. Whether a bladder infection could have been relieved by a procedure that pushed an unsterilized, often unwashed, needle through a girl's genital area, is unclear. It may have been the most efficacious treatment available, or it may have amounted to malpractice. In either case, the piercing of the young woman, together with the claim of submission, tells as important a story as the "science" of the approach.[8]

Nineteenth-century medicine is grimly fascinating. And these texts underscore how much, in the absence of solid knowledge, authorities are drawn to resist their helplessness by confabulating, a technique used continually when advising mothers. They (we, the culture, the *Zeitgeist*) invent answers and cures no doubt to feel competent and to create a certain facade of order, but often at the expense of the less powerful, like mothers. Looking back, it's easy to see how experts stretch to cover gaps in learning by asserting a ripe mix of unconscious sexual fantasy, of pseudofact shaped by cultural bias and stereotype.

The inevitable default position of ignorance is to prefer those falsehoods that mirror existing power structures. Some might compare assessing a 150-year-old medical text to the bad sportsmanship of shooting fish in a barrel. We know so much more now, embrace different biases, and make our own errors, so we should be gentle with the past, and respectful of its contexts.

Some also would argue that the rhetorical patterns, the authoritarian assertions by experts, have themselves been useful—even lifesaving. Simply following instructions, or rituals of cure, sometimes heals people, however unlikely the procedures. When you are ill, unsure, or frightened, and someone to whom you have assigned authority claims with certainty that he can make you or the situation better, you often relax and feel safer. There's little doubt, for example, that just such an ability was the source of Rasputin's destructive power in the Russian court of Czar Nicholas and his wife, Alexandra. The couple's hemophiliac son, Alexis, whom they adored, was often on death's edge. Alexandra felt completely desperate and helpless. The treacherous monk was able, apparently by hypnotically calming the terrified mother and child, to make the boy stop bleeding when no one else could.

Rasputin is a good example, for he also represents the harm of the charismatic and omniscient dimension of the expert's stance, the problematic giving over of the self that it invites, the misplaced worship, the sexual confusion, the hunger for relief, the foolish judgments that can then be exploited. Alexandra was so grateful to have Alexis spared that she trusted Rasputin too completely, to her detriment, her family's, and perhaps to her nation's. In his biography about Nicholas and Alexandra and the events that led up to the Russian Revolution, Robert K. Massie writes, "Gradually, Alexandra became convinced that [Rasputin] was a personal emissary from God to her, to her husband and to Russia."[9]

The czarina's sorry conviction illustrates exactly how intense anxiety and love for children can lead women to complicity with (even enthusiasm for) bad decisions and bogus experts. Discussing the appeal of fortunetellers, a character in Shirley Hazzard's novel *The Bay of Noon* observes, "What's alluring is the illusion, not even of power, but of authority. Isn't that what we want from gods, priests, poets, even from those columns in the newspaper that answer letters? The possibility that someone really knows, and has got the upper hand of it all."[10] Indeed, it is hard to think of a situation riper for experts than a mother desperate to keep a child alive and ready to blame herself if she cannot.

Professional expertise is based on the premise that knowledge builds legitimate authority. But the edges—what is actually known versus what is merely theorized and claimed, what is relevant but ignored—are messy. Meigs's account emphasizes female inferiority and submission.

Meigs's tone, his unearned certainty, also characterizes the burgeoning advice on child-rearing. With fewer children and less overwhelming physical work, nineteenth-century white middle-class mothers, in theory, had more time to focus on each child. Experts encouraged them to devote themselves to children. This shift of emphasis created a cultural expectation of intensified maternal focus, the absence of which, by the twentieth century, would become the basis for accusations of psychological harm.

Comparing Lydia Hill Almy, a woman raising children at the end of the eighteenth century, with Mary Hurlbut just thirty years later, Nancy Cott, in her now classic book *The Bonds of Womanhood,* offers an example of the early-nineteenth-century transition in mothering ideals and expectations. Cott notes how, in addition to mothering, the eighteenth-century Almy "not only kept house but let rooms, collected firewood, attended to livestock, and arranged to sell tanned skins."[11]

What is remarkable is that Lydia Almy felt that her two children were "grown out of the way" and "very little troble" when, as Cott observes, "the younger was not yet weaned." Her mothering work was considered to be mostly over when her children were maybe two and four years old! Cott writes, "Mary Hurlbut, in contrast, appeared solely concerned with her children's lives and prospects."

Mothers in America in the 1830s no doubt had a wide range of feelings about how much care and attentive rearing a child ought to get, and resources to realize their ideas varied as well. Cott's story does not necessarily mean that mothers suddenly worked harder rearing children, although some may have. It is possible that—made more self-conscious by the new ideology of motherhood—they conceptualized their efforts differently. For example, rather than teaching a boy his alphabet because it had to be done, you taught it to him because that made you a devoted mother and him a good citizen.

At the very moment some white women were urged to place more emphasis on mothering, more slave women were having children taken from them and sold. Their right to rear their babies was denied, even as they were beginning to be romanticized as surrogate "mammies." Read Harriet Jacobs's slave narrative and you will see that one focus of her extraordinary resistance is protecting her children; she struggles to outwit her master, who seeks to sell her son and daughter as a way of punishing her for not complying with his sexual demands. (The sociologist Arlie Russell Hochschild points out that the kind of callous substitution slave mothers faced continues; wealthy Americans import nannies from poorer countries forcing them to abandon their own children in order to earn the money to feed them. Few American employers make any provisions to help the nannies visit, live with, or even stay in touch with their own children.)[12]

Cott pinpoints a moment within the larger trend of the rising expectations of mothers, a phenomenon that has continued to the present.

Mothering moved into the spotlight. Child-rearing increasingly became the area (under the general rubric of homemaking) in which women were allowed to act and, at least covertly, to compete and excel. Experts rushed to define the endeavor, and many mothers signed on, enthusiastic to have a more worthy mission for their otherwise devalued lives.

The emphasis on the heightened importance of mothers, together with the sidelining of fathers, are trends that gather steam across the next 150 years. One odd symmetry is the way the father's lessening authority at home is mirrored by the emergence of new status for secular experts. Ann Hulbert, writing about "scientific motherhood," a movement, at the turn of the twentieth century, to make women better mothers by training them to behave scientifically, notes that the experts had become "the modern parent's modern parent." She might well have added "husband."[13]

And, as Hulbert notes, as the century progressed, science entered the mothering picture in a big way. If women were to produce improved children, suited for the new "scientific" world, they would have to learn how to mother better. And so they needed scientific experts. Hulbert quotes an almost giddy 1890s editorial in the *New York Times* which—amplifying the idealism Buchan had expressed a hundred years earlier—claimed that once scientists taught mothers, mothers would improve the world. "Given one generation of children properly born and wisely trained, and what a vast proportion of human ills would disappear from the face of the earth!" Theoretically enlightened by their knowledge of science, the experts could teach women new mothering for a new century. While husbands were at work, scientists would guide their wives and perfect their children.[14]

Unfortunately, the new scientific motherhood subscribed to the old system of threat. Rima D. Apple describes the message in a typical advertisement for baby food which deftly raises mothers' anxiety about infant mortality, while disguising its primary wish to sell a product:

> An 1885 Mellin's Food advertisement from the child-care journal *Babyhood* is headed "Advice to Mothers" and the body of the copy cautions readers: "The swelling tide of infantile disease and mortality, resulting

from injudicious feeding, the ignorant attempts to supply a substitute for human milk, can only be checked by enlightened parental care." The advertisement goes on to say most reassuringly: "Men of the highest scientific attainments of modern times, both physiologists and chemists, have devoted themselves to careful investigation and experiment in devising a suitable substitute for human milk." The result, of course, was Mellin's Food, a food "worthy the confidence of mothers."[15]

In other words, ignorant mothers are buying bad milk, which kills their babies. If women want their children to live, they must do what experts say, and buy formula from Mellin. Mothers, hoping to keep their children safe, scan the environment for information. Experts appear with authoritative answers. By the late nineteenth century, advertisers, piggybacking on the new interest in science, had joined in manipulating mothers' fears.

One significant voice in the scientific motherhood movement was that of Ellen Key (1849–1926), a single, childless Swedish feminist, who wrote a series of highly opinionated books about mothering and marriage, which were published in America in the first two decades of the twentieth century. Several recent writers have called *The Century of the Child* and *Love and Marriage* "bestsellers." Key became an icon, and her ideas had wide influence.

A 1914 *Harper's Weekly* piece referred to Ellen Key as the "intellectual chief" of the world feminist movement. *Collier's* claimed in 1916 that she was "known all over the world." In 1913 Putnam's Sons published a biography of Key translated from the Swedish with an introduction by Havelock Ellis, perhaps the best-known English psychologist of the era. Edward Bok, the famous editor of the *Ladies' Home Journal,* wrote a foreword to one of Key's books. The biography, together with the fact that these men associated themselves with her work, suggests her contemporary stature. Madeleine Z. Doty, a *Good Housekeeping* correspondent who interviewed Key in 1918, described her as the source of freedom for Swedish women. Newly minted Swedish laws—providing equal education for women, divorce, inheritance rights for illegitimate children, and maternity care for working women—were said to be the "greatest testimonial to Ellen Key."[16]

I quote some of the paeans to demonstrate Key's appeal and her accomplishments because her ideas about motherhood and eugenics in *The Century of the Child,* although occasionally insightful, are mostly confused and sometimes repugnant. Indeed, a few of her contemporaries were not fans. A *New York Times* reviewer of *Century* found her argument "sloppy in method and expression." Perhaps the most scathing—and perceptive—critique of Key was articulated by the British writer Rebecca West in a 1915 *New Republic* article entitled "Eroto-Priggery." Arguing that Key's view of motherhood ill-served real women, West grasped the fundamental problem: "this idea that the interests of the woman are equal and identical with that of the child is extremely reactionary." West alone comprehended that the equation negated mothers without necessarily doing anything for children; she challenged Key's construction of an ideal world based on a mystical level of maternal devotion and reverence for children.[17]

The Century of the Child expressed dubious sentiments about human perfectibility that would also bore into psychology and infect it for decades, while its title gave rise to the pernicious assumption that you could honor or aid the child without broadly concerning yourself with the mother as a person in her own right. In *Century,* earlier ideas, like Buchan's, narrowly idealizing mothers and basing salvation upon their devotion to infants, got new life and language for the twentieth century, and began to adopt a psychological form.

Key believed that "the future destiny of the human race" could be determined by understanding the "religion of development."[18] Advocating a mystical notion of social change based in perfectly devoted child-rearing, Key helped escalate demands upon mothers. She believed that mothers must give up everything for children, and that their dedication must be scientific as well as zealous. Moreover, by focusing on the mother-child relationship as the central source of social hope, she contributed to what would become the century's myopic and excruciating examination of imperfect mothering as the cause of human and social ills.

Key was infatuated with eugenics. She casually borrowed from its ideas about degeneracy to define new possibilities for harm—other than death—that mothers could inflict upon children. Some of her interpretations were quite idiosyncratic. For example, according to Key, women who conceived children without passionately loving their partners created a degenerate race. Embracing notions from "Darwinian writers" and the new science of psychology, Key insisted that specialists must teach citizens how to prevent depraved reproduction. "[T]he criminal must be prevented from handing on his characteristics to his posterity . . . Then comes the requirement that those with inherited physical or psychical diseases shall not transmit them to an offspring . . ." (Such ideas, widely popular in Europe and America before World War II, provided the rationale for Nazi doctors' killing 750,000 mentally and psychologically deficient "degenerates" in the 1940s.)[19]

Key believed degeneracy would be controlled, the world made new, if men and women united when they first fell deeply in love: "this race would be sound and strong, different from what our own race is now." Maternal devotion would be core. "The time will come in which the child will be looked upon as holy . . . all motherhood will be looked upon as holy, if it is caused by a deep emotion of love and if it has called forth the deep feelings of duty." Once mothers devoted themselves totally to pure love and child duty, life would progress to ever higher forms: "the completed man—the superman—will be bathed in . . . sunshine."[20]

While devoted mothers would provide the means toward salvation for the race, achieving such ends "requires an entirely new conception of the vocation of mother, a tremendous effort of will, continuous inspiration." Key added, "It needs tremendous power to do one's duty to a single child." This effort was so demanding that mothers should not work to earn a living or participate more than occasionally in social activities.[21]

Overall, Key articulated anew a polarization that placed women's autonomy at odds with the rights of the child. She wrote, "[I]t will be regarded as a crime for a young wife voluntarily to ill-treat her person, either by excessive study, or excessive attention to sports, by smoking or the use of stimulants, by sitting up at night, excessive work or by all the

thousan
ture, un

Key
defined
creating
in one's l
the cold
finds us i
truth tha
being use
smallest u
leave wou
the end ol
misfortun
part of the

To her
ficult for w
exploited w
an eight-ho
corporal pu
Sundays, an
how to refo
strengths of
to be treatec
child?"24

Neverthel
called "reacti
thrive if, and
omy, politica
ticipation in t
children woul
ted it with ne
wish that chil
with eugenics,
ity and to wha

still in my mind's eye are pictures from an old newspaper clipping I saw in an exhibition some years ago at Ellis Island. The photographs were of women "before and after" they received consultations from social workers helping them "Americanize." Their husbands had often immigrated years ahead of them, and, according to the reporter, felt embarrassed by their unassimilated wives. In the before pictures the women wore long hair and many layers of peasant skirts. Afterward, they smiled shyly, and modeled cute pixie cuts and fashionable outfits.)

Mobility and urban heterogeneity also interrupted transmission of relatively coherent communal ideas about child-rearing. The intergenerational flow of knowledge was both disrupted and devalued. At the same time, more women were attending high school and college, and, through education, coming to value information. Newspapers and magazines, like those that published Key, proliferated and helped to define (and respond to) a modern style of mothering with new requirements.

Finally, the American economy continued gradually to move away from traditional activities—like farming—to newer ones like factory and office work. How to rear a child, what skills and virtues to have her practice and master, became less obvious when no longer based in necessity. Whereas a little girl once might have imitated her mother spinning wool, and a little boy might have imitated his father plowing—and from a young age both would have learned skills by performing such tasks—modern adult work was becoming less visible, less concretely comprehensible, and less tolerant of youthful assistance. This transition contributed to mothers' feelings of uncertainty about how they should direct their efforts in child-rearing. For what adulthood were they preparing their children?

Many advice writers rushed to address the modern social disruption and capitalize on new interest in science and knowledge. But how helpful were their ideas? Just when a mother could begin to count on her child's living, she learned that she had better not feel relief. Chances were good that if she simply followed her instincts, or replicated the mothering she had experienced herself, she would create a degenerate or an emotional invalid.

John B. Watson was the maverick founder of behavioral psychology who worked as an early childhood researcher at Johns Hopkins University. Forced to leave when he decided he loved a female student more than his wife, he entered the field of advertising and made a fortune pioneering the use of psychology to create product "image" and raise sales. Watson then began writing popular psychology pieces for leading magazines and eventually wrote two successful, influential books, one on behaviorism, the other offering advice on child-rearing.[27]

Without describing the whole of John Watson's mostly horrific best-selling book *Psychological Care of Infant and Child* (1928), I want to look at the rationales he offers to mothers as to why they ought to follow his advice. First the threat: while, Watson suggested, mistakes in feeding a child can be fixed and ill health treated (note the new absence of death), "once a child's character has been spoiled by handling which can be done in a few days, who can say that the damage is ever repaired?"[28]

Then the gambit—which illustrates how carefully Watson worked to convince mothers that what they thought they knew, what they believed they had learned from their own mothers, was useless—and, indirectly, that resisting Watson's ideas would be harmful to their children:

> We have only just begun to believe that there is such a thing as the psychological care of infants and children.
>
> A great many mothers still resent being told how to feed their children. Didn't their grandmothers have fourteen children and raise ten of them? Didn't their own mothers have six and eight children and raise them all—and they never needed a doctor to tell them how to feed them? That many of the grandmother's children grew up with rickets, with poor teeth, with under-nourished bodies, generally prone to every kind of disease means little to the mother who doesn't want to be told how to feed her child scientifically . . .
>
> Parents—mothers especially—resent still more strenuously any advice or instructions on how to care psychologically for their children.[29]

In other words: Your grandmother and mother had it wrong. Their ignorance killed or harmed children. If you do as they did, if you resist the new science of psychology, you will do the same. And although you might wish to reject these ideas, your inclination simply offers more evidence that you are not a scientific mother, you are a damaging one.

Lest mothers miss it the first time, Watson repeated his threat often—as when he declared, "There are too many people in the world now—too many people with crippled personalities—tied up with such a load of infantile carry-overs (due to faulty bringing up) that they have no chance for happy lives." He added, "No one today knows enough to raise a child."[30]

Watson mostly attacked mothers' affection. He repeatedly declared that love ruined children. "In conclusion won't you then remember when you are tempted to pet your child that mother love is a dangerous instrument? An instrument which may inflict a never healing wound, a wound which may make infancy unhappy, adolescence a nightmare, an instrument which may wreck your adult son or daughter's vocational future and their chances for marital happiness."[31]

Watson played upon insecurities women felt about being part of a rapidly modernizing world. How should they raise children to help them manage this new order? He threatened awful consequences, undermined forcefully those feelings of nurturant tenderness central to many mother's identities—the precise feelings that most nineteenth-century advice givers had sought to intensify. However much women may have rejected some of his ideas, his approach illustrates well the way that mothers were continually shoved and elbowed—made to feel more uncertain, less knowledgeable—by the new scientific admonitions.

Watson modeled his book on L. Emmett Holt's extremely successful advice guide *The Care and Feeding of Children* (1894), which had focused primarily on physical and medical care. One example from Holt will give a good idea of how hard experts worked to devalue traditional maternal practices and push authoritative science. (To heighten *his* authority, Holt referred to his own text as "the Catechism" and presented it all in a question-and-answer format!) Here is his advice on infant bath temperature, something, need I say, that mothers had managed to work out for themselves since the beginning of time—often after they'd hauled the water, gathered the wood, and built the fire. And while Holt's warm bath was probably nicer for infants than the seventeenth century's "toughening" cold baths, the degree-by-degree precision can have no purpose but self-aggrandizement for the expert:

At what temperature should the bath be given?
     For the first few weeks at 100 F.; later, during early infancy, at 98 F.; after six months, at 95 F.; during the second year, from 85 to 90 F.[32]

By looking at one more bit of Holt's text, we can see, rather remarkably, another clear example of how the older death threat transitioned—between Holt and Watson—to the new psychological damage. To the question *"Are there any valid objections to kissing infants?"* Holt answered, "There are many serious objections. Tuberculosis, diphtheria, and many other grave diseases may be communicated in this way." Holt left ambiguous whether the mother herself might kiss the child. But he specifically disallowed kisses by nurses and children, and forbade all kisses on the mouth. For very young infants, his advice was doubtless sound, even sometimes lifesaving. Yet he made no distinctions by age, and the tone of the text suggests that his constraints on the practice had as much to do with philosophy as contagion. Thirty years later, Watson created a rationale of psychological harm for the same prohibition.[33]

When my first child was born in 1982, my grandmothers—one from Russia whom I never met, the other from Italy—were dead. But my mother and mother-in-law were alive and healthy. They each visited occasionally, cooked, helped out, enjoyed their grandchildren. We talked on the telephone. Yet neither they nor I assumed that they would teach me their hard-won mothering skills. There was no sense of vital traditions, nor of authority granted to them by the culture to hold or pass on crucial knowledge.

     I remember, growing up, that my mother had copies of child-rearing books by Benjamin Spock and Arnold Gesell. When as a parent I felt confused—daily—I sometimes read T. Berry Brazelton, Penelope Leach, an updated Spock, and others—often with mixed feelings. Or, I sought out neighbors or friends with children close enough in age, maybe just slightly older, who would answer questions or offer useful tidbits. (One kind neighbor had, in the course of her own toddler's long hospitalization for a life-threatening illness, learned to use a stethoscope. During the early years of our older son's life, whenever he caught a virus, I would start to worry. How sick was he? Did he need a doctor? And, of course, the unstated and absurd yet real fear: Could he have something exotic that would kill him? She, hearing my anxiety—and total ignorance—would rush across the street, listen carefully to the baby's breathing, count his pulse, put on a solemn, professional face, and reassure me that he was managing just fine. The stethoscope gave our ritual wonderful pomp. Then we'd sit down, laugh, have tea, and enjoy a good talk.)

Looking back, what seems interesting is my absence of confidence in the preceding generation's experiences. I don't think it is simply because both my mother and mother-in-law hold their knowledge modestly, or that neither woman lived in our town, that they didn't seek to convey more, though all these circumstances contributed. I think it is because we had all imbibed a societal gestalt, a feeling that too much was new and particular to the moment to make their experience of thirty years earlier terribly relevant. Part of this diffidence was doubtless from the insidious and pervasive devaluing of mothers that had characterized the era in which they raised us. But, also, I think we may have shared an unarticulated illusion that somehow, along with spectacular technological improvements, whether in spacecraft or food processors, there must have been a similar evolution in the requisite mothering techniques. What I needed to know I couldn't get from the last generation of mothers; it would be out there in the culture, discovered by psychologists, neurologists, biologists, and pediatricians.

It seems that each time a society changes, mothers, intimate transmitters of culture, are given new instructions about children, and new warnings about what constitutes failure. It's difficult to tease apart how much scientific advice to mothers benefited children and how much it simply draped a modern guise over efforts to direct maternal behavior. As we observed in the last chapter, a glaring problem with idealized motherhood as a source of esteem for mothers is that it tends to be unstable.

Once the inflated fantasy is disappointed, mothers become a large target for rabid blame. And defining maternal psychological failure became the order of the day in the twentieth century.[34]

So, to pick one example among many collected by Molly Ladd-Taylor and Lauri Umansky in their book *"Bad" Mothers: The Politics of Blame in Twentieth-Century America,* when racist America panicked about maintaining whiteness, particularly in the decades after World War II, white mothers "failed"—and had children taken from them by courts all around the country—if they divorced white men and remarried African American men. About the same time, other sociologists and psychologists blamed white Southern mothers (who were said to be too domineering) for *their* sons' racism. Ruth Feldstein summarizes the experts' analysis: "Racism in white men emerged as a result of feelings of sexual inadequacy and 'impotence' (a word that abounds in this discourse) and unresolved Oedipal conflicts—all of which white mothers helped to create." In other words, social science explorations focused so singularly on mothers that they managed to dismiss the complexity and reality of the political landscape.[35]

Overall, there emerged in the course of the twentieth century an enormous confusion about the limits, if any, of maternal responsibility: of what mothers should be able to offer children, and what children should expect to receive. If, suddenly, some women (more than the tiny elites of past centuries) had time, leisure, education, and relative prosperity, how much of themselves should they dedicate to their children to create mini "supermen"? What form should their dedication take? And what was good, what harmful, in their love?

Some of the new advice was enlightened and useful. But often, even the best of it arrived encased in threats. The result was an unfortunate synergy created by mixing heightened expectations with more precise scientific blame. New standards appeared making mothers accountable first for degeneracy and then for psychological harm, by loving wrong and creating psychological invalids or racists.

Close examination of advice books does not reveal overriding scientific worth in the experts' contribution. Indeed, the new professionals often trafficked in absurdity, self-aggrandizement, devaluation, and fear.

A lot of their pronouncements were pure gobbledygook dignified with words like "Darwin" or "Fahrenheit." Again, L. Emmett Holt, M.D.:

Do the emotions of the mother affect the milk?
    They have a very marked effect upon it; uncontrolled emotions such as grief, excitement, fright, passion, or excessive worry, or even extreme fatigue, may cause the milk, to disagree with an infant or even make it acutely ill.[36]

Mothers' passionate feelings alter breast milk to endanger babies? As we saw, several nineteenth-century medical men also thought so, but in Holt the threat is illness instead of death. It seems that the anxiety about the mother who, unchaperoned, might become passionate, feckless, and abandon the hearth was always present. To quiet her, experts simply—perhaps even unintentionally—equated with child loss and harm those of her inclinations that made them uneasy.

9

The Psychoanalytic Searchlight

THE IDEAS that define and confine mothers are like the wily god Proteus: they shift quickly, assume new shapes readily, so that both their enduring and more transient fallacies manage to remain well camouflaged. We can see the bias entangled in past advice, because time brings about such revelations. But as quickly as we recognize one presentation, the creature assumes another.

In the simplest sense, each new advice book (and I am using advice books to reflect and represent various webs of ideas and attitudes present in a culture at a given moment) holds its bit of power—more than a bit when it successfully helps to create and maintain an orthodoxy. Each at once addresses, soothes, and exploits the mother's primordial wish to protect, her fears of child loss, her accompanying uncertainties, and her awareness of her own limitations. What if she dies and abandons her children? What if she is inadequate, inattentive, or worse? What if she defies the rules? She won't get it right. What is right? Her children will suffer. It will somehow be her fault. She will turn away at the wrong moment, do the wrong thing, or feel the wrong feeling. Like the mother in *The Weir*, she might arrive at the swim meet a few minutes too late, delayed by work, perhaps by momentarily preferring to work, only to learn her daughter has died. If a child died, as one mother I spoke with said for many, "It would be the end of life as I know it."[1]

The writer Peggy Orenstein, who interviewed two hundred contemporary women, including many mothers, observed that "The phrase 'Bad Mother' affects women like kryptonite." Orenstein picked an apt metaphor. The threat of being revealed as a bad mother, of falling under the shadow of Agave, of feeling responsible for damaging a child, of inflicting harm without intending to do so, haunts mothers.[2]

The bad mother has been invoked throughout history; flattened into an ugly cartoon, she is a political commonplace. One of my sons, reading in a course about America during the Cold War, asked wryly if I knew that mothers in the 1950s made psychological errors that created Communism and homosexuality in their children? I offered him a few more items for his list. The nagging sense of badness so many mothers feel, the pleading look they give me when I say I'm writing a book, comes from being scraped raw by the endless public stories about the dire consequences of failing, the inflated notions of what mothers ought to do, and the ugly insinuations of how they can so quickly run a child off the rails: one wrong maternal love-move and your boy's Pink.

The bad mother is also summoned by mothers to describe other mothers. I remember gossiping with several women whom I barely knew while standing on the side of a soccer field one frigid November day almost a decade ago, watching our small children scramble in the slippery mud, the bunch of us miserable, comforting ourselves by guardedly clucking about a mother who never appeared, and whose son often had no way home if one of us did not drive him. At that moment, we were not interested in her story (or that of her equally no-show husband). She was useful only as our foil, our whipping mom. The cold, angled rain crept down our necks in spite of umbrellas. We wanted to feel better, to make sense of our own expenditure of unpleasant time by buffing its virtue with a handy comparison. Of course, one price of this moment was that ever after I felt worse when I missed my sons' games or performances. I became *her*, all the while knowing how *we* felt.

However much mothers may participate in passing the blame, many of the most significant and insidious ideas about the bad mother during the past century have come out of the world of psychology and psychotherapy. Lots of writers, myself included, have critiqued aspects of this view. Still it endures; blaming mothers dies hard.[3]

These new warnings from psychology followed precisely on the heels of the old religious and medical ones, just as the threat of death was diminishing. In part, the transition signals a burst of optimism, a kind of passionate progress, a wish to make a better world: now that children are living, we must make their lot better by examining the psychological qualities of mothering. But it's hard not to suspect equally that an old construct was seeking new fodder.

Women I spoke with mentioned repeatedly how they felt mothers as a group were made too responsible for their children's behavior. As one mother gently put it, if a child in her daughter's toddler daycare manifested any aggression, got into fights with other children, the adults talking about the situation, teachers, fathers, other mothers, would "gravitate toward judging the mom."[4] And what was being judged? In the past, a Puritan child, for example, might have been criticized on matters of conduct, and her mother for inadequately imbuing an awe of God and fear of hell. But now, without defining the particular contents of the compost pile of psychological notions that each of us has accumulated simply by living in this culture, people tend to assume in their judgments that the mother has made some psychological error that has led to a behavioral problem. Or, simply, that she is inadequate and cannot do right by her child.

The same woman, a sensitive and loving mother, offered an example of a bit of everyday painful judging she'd experienced. She had brought her almost two-year-old in for a routine visit to see their pediatrician. The parents, knowing that their daughter enjoyed the comfort of nursing from a bottle—and understanding from having lived abroad that it was okay in other countries to wean children later than Americans usually did—felt that it was appropriate to give the child a bottle in the morning and another at night. The pediatrician's response at checkup time was an angry condemnation, "I can't believe you have let this go this long!" The mother felt terrible—embarrassed and taken aback.[5]

A comment that sounds merely crotchety on a neutral subject humiliates when it touches on how a woman parents, particularly when it's an area in which a mother feels conflicted or uncertain: she knows the popular advice; she knows her child; she has feelings of her own; she is trying to find a balance. She wants badly to be a good mother—and to be recognized as one. Since as a society we give pediatricians power to judge mothering, the criticism packs a harder slap. The mother in such situations often reflexively feels shamed and incompetent. Her feelings may get misattributed to personal pathology, but are more usefully understood as the legacy and ongoing cost of group life. Indeed, the interaction reveals the function of shame in imbuing shared notions about how mothers should be.

Shame on you: In this tribe we don't . . . In this family we don't . . . In this pediatric office we don't . . . One way to understand shame is as a universal human mechanism for regulating individual behavior to conform to group practices for the sake of collective survival. Shame facilitates the quick and effective transmission of intimate standards and draws its power from the individual's wish to remain lovable. Its enormous benefits are in constructing coherent behaviors and attitudes in groups and minimizing conflict through semiconscious, often almost subliminal, consensus building. This act is acceptable to us; that one is not. Shame is one of the central mechanisms for inscribing gender behaviors. Boys don't cry . . . girls don't command . . . good mothers don't . . .

Shame is a powerful and primitive feeling. It becomes problematic in contemporary life in which groups are heterogeneous, in which members may aspire to greater autonomy and independence of practice, intimate and otherwise. Who is the referent "we"? Feelings of shame make people particularly susceptible to being cowed by authoritative statements on delicate matters. Shame doesn't quickly give quarter to eccentricity, to any largish quirk; it prefers that people go along, get along, and hide their differences. After ruminating and talking with others, a person can put the shaming statement in its place; but it often requires ongoing effort.

There are areas in which each mother is more readily embarrassed or humiliated, and areas in which she is less so. Some of the distinctions are private and quite personal, others are the legacy of communal life and social standards. The deep mandate to do right by children makes mothers super-responsive to certain kinds of shame statements, like the pediatrician's, or those of other mothers. Because the wish to be found lovable and worthy is at the center of shame, a standard of mothering based on correct love is perfectly designed to generate tremors and earthquakes of misery in women. For it first demands that the mother expose herself and live in the fullest vulnerability of loving, it then examines and finds her lacking, and, finally, it attributes the child's suffering to the imperfect way she offers love and guidance. Because our culture remains saturated with mother hating, mothers particularly—subliminally but continually—fear that a small lapse will reveal a large, shameful flaw.

We don't know the private or professional sources of the doctor's remark to the mother about weaning her child, but it seems she held strong opinions about nursing, dependence, independence, nutrition, tooth decay, and so on, and that her reaction was likely informed on some level by ideas she thought she had gleaned from psychology. A good mother weans her child by age . . . in order to foster appropriate . . . independence? Bad mothers . . . encourage unhealthy . . . dependence? (As if it were easy to tell which was what, as if such local values were sacrosanct.)

In a similar vein, another mother described a critical and condemning attitude she experienced from her son's elementary school teacher. "If your kids do have problems, then you *must* be doing something wrong," she offered. "That was certainly the message we got from the teacher: that we were doing things wrong at home. We were told, 'You need to have him take more responsibility. When he comes home have him put his coat away, put his shoes away . . .' And it was like they didn't ask what we did have him do."[6]

What is old, perhaps almost timeless, in these stories is the push and pull between community authorities and mothers/parents about how a child should act, and how to respond to his misbehavior. What is new, historically speaking, is the way that psychology, with its particular conventions of correct child development and its accompanying doubts about mothers, now provides the norms and informs the exchanges. In neither story did the professional ask the mother about her own thinking, a lapse that I believe is fairly characteristic—whether because of time constraints or attitude. Both mothers were surprised by the disrespect in the encounters, doubtless disappointed in themselves, as well as in their hope for real help. It isn't that teachers or doctors need always to "get it" right, nor to be perfectly gentle. Rather, because attributions of maternal badness are so pervasive, professionals are not only conditioned to see mothers (or, sometimes, parents) as the problem, but find themselves possessing undue power to evoke shame. The underlying social attitudes distort the individual exchanges.

For all the counseling that a mother "ought" to separate herself from her child so as to contemplate him with a little objectivity, most mothers find the effort at best a work in progress. Raising children and also working as a psychotherapist, I have lectured myself about keeping good boundaries with my kids—figuring out what is them, what is me. But this effort exists side by side with a deeper recognition that the task is impossible. Some days I don't know where they start or I end. I remember once when the boys were little and one got a haircut—perhaps a first haircut, perhaps not, but still, for some reason now forgotten, an intense emotional experience for us both—I realized the next day that when I approached the mirror, comb in hand, I was unsure whose hair had been cut, his or mine.

That confusion is one of many in a mother's mind, a given of generative love. And to demand that a good mother be both correctly attuned and separate is often unrealistic. I can be too critical of my kids; yet if one of the boys is criticized by someone else, my stomach starts to hurt. I feel empathy for him and protective; then I wonder what I could have done better to help him avoid the problem. Each occasion becomes an opportunity to review one's own failings: if only I'd been more patient, less hurried, calmer . . . a different person, more like . . .

Rather than reargue the whole history of the psychoanalytic view of the mother, a project that would take volumes, I want to look at a few representative bits of text from my professionally formative years that succinctly speak to these issues. Because the psychological expectations for mothers have not stayed within the confines of the discipline, because they have tinted many other cultural lenses, comprehending them is essential to understanding how popular culture now thinks about mothers, and the way contemporary threat is conveyed. The clinicians who read texts become the practitioners who treat people and disseminate authoritative views—within therapy, to other professionals, to the media, and to the larger society. Patients, themselves citizens wearing many hats, spread perspectives. Although psychopharmacology and evolutionary psychology may now be in popular ascendancy, the ruling orthodoxies of the past sixty to eighty years came out of psychoanalytic psychology, and were broadly translated into popular culture, in which their influence on notions of maternal harm and responsibility has been enormous. Some graffiti many years ago in my college library bathroom captured the absurdity and pervasiveness of the surreal attributions: Person 1: "My mother made me a homosexual. Person 2: "If I buy the wool, will she make me one, too?"

Much has been usefully offered by psychoanalytic thought. The best of it has made and continues to make an enlightening intellectual, emotional, and philosophical contribution. I admire Freud's writings, and I mostly agree with the psychoanalyst Stephen A. Mitchell when he writes about the "extraordinary, unprecedented exploration psychoanalysis provided in the first half of the twentieth century into the subtle textures, conscious and unconscious, of human fantasy and imagination."[7] At the same time, many of the psychoanalytic representations of mothers have been unconscionable. In truth, the psychological professions, my own included, owe formal apologies to mothers about the fields' historic practices. The worst of the overt mother bashing has been quietly dropped, yet many derivatives remain. And because the earlier focus has not been publicly disowned, because responsibility for harm has not been taken, the old ideas more than linger. Rather like the asbestos wrapped around pipes in the basement, overlooked when the rest of the house is updated, they continue quietly to make their claims.

If one current text could hold the title of "most important" in the world of psychotherapy when I was in graduate school in the late 1970s, arguably it would have been *The Psychological Birth of the Human Infant: Symbiosis and Individuation,* by Margaret Mahler (along with Fred Pine and Anni Bergman), one of the preeminent psychoanalytic theorists of the twentieth century. The book was published in 1975, and I wager that it was read, read in excerpt, or read about, by every graduate student in any clinical school for years after, even as other books and ideas replaced it. The text was treated with near reverence when I was training to become a clinical social worker. (It is worth mentioning that I was childless at the time, that the famous primary author was childless, and that, to the best of my memory, my professor was childless. Also contributing to our receptivity was the particular attitude of the field—at times useful, even exhilarating, at other times weird and bullying—which dictated that to become a therapist you had to be tough enough to look at people, yourself included, with an honesty that defied social convention. If you had trouble swallowing psychoanalytic "truths" about maternal deficiencies or anything else, you were soft; you lacked the right psychological stuff.)

Psychological Birth is still in print. As professional books go, this one is a classic. More sophisticated recent research and theoretical writing have cast doubt—even within psychoanalysis and developmental psychology—upon some of its assertions. But other ideas continue to hold sway. And, as such, it is a perfect text to demonstrate the conundrum of the mother's place in psychological thinking, as well as the historical continuity of "formulations" about mothers. We were told in graduate school (and we believed) that *Psychological Birth* would help us understand both children and adult psychopathology. In fact, when we evaluated patients we were to determine what part of their earliest development, as outlined by Mahler et al., had gone awry. At what moment had each mother been inadequate, or at least a bad match with her particular child? How bad? The deficits of the child would tell you about the failures of the mother, much as an x-ray would locate the place of fracture in a bone.

Mahler was Buchan's ideological granddaughter, Key's daughter. Their idealism is manifest in her work. Their grandiose notions of perfection have been tempered by the ugly events of the twentieth century—no one openly mentions eugenic breeding or "the superman" anymore—yet they also have been woven into the cultural fabric. Once airy assumptions—about creating better children, better mothers, and a better world through research and science—are now assumed to be substantial. Mahler and others seem to have accepted as baseline fact their predecessors' idealized constructions of mothering and maternal responsibility; they simply used psychology to measure women against these notions in new ways.

As much as anything, *The Psychological Birth of the Human Infant* became popular because it seemed to spell out—with a combination of interesting theory, close observation, speculation, fantastic confabulation, and bias—a view of how mothers love, relate to, and therefore help create the psychologically well-adjusted child. Furthermore, since psychoanalytic theories were traditionally drawn from single cases, the idea that the writers examined a number of children vastly heightened their credibility. In two studies between 1959 and 1968, they repeatedly interviewed thirty-eight children and their twenty-two mothers.[8]

By closely observing infants and toddlers with their mothers, the authors of *Psychological Birth* believed they had isolated a series of phase-specific steps in psychological maturation, all of which, given an adequately endowed baby, were best negotiated by a child receiving optimal mother love. We will look at some of their findings. As much as any bit of document can, they show how clinical writing serves both as a source and as a mirror of cultural feelings about mothers.

On one level, the book offers an interesting account of the behaviors of different toddlers and mothers. On another, it reflects a projective fantasy by the authors. As I reread portions of it, I alternated between finding it insightful and feeling it belonged in the theater of the absurd. The authors overlaid preexisting psychoanalytic fantasies about infant development upon the children and mothers they were observing, and then confirmed them or expanded upon them. But the theories were ungrounded to begin with, and thus the "research" findings were as precarious as a young child balancing on a swaying hammock.

According to the book's schema, in "The Third Subphase: Rapprochement," "the toddler reaches the first level of identity—that of being a separate individual entity." At this point the toddler is said to become more aware of his separateness from his mother, and thus more aware of his vulnerability and need for her. The authors write, "One cannot emphasize too strongly the importance of the optimal emotional availability of the mother during this subphase."[9] Two pages later, they add the following assertion.

> Depending on her own adjustment, the mother may react to the child's demands during this period either with continued emotional availability and playful participation or with a gamut of less desirable attitudes. It is, however, the mother's continued emotional availability, we have found, that is essential if the child's autonomous ego is to attain optimal functional capacity, while his reliance on magic omnipotence recedes. If the mother is "quietly available" with a ready supply of object libido, if she shares the toddling adventurer's exploits, playfully reciprocates, and thus facilitates his salutary attempts at imitation and *identification,* then internalization of the relationship between mother and toddler is able to progress to the point where, in time, verbal communication takes over.[10]

In other words, if the mother "adjusts" right and loves her child "right," the toddler identifies with her successfully, and matures to a higher level of functioning, so that, among other things, he can use words symbolically to express emotional states. By this account (to create a concrete example that is not in the text), if a toddler is given the correct attention—if feelings get meaningfully named, attached to words effectively—then eventually the sentence "I'm angry. I wanted the cookie *now, not later*" can replace a tantrum. For this to happen optimally, it is "essential" that his mother be "quietly available" and filled with ready "object libido." ("Object libido" is psychoanalysis's "scientific" way of naming the love energy one has for another person.)

Their research offers no evidence that this scenario is true. Nor does it identify the extent to which "optimal mothering" is essential to feeling-language acquisition. It simply takes optimal mothering whole hog from the mother-idealizing texts of the nineteenth century and then science-coats it. The researchers knew the kind of mother they preferred, and they wanted their findings to be true. More than that is difficult to say.

Certainly, much of mothering seems to me to be about civilizing children. Helping them to suitably express, name, and control their feelings and actions is a long work in progress. Controlling one's own feelings and actions throughout these encounters is equally arduous, and sometimes impossible, especially when faced with toddlers or teenagers, both of whom are often creatures of strong volition unaccompanied by any trace of sense. (As I write, an image floats back of our younger son, perhaps a year old, determined to surf himself in his walker down a steep flight of stairs in order to go outside at night during a rainstorm, and becoming infuriated when thwarted. Memory does not record whether the mother-serving-as-barrier kept her cool upon this occasion or not.)

In his lectures to young clinicians, Leston Havens, a psychiatrist colleague, writer, and clinical professor at Harvard Medical School, often—with an enlightened outlook too rare in the field—harps upon the fact that psychiatry has never established a sound idea of normal adulthood; and that this absence is a problem. Psychiatry prefers to describe pathologies. When pressed for a definition of mental health, practitioners refer back to Freud's admonition, that one should be able to "love and work." But were that the standard, many existing diagnoses would become irrelevant.

So too, the field has rarely been adequately curious about the vicissitudes and subjectivity of the normal mother. Once again, clinicians have long used shorthand to avoid the question. They have repeatedly referred to the writings of D. W. Winnicott, the British pediatrician and psychoanalyst, who coined the term "good-enough mother." You don't have to be perfect, only good enough. On first glance, the idea is comforting. However, rather than offering respect, the expression has often been used as a glib way for the psychological professions to dismiss facing the tautological problems within their own standards. In at least the first decade and a half of my work in the field, when the epithet was used constantly, I never heard a patient's mother described as "good enough."

The mother Mahler favors brings to mind Leonardo da Vinci's idealized portrait of *The Virgin and Child with Saint Anne,* which pictures two women mothering a child, each in a state of what I can only call passive beatitude. In the gorgeous late Renaissance painting, the adolescent Saint Anne sits on the Virgin's lap and bends rapturously toward the toddler Jesus, while the Virgin rests benignly just slightly behind them. The Virgin and Saint Anne gaze lovingly at the toddler, who gazes back at Saint Anne. Content to sit receptively, the women lack all worries, obligations, or competing desires. Their idealized quiescence, their gently blissful love, is glorious. Who would not want to sit on this Virgin's lap? We know as viewers familiar with their story that they have seen trouble, and that terrible suffering lies ahead. But that knowledge only heightens the exquisite tranquillity of the moment.

Mahler's observation strikes me as being based, like Leonardo's painting, upon the idealized fantasy of a mother. She and her coauthors assert that optimal maternal emotional availability is "essential," but they offer no useful definition: no thoughts about relative quantities (one hour in a day, or ten); no account of how it feels to the mother or other caretaker; no list of the resources needed to support it (note Leonardo's sensible two-women-to-one-child ratio); no measure of whether it can actually be delivered by the majority of "normal" mothers; no proof that its purity makes a significant difference to a child; and no way to assess its particular usefulness to children relative to such other variables as sound health, sibling love, father love, kin love, friendship, mother's wealth and social class, or safe housing. For all the acuity of some of its observations, this famous psychological study is not science: it's religion.

Still, most of us would agree that mother love is important. (The psychologist Judith Rich Harris disagrees; in *The Nurture Assumption* (1998), she claims that children's paths are determined by genetics, neighborhood, and peer group; and while her book offers a long overdue, refreshing corrective, it ultimately protests too much.) As mothers, we watch our loving efforts giving pleasure and comfort. We know that the deep, struggling engagement that love promotes helps children grow. As children, we want to feel our parents loving us. As children or adults, we go into the world with more confidence and stamina if we believe that someone is really on our side, that a person close to us, despite static and failings, understands us, treasures us, appreciates our talents and perspective.

My debate with Mahler, Pine, and Bergman is about the qualities within love that make it useful, about the authors' penchant for leaving the conditions of the world or mothers' feelings out of such a story, and about whether a profound human wish for optimal love should be set in concrete as the standard against which real mothers must fail. What's more, Harris's assertions rightly remind us that the better feeling of living as someone who is loved does not necessarily lead to a better outcome in worldly measures.

Discussing child behaviors, including the way the toddler sometimes "shadows" the mother, the authors add a parenthesis: "Some mothers, by their protracted doting and intrusiveness, rooted in their own anxieties and often in their own symbiotic parasitic needs, become themselves the 'shadowers' of the child."[11] What can any reader say to such an assertion, but "God forbid." Up until this point, the discussion has maintained a fairly reasonable surface and civil tone. Then: *their own symbiotic parasitic needs.* All of a sudden, the mothers whose approach the authors don't like have leprosy or something; they behave like invasive, dependent worms. These mothers have unacceptable unconscious impulses and sometimes relate to their children out of their own anxieties. They must be very bad, or certainly the authors would have found nicer words.

Anxious mothers can be a drag. I know because I am one. I don't think my kids experience me as a worm, but I don't think I'll ask them. My older son, whom I helped teach to drive on the unbearably dangerous roads around Boston (we will not mention his equally anxious father who would have preferred not to participate at all), didn't want me back in the car for the first year he was at the wheel, because he didn't like the strangulating sounds I made or the urgency with which I pumped my imaginary brake. But he was mostly sweet about it, and we laughed together. The word *parasite* didn't come up once.

A page later in *Psychological Birth,* the authors discuss the way the "rapprochement subphase" goes awry when mothers are "unable to adjust to the progressive disengagement and/or the increased demandingness of the growing child." They write, "From such relatively direct expressions of the need for mother as bringing a book to be read to them or hitting at the books or needlework their mothers were habitually preoccupied with, they turned to more desperate measures, such as falling or spilling cookies on the floor and stamping on them in temper tantrums—always with an eye to gaining their mothers' attention, if not involvement."[12]

When mothers' eyes turn away at the wrong moments, or chronically turn away, children become upset, sometimes with cause. The word *habitually* is central here, as it is the authors' way of using language to insist beyond argument that these mothers are inadequate and look away too much. Should we trust their account? Perhaps. Most mothers recognize that there are times they can't muster desired attention. A more interesting discussion would be one that included the mother's opinion about how much looking she'd already done that day, and how she thought about the balance between meeting the child's emotional wishes and performing other tasks or simply sustaining herself—and how the absence of cultural respect, economic recompense, or companionship in her work might actually be depleting or depressing her. Of course, maternal eyes convey many feelings; children long most for loving, engaged looks, dread shaming, critical, or angry surveillance, and fear gross inattention.

Maybe Mahler's mothers felt isolated, devalued, frustrated, or bored. Only recently has anyone assumed that an adult woman should devote her day to caring for a single child. In *Women's Work: The First 20,000 Years*, Elizabeth Wayland Barber describes a common female practice for millennia: mothers collectively weaving textiles, able to talk and work, while together keeping an eye on the kids.[13] I suspect such situations shouldn't be romanticized, but they were likely less isolating. Maybe Mahler's children suffered from having too much expectation of exclusive focus directed at their mothers, and too much intense contact with a single caretaker, whose limitations thus were writ larger.

Mahler's respectable but neglectful mother, who might have her eyes on a book rather than on her child, is most immediately the descendant of the eighteenth-century woman who made her contemporaries anxious when she learned to read. As we noted earlier, a woman with a book has often been considered dangerous. When novels were first published in eighteenth-century America, many people condemned them—including national heroes like John Adams and Thomas Jefferson. Critics warned that fiction would give women notions, encourage them to fantasize about a world beyond domestic duty, take them away from their children—and imaginatively away from their spouse's control.[14]

When knitting instead of reading, Mahler's inattentive mother becomes a bourgeois Penelope who fails because she doesn't raise her eyes often enough from her needles. In truth, the text recapitulates much of what we've seen from the past. The good mother who follows the rules (in this case the psychoanalytic rules of optimal availability) is to be praised. All other mothers are damaging and can be either politely devalued or called awful names with impunity. Nowhere in Mahler's book do the mothers have a direct voice. In fact, mothers' perspectives, except as they represent pathology, have historically been of as little interest in the world of psychology as elsewhere.

When one thinks of all the mothers in the world today, half of whom are trying at any moment to keep children from starving, or are struggling to keep children minimally safe, it is remarkable that a professional discipline could assume so casually the right to assess stringently the unconscious minds of the relatively privileged and lucky few, and use pseudoscientific yet exacting calipers to measure the way these mothers fail at love. That they then find the women so often unsatisfactory is itself some combination of marvelous—a feat of extraordinary idealism—and dumbly astounding. Part of what must be admired about the premise of psychoanalytic psychology is how boldly, almost wantonly, it has championed precisely attuned love. Unfortunately, real mothers are the candles, burned at both ends, melted upon this altar.

The minute a twentieth-century mother made her way into relative safety, survived childbearing herself and gave birth to children who usually lived, she was confronted with a new standard of care that examined her unconscious life, her object libido, her emotional devotion, with fanatical critical intensity. To the degree that psychology, and studies like Mahler's, have contributed to making society recognize children as impressionable creatures with sensibilities, the field deserves praise. When psychology speaks out against beating children, humiliating, terrorizing, enslaving, and sexually abusing them, it is serving a humane and substantial function. So too when it describes methods of helping adults and children heal and prosper. Unfortunately, each time experts observe or postulate about children's psyches, their usual accompanying reflex is to measure mothers and find them lacking.

Furthermore, much of what psychology pinned on the ailing mother was deemed to be beyond conscious control. The signs of her pathology were readily visible—sometimes only visible—to carefully trained clinicians who could instantly recognize a case of parasitic-symbiotic mothering when they saw it. This type of critique is particularly demoralizing because of the way it seeks to make an expert's power unassailable by laypeople. In seventeenth-century New England only judges and ministers could decide which women were witches; the woman's own protestation held little worth. Furthermore, one of the basic ways of triggering shame in people is observing something intimate about them that they have not themselves noticed: your zipper is unzipped, you're blushing, your unconscious parasitic dependency is harming your child. And finally, even when a specific description has merit, as it enters a misogynistic society the details of meaning bleed into the larger sea of prejudice, deepening its color as they give way to it.

Texts in the field generally interpreted the workings of the mother's unconscious mind retrospectively—through the eyes of her adult child. To their credit, the best theorists and therapists have always been willing to take the child's story as important apart from any decisions about its real-world truth. They understand that the commingling of fantasy and memory is complex. For example, the fact that a therapist might say to a patient, "How painful for you that your mother wouldn't look up from her knitting/book when you so longed for her to do so," does not translate into a belief in each therapist that the mother was necessarily deficient for not looking, or that the child's desire ought to become a new rule for maternal behavior. Often, the concrete notion of badness attaches itself in other places—texts, case conferences, evaluations—through trickle-down effect as the story makes its way into professional discussion and the popular media. More subtle and richer narratives are flattened into stereotypes: The mother "failed to . . ."

Still and all, how much society ought to try to create improved children by endlessly examining mothers, attempting to hammer them and their psyches into better shape, is a real question. I find myself thinking of Buchan's equation of mothers and cattle, and the way science now breeds Frankenstein-like cattle that stand in their stalls all day, swallowing hormones, udders swollen, as milking machines pump from them absurd but profitable quantities of milk. The problem of mother love is neither in the wish, nor the distance between the wish and the reality, but in the texts and ideologies that confuse wish with reality, dehumanize women, inflate expectations, and artificially sever the personal from the social and political.

D. W. Winnicott's famous "good-enough" mother embodies these confusions. It has had enormous historic impact in the world of psychotherapy and is still current. So let us look at it a little more closely. The substance of Winnicott's beliefs can be seen developing in a series of radio lectures he gave for mothers in the 1940s. In them, he coined the term "ordinary devoted mother." Why didn't he simply say "ordinary mother" or even "mother?"

The earliest reference I found to the "good-enough mother" was in an essay Winnicott published in 1949. "The need for a good environment, which is absolute at first, rapidly becomes relative. *The ordinary good mother is good enough.* If she is good enough the infant becomes able to allow for her deficiencies by mental activity." In two better-known essays from the 1960s, the good-enough mother serves one specific function—and one only. Her job is to be able "to meet the needs of her infant at the beginning, and to meet these needs so well that the infant, as emergence from the matrix of the infant-mother relationship takes place, is able to have a brief experience of omnipotence." According to Winnicott's theory, the infant's emotional/fantasy experience of temporary omnipotence becomes the basis of his later ability to accommodate reality. By initially offering *exactly* what the infant needs, the mother creates a crucial spark of psychological vitality that becomes the basis of all the child's future development and authenticity. This theory, while neat, is fantastic.[15]

On the surface, Winnicott's declaration sanctioning the "ordinary good mother" sounds plausible, even benign — until you look at the consequences of failure, which, he believed, produced psychosis. While in the radio talks he only lightly mentioned psychotic outcomes from maternal missteps, in a famous essay addressed to a professional audience, "Primary Maternal Preoccupation" (1956), Winnicott spelled out more of what he meant. He explained that he used the phrase "ordinary devoted mother" because ordinary mothers might be inadequately devoted in this first phase of infant care to abandon the world as completely as he insisted their infant's psychological development required. He noted, "When a woman has a strong male identification she finds this part of her mothering function most difficult to achieve, and repressed penis envy leaves but little room for primary maternal preoccupation."[16]

Furthermore, Winnicott suggested that if mothers missed this opportunity to do as he dictated, parents must spend the rest of the child's growing up making attempts at repair, though "it is not certain that they can succeed in mending the early distortion." Winnicott then referred to others who have noted the same problem while attempting "to describe the type of mother who is liable to produce an 'autistic child'"! In other words, an active woman (one who wants to have a voice, or perhaps occasionally loses herself in a novel, or in her fantasies) who doesn't adequately abandon all her desires in the world will harm her infant so much that he is likely to become autistic. (In "Ego Integration in Child Development," the list of afflictions Winnicott claimed were caused by this early failing include "Infantile schizophrenia or autism, latent schizophrenia, false-self defense, and Schizoid personality.")[17]

Reading through a number of Winnicott's radio talks, the pieces in which he directly offered mothers advice and which were first delivered in the postwar years in England, I am struck by his affinity with Jean-Jacques Rousseau. Winnicott believes he must strip away the constricting social conventions, the bad advice of earlier advisers, and allow mothers to get in touch with their "natural" instincts. ("A mother who has been schooled into training her infant to regular habits, starting with regular three-hourly feeds, feels actually wicked if told to feed her baby just like a gipsy . . . she easily feels scared of the very great pleasure involved in this, and feels she will be blamed by her in-laws and the neighbours for whatever else goes wrong from that day forward.")[18]

Winnicott portrays himself as a free spirit, a Pan with pipes, who wants to liberate mothers from rigid schedules and pleasureless care-giving; he wants to shield them from bourgeois blame. His advice will create natural women and lead them back to the native sensuality and gratification of total devotion to their infants' psyches. In his story, the repressive forces are represented by neighbors; also sometimes in-laws, nurses, and doctors—though never psychiatrists. (Like other advice givers, he discredits women's belief in local female knowledge. In one lecture, the potentially troublesome parties are "the matron of the hospital, or the midwife, or her own mother or mother-in-law." While, doubtless, these women could pass on both benighted and good ideas, the generalization is striking.)[19]

In the past, according to Winnicott, high infant mortality frightened and cowed mothers, so they listened to too much bad advice. ("Infant disease and death make mothers lose confidence in themselves, and make them look for authoritative advice.") Now that doctors have cured many childhood illnesses, Winnicott believes that "it has suddenly become urgent for those of us who concern ourselves chiefly with feelings to state as accurately as we can the psychological problem which confronts every mother, however complete the absence of bodily disease and disorder due to the doctors' skill."[20]

Several points are striking in this passage. First, it contains an unusually direct statement about the urgency psychology felt to "cure" children's psyches once medicine had "cured" infant mortality. But acts of doctoring, as we pointed out earlier, were probably not responsible for lowering mortality rates, however wonderful the later benefits of medicine. So it seems that Winnicott is first making an inflated claim for medicine's achievements, and then hitching his psychoanalytic wagon to its star, to lift his own authority. Furthermore, at the same time that he tells women repeatedly to ignore advice, even suggests that they correct his assertions when mistaken, he implies that he has invaluable knowledge to communicate which will save their infant from psychological harm, knowledge which mothers are in no position to assess because it is scientific and gleaned from psychoanalytic sessions.

What's more, we know that it wasn't simply infant mortality that made mothers lose confidence in themselves. While I'm sure mothers did wrongly blame themselves, and felt terribly demoralized when children died, it was infant mortality culturally framed or reinforced as maternal failure that seems to have done the damage. Uninterested in noticing this distinction, Winnicott reenacts it. For mothers, a central dilemma—arguably *the* central dilemma—of the ages has been how to bear child love in the face of loss. Winnicott briefly nods in the direction of this fact. But rather than appreciating its significance, he un-self-consciously puts pressure on mothers to move the fulcrum point: to respond immediately to a little more safety by giving of themselves more completely. Not only does his suggestion come with the usual threat, but sadly it misunderstands the more subtle consequences: the increased—but unmet and unsupported—vulnerability of mothers who love so fully in a world indifferent to their concerns.

I have long admired many of Winnicott's rather cryptic essays. He is at heart a poet; and he has offered beautifully written descriptive and metaphoric contributions to psychoanalytic thinking. I have no wish to "throw out the baby with the bath water," nor to attempt here to assess his whole contribution. (His invitation to nurse "like a gipsy," to freely take pleasure in the relationship with infants, is certainly more sensual than the scientific approach of Holt, or the utterly distanced approach of Watson.) However, his writing is not scientific, and when he claims that it is, he harms his credibility—and he harms mothers. To demonstrate just how problematic and convoluted his stance can become, consider his comments on breastfeeding.

> It is said that there is nothing in human relationships that is more powerful than the bond between a baby and the mother (or the breast) during the excitement of a breast-feeding experience. I cannot expect

this to be easily believed; nevertheless it is necessary at least to have the *possibility* of this in mind when considering such a problem as the value of breast feeding as compared with bottle feeding. It is true . . . particularly of the psychology of early infancy, that the truth of truths cannot be fully and immediately felt. In other sciences if something is found to be true it can usually be accepted without emotional strain, but in psychology there is always this matter of strain, so that something which is not quite true is more easily accepted than the truth itself.[21]

What a confusing use of words. The unique intensity of the infant-breast bond is asserted as scientific fact, and skeptics are chastised as doubters. Furthermore, Winnicott has stated earlier that his basis of measurement is from psychoanalytic work with psychotic patients! (The first line of the essay reads, "The intensity of infant feelings recurs in the intensity of the suffering associated with psychotic symptoms.")[22] In other words, in this essay, Winnicott deduced the psychology of infancy from adult psychosis, claimed his observations were scientific, and declared that anyone who doubted his science was simply a person unable to accept truth.

These examples of Winnicott's and Mahler's writing are problematic in their prejudices. At the same time, aspects of their descriptions and assertions are enlightening. Mothers have formative power with infants, though it is unclear how much, and they have power in intimate relationships even as they may often be devalued within their family structures and in their societies. But these contradictions lead us to the heart of the larger social problem created by the formulation of maternal damage within psychology and psychoanalytic texts: close observation can easily be used in the service of social repression.

This fact is best comprehended when we examine a powerful mechanism of propaganda, which the literary critic Erich Auerbach calls the "searchlight device." Indeed, Auerbach, who fled the Nazis and understood totalitarian power tactics, offers astounding insight into how the mechanism functions to create an appearance of truth while destroying truth in the process.

The searchlight device, he writes, does its damage by "overilluminating one small part of an extensive complex, while everything else which might explain, derive, and possibly counterbalance the thing emphasized is left in the dark; so that apparently the truth is stated, for what is said cannot be denied; and yet everything is falsified, for truth requires the whole truth and the proper interrelation of its elements."[23]

When you shine the searchlight on the mother-child relationship, as psychology has now done for the better part of a century, the sum of the observations comes to possess some descriptive accuracy, or truth. But because that examination of a small part of a larger, much more complex whole *never* fully or respectfully takes into account the interplay between the mother's subjectivity, the child's or her social reality, and the child's experience, the truth is imbedded in a larger lie, for truth "*requires the whole truth and the proper interrelation of its elements*"!

Not only were the psychoanalytic and psychological observations of infants and children inaccurate when they claimed a scientific status they had not earned, but by framing their questions so narrowly, they gave new energy to an older lie: that mothers' behavior that defied either convention or the adult fantasies of the child's desire was a primary source of child harm. For psychoanalysts to have done their investigations with a greater possibility of capturing useful maternal truth, the investigators would have had to notice and take into visible account the second-class status of mothers. A claim that the mothers they studied were relatively privileged and removed from the most immediate dilemmas of survival and enslavement, finesses, obscures, and otherwise overlooks the enormous impact upon all women of their shared history, objectification, enforced dependency, fragile political status, and economic inequality.

Furthermore, psychology prospered—gathered audiences, sold books, disseminated opinions into the broader culture—in part because its prejudices about women mirrored and confirmed the society's, and in part from the mother's very urgency—never adequately recognized in the field—to do right by her children and keep them safe. (We have reason to wonder how much of the social science research of the twentieth century across the board functioned to amplify existing prejudices and support the status quo.)

Finally, as well as devaluing, the psychological literature has also been grossly silent on the enormous competitiveness its own practitioners feel and enact with mothers. Therapists often want so badly to be the better mothers that they aggressively, sometimes unconsciously, elbow real mothers to clear the field. Needless to say, this practice contributes to distorted theories and generally makes its own mess. Were the competitiveness owned directly it would be less damaging.

Distorted standards of all kinds devalue mothers' everyday struggles to care for children. Or, to put it another way, the more children grow up in a culture that tells them that their mothers are falling short (even as, statistically, in many countries most mothers still get less nutrition and do more hours of labor a day than fathers),[24] the more each child feels personally deprived, disappointed in the particular mothering he received. A healthy social standard would be that all children and young adults—however well parented—would naturally expect to have additional emotional needs supplied by other adults. All deserve and could benefit from close mentoring, avuncular love, guidance, and/or "good-enough" psychotherapy.

Looking back at childhood can be worthwhile for self-knowledge and emotional growth. To appreciate one's particular history and bounty, to experience additional nurturing, and to mourn losses and disappointments can help to crystallize identity, desires, and the ability to act in the world. But the current public message, that somehow, because of bad parenting and dysfunctional families, any poor soul with residual hungers, depression, or dependencies must have *particularly* missed out, is inaccurate and insidious. In this sense, in America, mothers are sacrificed to preserve a myth of human perfection, of the possibility of life without suffering, chance, or tragedy. One summer night, walking in the dark with my husband, our younger son, and a crowd of strangers, all of us making our way to a big field to watch July Fourth fireworks, I overheard a mother heatedly answering a teenage daughter, "Compared to other families, *we're just not that dysfunctional!*"

Children deserve parents who want them and love them. But they also deserve a just world. It is not right to put so much and such urgent emphasis on the quality of mothering, and so little on everything else.

While some mothers are oblivious and unequivocally destructive to children, most will sacrifice continually to live up to difficult standards, at significant personal cost. It is long since time to stop exploiting this maternal tendency so as to avoid the larger societal responsibility to care for children. And, as we've observed, the most important question remains unasked: What do mothers need in order to do their part in child-rearing work? In a chapter of a book by leading scholars on the mental health of women worldwide, the authors point out that traditional aid or development programs for "mother-child health" have tended not to think about the mothers' needs at all![25]

In a restaurant at dinner one night I watched a nearby table at which four adults in their early thirties tried to eat *and* contend with a tired toddler. The boy, blond and beautiful, perhaps fourteen to sixteen months old, was a squirming handful. The adults were terrific with him. I would say the mother focused the most on the boy's needs, but the father was a close second, and one of the other men at the table also helped out.

The adults shadowed and retrieved the child as he wandered the restaurant. They took him outside when he got too restless, fed him when he wanted to sample the food, distracted him, gave him his bottle, entertained him, and helped him survive a difficult environment. They appreciated his abilities and his limits and made a steady effort on his behalf. They still had time to eat, talk, and laugh together. It was pleasing to watch the perceptive way that they switched off, sensing fatigue and spelling one another smoothly. Three-to-one (with the fourth able to organize the food-ordering and keep some focus on the conversation) seemed to work pretty well. But I don't think it would ever have occurred to Mahler and her colleagues that such a ratio was the real secret of optimal availability.

So, too, I like the notion of psychotherapy as a process that lends a hand, that helps people manage what the fabulously complex contemporary society now demands, rather than one that simply purports to do what some inadequate parents could not do. In an everyday way, the well-meaning diners juggling the toddler may be as good as it gets.

· PART III ·

"A

PAIN

SO

DURABLE"

10

The Free Mother

LET'S PAUSE in our discussion of texts, turn history on its head, and suggest that what a child needs most in the world is a free and happy mother. Having used the word *happy*, I will immediately qualify it, since I believe much happiness is local—an unsteady state often beyond our control. Pleasurably anticipating lunch with a friend, I might in fact enjoy the day's best moments while sipping coffee waiting to greet her. What if she confides a troubling story that makes us feel close but sad? Feeling is unpredictable, and happiness is delicious but too fickle to serve as a foundation for any edifice. Years working as a therapist have taught me that part of what creates misery is the false assumption that one ought to be consistently happy. Furthermore, the relationship of people's circumstances to their quotient of daily good feeling is no simple equation.

So let me qualify my assertion: what a child needs most is a free mother, one who feels that she is in fact living *her* life, and has adequate food, sleep, wages, education, safety, opportunity, institutional support, health care, child care, and loving relationships. "Adequate" means enough to allow her to participate in the world—and in mothering— without starving, or feeling economically trapped or uncompensated, continually exploited, terrorized, devalued, battered, chronically exhausted, or virtually enslaved (and for some, still, actually enslaved).

A child most needs a mother who has resources to enable her to make real choices, but also to create a feeling of adequate control—a state of mind that encourages a sense of agency, thus a good basis of maternal well-being, and a good foundation on which to stand while raising a child. Surely, child care prospers in this soil as well as, if not better than, in any other. What is more, such a mother can imagine a life of possibility and hope, and so can offer this perspective to a child.

Let me add one other condition. A child needs a mother who lives and works within a context that respects her labor, and that realistically supports it without rationalizing oppression in the name of safety, or substituting idealization or sentimentality for resources. A child needs a mother who is not constantly abraded by philosophies that inflate her accountability while obscuring her effort.

No society that I know of has ever voluntarily turned its laws and riches toward liberating mothers. I find that remarkable. Yes, under pressure, legal and social concessions have been made. But often they have been partial . . . and grudging. Why concede what isn't demanded? Societies can take for granted much of the work of mothering, make it invisible. Mothers will do it anyway. The desire to raise a child, the inexorable pull of sexual pleasure and reproduction, the wish to nurture, are all compelling. Moreover, it is easy to impregnate a woman, and then, however gentle and loving the particular relationship, to have the unequal laws and unspoken rules of the culture control her once she has children and is worried for their well-being. Of course, there are always exceptions, but in general, these realities have served across the ages to thwart maternal freedom.

Though we find ourselves in the postmodern era, in fact even the luckiest among us continue to be living in and trying to make personal sense of the modern, particularly the emphasis it places on romantic love as a hypergood—a condition so valuable it supersedes competing goods.[1] American popular culture and, increasingly, American law, consider this love to be a transcendent experience that provides the best basis for intimate human relationships. We generally possess (at least informally) a shared system of values wherein love is allowed to alter other priorities—be they genetic, ethnic, kin-based, gender-based, religious, or class-bound. There have always been loving marriages and families—even if guessing the proportion is impossible. People who get along at all, and who are together at close quarters, tend to become attached. Proximity, joint labor, and mutual dependence, when violence and derision are kept in relative check, breed deep fondness. But until a few hundred years ago in much of Western Europe, putting love before class, religion, race, dowry, prospects, or duty and obedience as a basis for marriage was often deemed feckless; and, in some circles and cultures, it still is.

Conversely, today many people subscribe to the notion that love is the freight elevator onto which we may load our wishes for congenial family life and our hope for well-being. Choosing relationships according to feelings of love is, by many, now considered a right. Furthermore, through psychoanalytic thinking and developmental psychology we have systematized the belief that love is essential to psychological growth, a catalyst and basic ingredient of emotional development.

There is a scene in Stendhal's novel *The Red and the Black,* published in 1830, that succinctly captures this point. Julien, the young and awkward protagonist, conversing with a priest whom he knows well, notices tears of concern in the priest's eyes. Stendhal writes, "Julien was ashamed of the emotion he felt; for the first time in his life, he could see that someone cared for him; he savoured his tears." Feeling loved becomes the basis of Julien's increased sensitivity to experience, and to himself as a sentient creature, his emotional awakening. However overused and under scrutiny notions about "self" or "identity" may be, it seems true that experiences like Julien's contribute to creating a psychological feeling of aliveness in a person, and a sense of inner self-possession and volition. Furthermore, almost two hundred years after the book was published, we continue to share with Stendhal an expansive—if often ill-defined—philosophical stance, which honors the pursuit of a more sophisticated and self-conscious individual identity and bases it in awareness of feelings—as well as in actions.[2]

The conversation that deeply moves Julien demonstrates an aspect of what psychologists—and the hard-to-pinpoint voice of popular culture—now assume children ought to feel from their mothers regularly, if not continuously. (Stendhal's description demonstrates how we can, of course, expect it equally from fathers, uncles, mentors, how it may be most potent when taken as a gift, not an entitlement. But that view hasn't so much been the way of American texts or popular stereotype.) No longer content with a standard that considered a mother to have discharged her duty if she delivered affectionate guidance, piety, porridge, and the annual shirt, child-rearing experts now feel that each child should experience empathic love as part of his or her birthright. In a sense, we have tried to systematize and make more steady and abundant something that has been long present but not previously highlighted, nor glorified so particularly. (The psychologist Jerome Kagan has suggested that this new emphasis on love may also have developed as children came to have fewer daily chores to perform: "the economically parasitic role of modern children renders them more needy of reassurance that they are loved.")[3]

Contemporary psychology is also based in this same premise—that is, that many years of attuned love should be a child's birthright. On one level, the proposition is radical and interesting. On another, it has been put forth with unconsidered fervency, adopted blindly from the nineteenth- and twentieth-century idealized writings of the sort we examined from Buchan, Key, and Mahler, and imposed upon mothers with almost total indifference to their contexts or experience. What priest ever listened to Julien's mother with tears of empathy in his eyes, or in any way let her know that she was an individual of worth and that her ambitions were valued? Assuming that empathic love (love that seeks to understand and recognize the other person's subjectivity) is a worthwhile, even profound thing for people to experience, how can a mother fairly be asked to give it fully if society imagines her one-dimensionally? That some mothers do so is grace—not the society's entitlement. The fantastic assumption has been that there is a strand of goodmotherlove that replicates continually apart from any larger reality and thus needs no attention.

In *Disposable People* (1999), Kevin Bales's carefully researched and scathing book about contemporary world slavery and the 27 million people living as slaves today, the author discusses how poor mothers and fathers in Thailand will readily sell daughters into sex slavery. A not uncommon trade is one daughter for one color television set. While the parents may deceive themselves and deny the full torturousness of the child's experience, they do know the general meaning of selling the girls, and they are aware that their daughters are likely to die of AIDS.

Bales's research leads him to conclude that there are a number of reasons mothers agree to this arrangement. The central one is that in Thailand women are considered worthless compared to men, are denied power, are generally not educated nor able to create independent lives. Extreme male hegemony and sexual promiscuity are widely sanctioned. Furthermore, a central belief in the country is that each child owes her parents a debt for raising her which she needs to pay off any way she can. The enslavement of female children by very poor families has a long tradition and comes out of desperation mixed with severe gender bias.[4]

Perhaps by gaining a color TV set, the family's status will increase enough to help a son make a better marriage—so *his* children will survive. I wouldn't be surprised if some such triage exists. A virtually enslaved mother may feel forced to trade a devalued girl's safety for a higher status boy's benefit. But still, how can we claim that attached mothers protect their children and sorrow for them if such atrocities can occur? Bales points out that prostitution is glamorized; a mother might be able to deceive herself that she is actually helping her daughter get a little money, some autonomy, and a lift from dire poverty.

Whatever her illusions, the deeper question is: Why are women all over the world, century after century, denied resources and treated so unequally? Most oppressive systems sustain themselves by terrorizing anyone who doesn't comply. Women who wish to resist, physically less strong than men, may well be overpowered. A World Health Organization study (2000) of the percentage of adult women assaulted by their intimate partners suggests that violence enforces the status quo. And the numbers are stark: in Egypt 34.4 percent, Bangladesh 42 percent, Turkey 57.9 percent, Canada 29 percent, the United States 22.1 percent, and in the United Kingdom 30 percent of women have been assaulted at some point in their marriage or partnership. A Unicef report from the same year suggests that "up to half the female population comes under attack by those closest to them at some time in their lives."[5]

A vivid example of the way violence and the greater immobility of caring for children can come together to impede and endanger mothers is offered by the family violence expert, and graduate of Harvard Law School, Sarah Buel, describing her own great difficulty leaving a very dangerous, battering marriage. When her son and foster children were young, she had no high school degree, much less a profession, and though she fled her husband's murderous violence toward her, because of her children she returned to him a number of times before she was finally able to leave. "The first job I could get was in a shoe factory. Well, it took me all of three weeks to find out I could not both pay the rent and pay the babysitter. So, yes, you go back."[6]

By making independence based in law and equally paid work difficult for mothers to achieve, and by reminding them through the threat of violence of their twice-vulnerable status, the world has developed a quiet, elegant, and effective way of controlling women, while maintaining inequality.

Two stories that are organically linked have been wrongly separated: the child's experience and the mother's. On the one hand, legitimate conflicts of interest between the two about the use of emotional resources have been collapsed; on the other, unities of concern have been hidden. And, as we examined in the last chapter, one result in America of this significant disconnect is the absurd amount of effort that has been spent documenting the failures of mothers—the primary legatees of the ever more refined imperative to express love in the correct form and amount. The frequent retelling of this story has saturated the atmosphere with mother blame; the resulting pollution has joined with the large, pre-existing inequality and choked and hampered women who might otherwise have possessed deeper satisfaction and confidence in their own efforts. Consequently, even those mothers who actually are freer, feel uncertain and unsafe. They are surrounded by threats detailing how their inadequate care might have damaged their children, and they can find few ways to limit the attributions of harm, nor the multiplying of criteria against which they must judge themselves, nor their own worry.

The unstated, punitive conclusion is that maternal effort, while crucial, may bring little redemption. Mothers will fail if they do not work hard enough at mothering in a psychologically correct way. But if they do, they may fail anyway, as their deep character flaws, incorrect psychic structure, or other diverse blemishes, like so many slips showing below the hems of dresses, will betray them. They will love wrong. At the same time, love makes it almost impossible for mothers to detach their feelings from social standards, and vulnerable to being judged as deficient.

One spring day I went to buy some lobelia and petunias for a pot garden I had decided to plant. I was standing in line at a local nursery waiting for the two women ahead of me to pay. One spotted a flat of young lettuce plants on the counter. "How much are these?" she asked. "My son has planted lettuce seeds. They're not coming up. I want to stick these in to surprise him. It will feel magical."

The woman with her and the saleswoman oohed with delight. One said, "Your son will always remember this. And later, when he knows the story, he'll make an exception for all you didn't give him. 'Mom,' he'll say, 'you didn't do xyz, but there was the lettuce.'" Everyone laughed. The saleswoman was so pleased at the fantasy prospect that she made a gift of the flat.

Overhearing the story, I squirmed a little. Not only did I never plant lettuce with either of my children (bless their father and their first-grade teachers), but had I done so I would have lacked the wherewithal to delight them by substituting plants for sterile seeds. The rigid Girl Scout in me would have felt it wrong to mislead innocents about the fickle ways of nature. Quickly, even as I laughed, I construed my own position as a flaw and knew that my unconscious search for redemption was again thwarted. But that's the lesser point.

More interesting is how the story mixes gestures of love with the women's expectation of failure. The mothers agreed without hesitation that while they hoped for forgiveness, hoped they could pile enough magic on the positive side of the ledger to offset some debt, they did not dream of absolution. What they did—how they lovingly thought about a child in the child's absence, considered and chose a way to please him—was not simply to their credit. It was to pay down a mortgage of harm, or at least to mitigate their assumption that they were inevitably also injury's agents.

And of course in a sense they are right. But not so exclusively in the personal, self-critical, and picky way they imagined. As the brokers of intimate care, as the hands that most often rock the cradle, their fingerprints can be found everywhere. Yet the smudges they leave are overscrutinized by zealous detectives who mistake the inevitable for malicious design. Mothers will always give children some things and not others; will harm them as well as sustain them; and mothers will fail in smaller or larger ways depending on their own qualities, but even more on where society sets the standard, and how much and in what ways it supports the effort to raise children.

In turn, society—including mothers—will likely raise the bar as high as it possibly can, for it sees no reason to do otherwise. Parental concern, specifically the mother's anxieties, her wish to do right by her children, is too large not to invite both well-meaning and cynical responses from all quarters. Putting pressure too singularly on mothers is an elegant but immoral resolution to the huge social problem of how to assure adequate devotion to the next generation. It forces undue responsibility upon mothers and exploits their willingness to care for children.

Furthermore, because mothers have been so consistently flattened, seen not as whole people, but judged too narrowly by their capacity to nurture children and men, society has felt free to objectify them and treat them like nonhuman commodities. The real mother is devalued in favor of the fantasy standard of an optimally loaded model who could make life one big joy ride for the child.

We must wonder how so much devotion can have been asked, even demanded, of mothers when the world has not treasured them—has mostly, in fact, devalued their capacities, seen them as property and chattel. With so much of hope hanging on love, and particularly on a purified, educated, or informed mother love, it would seem that societies would have thought carefully about how to provide them with fair resources. But that has not usually been the case.

Let me qualify what I've just said. Protection *has* been offered to mothers, tenderness too, occasionally between equals, but often of a particular kind for a considerable price: in return for their staying personally, economically, and politically subordinate. Whenever women have been tempted to push for their own rights, one tacit threat has been that their self-assertion would break the accord, and . . . endanger children. I don't believe that women are nicer, or easier in relationships, than men. They have simply, historically and politically, been more dominated, enslaved, and oppressed.

So, once again, let me suggest that the best mother is a free woman. What is odd about writing this sentence is how bland it is, and yet how radical when held up to the historical reality of women's lives—a sandblasted facade surrounded by its sooty counterparts. Remarkably, once again, as far as I can tell, no country has ever felt that mobilizing its resources to help create freedom for women was of much importance. Quite the opposite. I can think of none that has voluntarily offered women political, economic, and social equality. Why not?

Freedom for mothers is simply too frightening to contemplate. I deduce this from the lack of a ready definition of the idea, the rarity of stories about it, the paucity of creative social thinking, and the "you must be kidding" reactions I get from mothers when I mention the word—even from women who for all intents and purposes would seem to have some. The concept makes everyone anxious.

A glimpse at a free mother is reflexively processed as an experience of abandonment. The mother who has choice will turn toward license. Pentheus suspected this in *Bacchae* when his mother and other Maenads danced in the mountains. John Flavel, with a paradoxical keenness worth crediting, felt the only freedom for mothers was to be found in complete submission to God. William Buchan, for *their* health, forbade pregnant women to dance. Charles Meigs solved the problem by declaring women incompetent in all realms other than family love. Ellen Key demanded total devotion to children. Margaret Mahler criticized in psychiatry-speak when mothers dared knit or read books. Only John Watson took a different view. He disdained mothers so much that he suggested children should be raised outside the home—by a steady rotation of professional nurses, quick turnover serving, he declared, to obstruct the damage of attachment.

But weren't the ancient Greek playwright, the minister, and the experts referring to something far more unconsciously dangerous as they sought to inculcate obedience: the unsettling fantasy of the mother's departure from narrow practices, because of their own wishes for safety? From the men themselves as well as their offspring? A secondary meaning of *abandon* in *Webster's* is "to give (oneself) over to a feeling or emotion without check, restraint or control." This definition outlines the maternal state that so many texts obliquely describe as taboo for mothers; abandon is the opposite of maternal behavior deemed good for her infant or child. Because the mother's attention is turned away, because she is lost in her own feelings, perhaps lost to herself, she becomes unreliable and even life-threatening.

This tension, this conflict of focus, is intense. Mabel, an adolescent girl training to swim the English channel in Tina Howe's play *Pride's Crossing*, castigates her mother for showing no interest, for not noticing, for never watching her swim. "[B]ut it was *your* gaze I was desperate for. I kept looking at the window, willing you to lift the shade and finally see me."[7]

The wish to be kept safe, treasured in the eyes of someone who loves you, the sense that you become more able, more alive, when she watches you *with love*, is widely shared, perhaps universally felt. (It's the basis of the transformative moment Julien experiences in *The Red and the Black*.) When a mother's eyes are not where the child wants them to be, the result can be painful. "[Y]ou were so wrapped up in your own misery, you never raised the blinds to look," Mabel accuses.[8]

In the play, the mother, Maud, is difficult to bear, obsessed with appearance, shallow. Rather than supporting her daughter's wishes for freedom—to participate in the world more broadly, even to exult and triumph—Maud is the voice of convention and constraint. Instead of taking the daughter's side against the social forces that limit her, Maud becomes the bearer of the culture's bad news, the enforcer of its repression. Unfree herself, perhaps unaware of her lack of freedom—she ushers her daughter into her own darkened room.

From a mother's point of view, such actions are often construed as protective. She fears the child will be harmed or destroyed if she is not taught to comply. Having her daughter do as she did also discharges rage against her own confinement, offers a defense against loss, and protects her from grieving sacrifices that, while locally urgent, from a larger perspective may not have been necessary. Years ago, I used the image of Chinese mothers giving *their* daughters over to foot binding to try to capture this dilemma. I've been fascinated by how many other writers separately settled on the same metaphor—how it has become a cliché of our era. Mothers bound feet, I assume, often without conscious intent to inflict cruelty—however much unconscious rage and sadism they may have discharged—but in order to make daughters attractive and eligible for marriage, virtually the only possibility available to them.

To a degree, this maternal "duty" is an inevitable, central part of being a parent, of raising children to enter the world as it is. How the mother guides the child, what she watches with enthusiasm, what she encourages or prohibits, depends heavily on her own sense of hope, her own experience of the world, her feelings of choice and opportunity.

Maud, who also attempts to preserve status for a daughter through marriage, may have acted with similarly misguided maternal protectiveness. Each mother looks around and takes her best guess. If her experience is of locked doors and landscapes without vistas, of danger or oppression, how can she, in good conscience, prepare the child for anything else? If the only egress demands a contortionist, mothers will attempt to force their children into the requisite shape. Part of the reason so many women in my generation contemplated the story of foot binding is exactly because society changed a little. What had been made mundane by presumed necessity, suddenly, viewed from a new perspective, seemed like complicity or a betrayal. Mabel expresses that feeling.

But even as the daughter's wish for greater freedom becomes acceptable, there is more to the disagreement between Mabel and Maud than simply a heated exchange that exposes another disappointing mother. In a larger sense, the dialogue describes a tension about resources. The places mothers rest their eyes, the emotions they project, the amount of time they watch, is closely scrutinized by children. It can be a matter of life and death, emotional sustenance, identity creation, social direction, or simply of whimsy.

From the mother's perspective, watching a child can be urgent, deeply satisfying, delightful, calming, loving, terrifying, part of the necessary work; or it can be tedious and self-depriving. Depending on competing tasks and desires, it can be a priority or not, even possible or not.

Informal standards, varied by era or neighborhood, broker ideas about how much watching constitutes good care. As we have seen, some psychoanalytic texts condemn heartily the mother whose eyes are inconstant. Not long ago, mothers may have watched mostly to assure safety, oversee tasks, and to witness moments of delight. Children were watched less exclusively by mothers, and more by other family members, servants, neighbors, and by God. Nancy Scheper-Hughes tells of one slave master in nineteenth-century Brazil who had mothers bury mobile toddlers up to their chests in holes dug in the ground "so as to curtail movements over long stretches of time" while the women labored in the fields.[9]

Still, the "eye problem" creates part of the reluctance to join the words *freedom* and *mothers*. A mother may turn away to care for another child, or do necessary housework, but not to indulge more than an occasional fancy or do too much of her own work; that is deemed selfish. So too, if she is a single mother who must work, she is too readily frowned upon. In turn, often half-obscured but consistently present voices in society whisper that a free mother may not wish to watch.

Certainly, there are few more basic or frightening human emotions than the feeling of being left by someone who sustains you. What makes abandonment different from a more sanctioned departure is the sense of helplessness. Abandonment revolves around a core of unreadiness. One feels dependent upon the other for psychological well-being—if not life itself—and thus endangered by a mother's absence, bereft of resources. It is difficult to overstate the intensity and overwhelming urgency of the feeling.

Current research in the United States indicates that somewhere between 30 and 70 percent of murdered women are killed by male partners and lovers (as opposed to 4 percent of murdered men who are killed by women partners or lovers). The overwhelming number of murders occur either when the women decide to leave, or within a year of their departures. A psychologist discussing the phenomenon suggests that the men "often have a terror of being abandoned and express their dependency in extreme jealousy and controlling behavior." No longer in the United States supported by codes of law that in the past made it almost impossible for women to leave, some men kill rather than suffer their feelings. That this experience is intense enough in adults to provoke murder is testimony to its psychic centrality.[10]

Implicit in these statistics is an interesting psychological point. It would seem that the fear of maternal abandonment is an unnamed meeting ground for the whole family. Men, women, and children share a dread of the mother's leaving, which then gets superimposed on ideas about freedom. The mother fears the "bad" part of herself that might wish to leave, and feels as well the daughter's fear of being left. Since everyone has been a child, and only some have become mothers, the odds favor the child's perspective as it lives on in adults.

A woman who sometimes looked after me when I was a teenager in Vermont, herself childless and divorced, told how, when she was little, her wealthy mother went on a tour of Europe that lasted many months. The day the traveler (should we call her a female Odysseus?) finally walked back in the door, her three-year-old daughter did not recognize her, and asked, "Who's that?" The story chilled me when I first heard it thirty-five years ago, and is sad now. *My poor sitter had a bad mother,* I thought. Yet, it never occurred to me to wonder where her father was, why her mother left, who took care of the children while she was gone, or how the mother felt about the separation and how she acted throughout the rest of her daughter's childhood.

I suspect the story returns now because it captures something about the anxiety and the resulting distorted tableau summoned by imagining a free mother. Our first reflex is to see her as indifferent, abandoning, and self-consumed. Our second is to identify with the child's sense of loss, and to feel diminished by the mother's actions. She's walked out; she has better things to do than care for us; she has seen our essential badness and fled. We will be harmed for life. To raise Telemachus, Penelope must stay at her loom while Odysseus battles. We favor this version.

In her powerful story "The Children Stay," the writer Alice Munro describes how Pauline, the mother of two very young children, comes suddenly to leave them and her husband to go off with another man. Pauline is a loving mother, preoccupied with her children, and attentive. Sitting beside the ocean, she puts down a script she is memorizing. "She was afraid that she would get too absorbed in it and take her eye off the children for a moment too long." Pauline is hesitant, eager to please. Before she leaves, we are told how—to cross the short distance from cottage to beach—she dutifully wears shorts over her bathing suit so as not to displease her in-laws. So, too, she carefully finds shade to sit in on the beach because Jeff, her lover, wants her skin pale for her role in the play he is directing. She is inclined toward loyalty; the shift from one man to the other seems to be the most freedom she can imagine for herself.[11]

Yet she leaves her husband and children. The story implies that Pauline is partly pursuing sexual passion, partly attempting to flee from deadening feelings of emptiness that might be caused by her marriage. Or maybe not. Motives remain mysterious. Suggestions about her reasons for going are made indirectly, lightly and ambiguously; no pat explanation is offered. A lover declares his need for her; she goes to him.

The next day, her husband, helpless, miserable, enraged, talks with her on the telephone:

> "The children stay," Brian said. "Pauline. Did you hear me?"
> "No," said Pauline. "Yes. I heard you, but—"
> "All right. You heard me. Remember. The children stay."
> It was all he could do. To make her see what she was doing, what she was ending, and to punish her if she did so. Nobody would blame him.[12]

In the single sentence "Nobody would blame him," Munro succinctly summarizes the social and legal code of Western history dating back at least to Euripides. Pauline experiences Brian's words and the reality they communicate about the loss of her children "like a round cold stone in her gullet, like a cannonball."[13]

Will she go back to be with them? She feels she cannot. So she lives without her children. Munro ends the story with a discussion of emotional pain and how it is managed. She has referred earlier to Anna Karenina and Madame Bovary, as well as to Euridice and Orphée and the perils of looking back. She conveys that she understands perfectly the tragic ending that history expects.

Describing the extent of maternal suffering Pauline has incurred, the narrator postulates that her lover, Jeff, has no idea of what she is experiencing, but adds: "It isn't his fault. He's still an innocent or a savage, who doesn't know there's a pain so durable in the world."[14] Neither diminishing the attachment, nor creating a feelingless mother, Munro honors the depth of pain and still maintains the possibility of everyone's survival. No man murders. No child dies. No ruined woman swallows arsenic or jumps in front of a train. They all go on.

At the end of the story Munro writes, "Her children have grown up. They don't hate her. For going away or staying away. They don't forgive her, either. Perhaps they wouldn't have forgiven her anyway; but it would have been about something different."[15] These understated sentences, with their careful honesty and qualified feeling stand coolly beside the whole long history of deadly cautionary tales and sensational debacles. By leaving and defying her husband's assumption that she should stay, Pauline loses her children, although the completeness of their separation is unclear. Is she allowed to see them when they're little, or must she wait until they're grown? We don't know.

On one level, the template of defiance and child loss is the same one we've been observing in other texts. However, Munro breaks the mold. This story brilliantly revisits the constellation of mythologies about mothers. What has history led us to expect for Pauline? Either such a woman doesn't really love her children, or she stays and obeys at all costs, or she leaves and destroys her family. (As I first wrote this in the year 2000, the *New York Times* carried an account of a mother of seven children in Mazar-e-Sharif, Afghanistan, in a stadium in front of several thousand onlookers, publicly stoned to death as punishment for adultery.)[16]

"The Children Stay" quietly presents another possibility. The mother does not have to pay with her child's life or her own. Munro challenges the sense of ultimate badness many associate with a mother defying her husband, having illicit sex, or leaving. Without minimizing harm or pain, she deftly places the particular suffering fairly within a larger firmament, as a star among stars, rather than a singled-out, overwhelming, burning sun. Fittingly, the story is lit, the reader's tension electrified, by energy from our own expectations, and our fears, perhaps even our anxiety about her assertion.

A common reflex and unconscious fantasy about a "free" mother is that if she is leaving by choice, she must be going to a lover. However forbidden such a departure, other kinds are held to be less comprehensible. (If, for instance, we hear of a mother abandoning her children so that she can read magazines all day in a library, we assume she is mad.) Whereas, in the past (also as it endures into the present), the adulterous woman feared violent retribution from others, in this contemporary tale she is faced with the more everyday consequences of her own agency. The story shifts the locus of harm, so that she experiences the pain she inflicts, plus the self-incurred psychological loss at choosing to depart (at least from her husband), of becoming the abandoner. Taboo and almost impossible to imagine is a narrative that plausibly or sympathetically describes a mother gaining something significantly more emotionally valuable than the children she has left. (For fathers, the common—though often false—assumption is that the new, better relationship implicitly makes up for the loss of children.)

Whatever the angle, it seems that people are unlikely to think about a free mother without fusing the fantasy with notions of adulterous sex and abandoned children. Unobvious, even lost in so many accounts, is the free woman who *offers* steady proximity, *offers* fidelity, nurturance, and love because she chooses, and because she has enough resources to make her intentions possible without demanding disproportionate sacrifice. One reason we hesitate to see her accurately is that by obscuring her behind other camouflage, we may not have to assist her, or to create laws, working conditions, and institutions to better support her efforts.

*   *   *

The larger false proposition is that mothering is simply what mothers do. So societies are entitled to minimize its real contribution, shirk their responsibility to offer adequate supporting resources, yet freely criticize those who do it. Interestingly, while men may be criticized as bad fathers, there is no equivalent cultural assumption that fathering is simply what fathers do. Men work.

What, contemporary America seems to be asking, is fathering anyway? Recent bestsellers like David McCullough's biography of John Adams, or Mitch Albom's *Tuesdays with Morrie,* or the spate of books about World War II heroes, suggest that we collectively have a longing for wise, honest, brave, self-sacrificing, and loving fathers.[17] But we're not sure how these heroes fit with the everyday lives of most men. Probably in the past much of fathering involved hands-on teaching of tasks—like plowing, hunting, or carpentry, and the setting of behavior and values. The current public notion is vague. Is it like mothering, or different?

Within some families this confusion is the result of real role integration, because mothers and fathers increasingly share income-earning work, child care, and housework. But such families are not the majority. Nor is it easy to spot a healthy public articulation (that is, one devoid of either terminal idiocy or an insistence upon undue authority) of a version of fatherhood that gives men an expansive part in family life. While such fathers exist, they tend not to get much press. In general, even as some men participate fully and with deep devotion in nurturing children, we seem to lack a solid, clearly defined idea or expectation of meaningful emotional, practical, and moral contributions to children by fathers. And many men's sole participation is defined by their paychecks. Certainly, one reason for downplaying paternal importance is its economic convenience to employers.

In a magazine article about work, a successful corporate lawyer recounts how his wife telephoned him at the office to tell him that their three-year-old son had just misidentified a morning talk show host as "Daddy." The lawyer told the reporter, "My own son didn't recognize me. Then I pledged to stop working weekends, and I've managed to do that to some extent."[18] However uneasy such a father makes us, many would also accept his absence as a given of his success—perversely, almost a badge of honor and sacrifice. His contributions to his family, money, status, and all their accompanying benefits, are seen as enviable, apparently overriding his lack of physical presence and emotional participation. As long as the mother is at home, he can be unknown to his children. Conversely, no mother would allow herself to be quoted in a magazine describing a like situation; the shame would be intense, the condemnation enormous.

Many children have loving, dedicated fathers. Some thrive because their father's love is primary, or because their fathers protect them from their mothers. Yet, sadly, the relational aspects of fathering are not widely seen as a core part of maleness, nor as a readily defined contribution to the well-being of children. The cultural disconnect deprives boys and men of a healthy entitlement: that their adult role includes the right to nurture and guide the next generation in intimate ways. Equally noxious is its opposite: that the efforts of mothering are construed as innate and naturally laid out for women. This ongoing polarization of assumptions strains both sexes.[19]

Yet another reason that equating freedom and motherhood is difficult is that we're so unused to the idea. Most of us arrived on earth because our ur-mothers, our grandmothers, even our mothers, could not count on anything close to "safe" sex or reliable contraception, or safe abortion. Even abstinence often has not been in a woman's control, certainly not once she married. With some variation of place and time, and assuming both partners were fertile, a married woman was likely to find a good chunk of her often short adulthood given over to pregnancy, childbirth, child death, unremitting work to care for living children—and possibly her own death in the process. Even now, the truth is that political and economic equality between the sexes is still far from realized. Some women have opportunities. However big the local numbers, in a broader sense the situation is novel. Whether we will hold on to these gains, whether we'll manage to expand them so that they become available to women the world over who wish to participate, is uncertain. It is simply ridiculous to suggest, as too many do, that mothers have achieved equality.

All that has occurred for some middle-class American women during the twentieth century—most particularly the increased availability of contraception, the possibility for legal abortion, improvements in maternal and child mortality rates, better nutrition, access to higher education and jobs, the slight decrease in wage differences between women and men, liberalized divorce laws, and the right to vote—has created a sea change, a historic anomaly. But the resulting circumstances—not yet available to all women—are fundamentally unexplored even for the most fortunate. We have barely had occasion to consider what they mean now, and we certainly don't know how they will unfold across time.

How ironic, and yet perhaps predictable, that the truly new would so quickly be framed as associated with some fantasy of extreme feminism and therefore inconsequential, unsexed, or tired. But the *Zeitgeist,* which dictates fashion, can be a fickle friend.

Lately, for instance, attributing behavior to our genes, to mental hard-wiring, and to varieties of evolutionary psychology has been fashionable. Pundits have observed that popularized notions of Darwinian thought ("biobabble," as one writer put it) have replaced popularized notions of Freudian thought ("psychobabble") as the basis of public discourse.[20] And indeed, genome research, neurological discoveries, and new psychological theories based on Darwin's ideas and animal behavior are informing, even revolutionizing, our views of human behavior.

Unfortunately, the resulting theories have often been framed in ways oppressive to mothers. They have encouraged reductive views of behavior, particularly female and maternal. Popularized notions from sociobiology over the past twenty-five years, only lately and partially challenged, insisted on portraying women as breasts and uteruses in search of the perfect sperm. So too, whether or not members of the field intend it, and many make disclaimers, sociobiology and evolutionary psychology have frequently perpetuated deterministic and simplistic interpretations that suggest "my DNA made me do it." While I'm ready to embrace suggestions that our biology may sometimes incline us to behave in certain ways—and indeed I partly argue this book from just such a stance—I find it crucial to take such ideas and examine them with an eye toward enhancing freedom and social justice.

The sociobiologist Sarah Blaffer Hrdy has published a substantial treatise on mothering called *Mother Nature,* in which she not only provides endless fascinating anecdotes about human and animal mothers, but also successfully challenges some of the more conservative misogynistic ideas that haunt sociobiology. Nevertheless, Hrdy is also trying—and says so—to come to terms with her own belief that her mother was inadequately present in her life, and, worse, that she fired each governess Hrdy grew to like, disrupting her attachments. (Was her mother dutifully following the advice of John Watson?) Hrdy returns repeatedly to questions of infant-mother attachment and struggles to make up her mind about where she stands. Using science as her lens, her analysis ends up supporting the idea that children can thrive with multiple attachments, especially when they're steady.

But she also sometimes uses her "science" to talk, for example, about how difficult it is to find adequate human "allomothers," that is, caretakers. While she speculates about the Darwinian reasons for this dearth, I saw no mention of the obvious and extraordinarily important political and economic variables: that the work of foster parent and day care provider is underpaid and undersubsidized in the United States. However much Darwin's theories may shed light on the causes, we make a mistake if we let them justify the way bad practices endure.[21]

Ideas spread best in the mass media when they support underlying power structures. As the divide grows between rich and poor in America, there is a covert reglorifying, a Technicolor remaking, of something like "survival of the fittest," which attempts to justify outrageous inequalities, and more particularly to silence as scientifically naïve those who might put forward opposing ideals of social justice. As the Harvard geneticist R. C. Lewontin observes, "The claim that all of human existence is controlled by our DNA is a popular one. It has the effect of legitimizing the structures of society in which we live . . . It also claims that the political structure of society . . . is determined by our DNA, and that it is, therefore, unchangeable."[22]

Another reason I bring up genes and DNA, and the persistence of different kinds of deterministic thinking, is to highlight a vexing, broader problem in our discussion of mothers and freedom. So much new information—whether it becomes the basis of myths about the critical need for particular kinds of early stimulation of infants, or fatalistic ideas about how nature constructs us—gets used prematurely to "advise" mothers about what they ought to do, or how, or why. Just as iron filings will organize to follow a magnet, social science ideas as they enter the popular media cannot seem to resist following oppressive, faulty notions about women and maternity.

Specifically, maternal sensitivity to child loss and enhanced vulnerability, the ways that becoming a mother casts a potent spell over women, could be construed by some as simple biology: a mix of wiring and oxytocin that inexorably defines behavior and so justifies a history of inequality. Such a conclusion would miss my point entirely. However large biology's contribution to this potent spell, what matters is how we collectively recognize, socially reinforce, and ultimately handle the resulting mental states in mothers. My wish is to underscore the need for social changes that would allow all mothers to live more fully within our necessarily enhanced, protective emotions without having to accept second-rate citizenship for the effort.

Women deserve—and need to advocate for—public narratives that do not use threats of child harm as a means of social control. Whether disguised as religion, law, medicine, psychiatry, sociobiology, or genetics, these theories are imprisoning and harmful. If we are really interested in improving the lot of children, our best method would be laws and policy that support mothers and mothering.

Let me reiterate: the best mother is a free woman. Simply stated, a mother who feels valued and supported by her family, neighborhood, workplace, and society will have an easier time communicating to her children a sense that they are loved and valued. Conversely, a society cannot care adequately for children without respecting and caring for mothers. This point is at once so simple and so chronically overlooked as to be almost unbearable. Should we laugh or cry? Though many sentimentalize and make heroines of mothers by admiring their capacity to sustain children in adverse circumstances and to abdicate all else in the process, such a necessity is not to be idealized. Women stretch themselves too thin attempting to fill the gap between what they believe their children need and what the nation supports.

The most deeply immoral ideal we continually impose on mothers is the notion that they should be so singularly and asymmetrically accountable. Or, to put it another way, the demand for quantities of empathic love from mothers to children is the last place where science still tolerates the mistaken notion of spontaneous generation. We believe mothers should produce copious empathy without experiencing it from the larger culture, other than in the solicitous, protective kindness sometimes accorded to the weak.

The more we are able to imagine women and men as diverse and complex, the more parents will be able to pass these qualities on to their children. To hold such a power simply within the narrow mother-child or even father-child relationship is naïve and destructive. Humanness at its best is an imaginative act. And it expands when powerful forces within the culture gather to its cause. Discussing early childhood development and some of the differences between humans and other primates, the cognitive scientist Jerome Bruner succinctly observed that "in some deep sense 'becoming human' depends upon being with others who treat you as subjectively human."[23]

What comes to mind in response to Bruner are two stories a friend told me long ago about children who lived in or near her village in France in the first half of the twentieth century. One was a deaf-mute boy. His parents, apparently unable to imagine a child who lacked language and hearing, treated him like a farm animal and harnessed him to a plow to till their fields. My friend encountered the other child later, as a man who kept dogs but did not feed them adequately, so they slowly starved. As a boy, his own parents, very poor day laborers, confined him in a wine barrel, guarded by a dog, when they went off to work each morning.

Bruner briefly describes the process that creates psychological humanness thus: "So parents treat kids as if they had human intentions, desires, and beliefs, and expect their babies to treat them in just the same way. And in response, kids become increasingly sensitive to mental states in others over the first year." The more nuance, the wider array of possibilities loving adults imagine and name within an infant's responses, the more completely a child will come to have words and ideas about herself that are diverse and embody a broad sense of possibility. If this kind of sensibility in a child is desirable, and I would think it is, then what is the best way to help promote such emotional richness?[24]

Usually, when ideas like this one are put forward, they are imagined rather narrowly as created by individual love, typically maternal. But there's an important fallacy in this construction. For it leaves out the way the larger world treats people. Even if numerous loving mothers and fathers manage to transmit caring, to perform in the face of all impediments the imaginative act that Bruner describes—if their work is obscured and devalued by the larger society, if they are victimized by oppression, violence, and inequality, it is inevitably impeded and eroded. How "the boss" or the society treats the parents is a critical part of the narrative. Furthermore, the many parents around the world who must—metaphorically or actually—leave the child in the wine barrel in order to labor for survival, cannot then, justly, be singularly held accountable for the child's suffering. Lost in the way the story is usually told is how psychic life and legal, social, and economic justice are entwined.

The best mother is a free woman.

11

Worrying Mothers

IN HIS CLASSIC STUDY *Attachment,* a book first published in the 1960s and revised in the 1980s, John Bowlby several times describes behavior that occurs when a creature is "alarmed." So, for instance, when a young gosling is alarmed, its actions change dramatically. Or when, among baboons, "either mother or infant is alarmed, they seek each other out; and, when her infant is in trouble with peers or with adult males, mother tries to protect it." Human mothers are not goslings or baboons. Indeed, we devote a lot of intelligent energy to making distinctions—to talking back to an alarm system, and weighing its imperatives against other information and values.[1]

However, Bowlby's descriptions capture something—whether metaphorical or actual—about the response I have been trying to describe. A woman wakes one day, babe in arms, and finds herself having signed up to repeatedly become alarmed on her offspring's behalf. Without adequately naming this phenomenon, without exploring its importance, or mothers' feelings about it, cultures from the beginning of time have made relationships to this visceral, powerful, and primitive part of the mothers' experience, and to all the more complex or derivative responses that originate within it. They have—unintentionally and intentionally—discovered endless ways to stimulate and manipulate them.

Women become alarmed when their infants and children are threat-

ened. These threats can be life-and-death, or relatively inconsequential
—small tremors that somehow evoke larger worries about physical, psychological, or social harm. The feeling's effectiveness comes from the
fact that child loss and the accompanying grief are extraordinarily painful experiences for attached mothers. Mothers know about this pain in-
tuitively, from near misses if not first-hand, and take it for granted as a
background against which we live our lives. When something occurs
that puts the wire to the battery, we stay buzzed until we know our children are out of danger.

Sylvia, a mother I interviewed, described her long night waiting for
her fifteen-year-old to return from a church outing. Her son joined
some friends from another church who were traveling to an amusement
park several hours away. Sylvia sanctioned the trip. But after they left
she realized that she knew the minister's first name only and wasn't sure
of the name of his church. What if he wasn't who he said he was? What
if—as one hears in so many news stories—he had bad intentions? She
worried that she had not checked everything out carefully enough. They
were due back at 9:30. Arriving early, she waited with other parents in
the dark parking lot. No church vans appeared for almost an hour. Finally, they learned that one van had broken down, and all would be several hours late, arriving after midnight.

Worn out, back home, attempting to stay awake while her husband
—tired from his long day—slept, Sylvia fought off panic. "By one A.M.,
I was out of my skin. So at one-twenty when the phone started to ring,
I picked it up before the first click and said hello. 'Mom, it's Andy. I'm
fine. Are you okay?' It was like I was hysterical. I became unglued and
started crying." Heightening Sylvia's worries about trying to keep an adolescent safe was her constant awareness that as a "black male and tall,"
her boy was more endangered than his white peers—at risk simply because strangers would not see the "innocence of the youth . . . but more
just see that stereotype."[2]

In order to balance fear against concern for children's needs for independence, mothers struggle with their emotions, and (as Sara Ruddick
describes in her book *Maternal Thinking*) think hard. One evening, I
was seated at a dinner across from a woman in her sixties or seventies

whom I had not met before. She politely asked me about my book, and I started to describe the topic. Her eyes filled with tears, and she told this story, which I have since heard in many variants: When her two daughters, now grown, were little, they decided that they wanted to walk to school. The prospect worried her. Their neighborhood was okay, but who knew? Her instinct was to say no, to insist on driving them. At the same time, she felt that it was important that they have opportunities to explore on their own, and thus gain self-confidence. So she agreed to let them walk. But what if they got hurt? Could she live with her decision? She compromised. She said yes. But secretly, each day, as soon as they departed and she waved good-bye from the front door, she ran to her car to drive after them, trailing at a distance until she saw them arrive safely at the school.

In the same vein, Cathy, a mother of four children, described her worry, and her way of monitoring safety while letting her ten-year-old daughter walk alone to the local library: When her daughter announced that she was leaving, Cathy checked the time and made a mental note of how long the outing ought to take. As soon as the little girl left the house, Cathy ran up the stairs from the cellar, where she had been doing housework, to the living room so she could watch from the window as her daughter walked up the street toward the library. "And then I went to the living room because I knew exactly timing-wise I could watch her walk up to probably about the third house . . . and then I wouldn't be able to see her anymore. But you know what I mean? . . . It's such a fear."[3]

Joan, a young mother with a two-year-old daughter, further spelled out the intense, everyday effort of trying to find a balance between independence and safety for her child:

> But right now my struggle is to provide her enough space for her to grow. And what I'm most afraid of is losing sight of her. It's hard, too. I think it's mostly unconscious because I am not thinking that somebody will nab her or somebody will grab her. But it's just that there is a moment of real terror for the few times I lost sight of her and couldn't find her. In fairly safe settings. Like once I was at a facility for toddlers.

There were lots of people around but, you know . . . I had a real physiological reaction. I walked by where she had turned around and run into a structure . . . a little playhouse with stairs and little rooms and slides . . . I was pretty sure that was where she was, but it was really a moment of terror and I think that the fear must be that I am afraid of losing her and not that she would fall down two stairs and hurt herself.[4]

Each mother has stories about how she anticipates danger and constructs safe routes—concretely and metaphorically. The women I spoke with or interviewed often initially felt embarrassed to describe them (even as they poured out), unaware of how universal they are. But why do they matter? In a way, it would be easy to dismiss or trivialize them, yet that would be a mistake. The stories matter because they are the expressions we can see most readily, the narrative embedding and sequencing of a central maternal experience. They describe the way women's core fears of child loss or harm—their need to protect children—get woven with love into our everyday lives; the way that each woman knows the place where terror waits, and focuses continual effort, conscious and subliminal, on outmaneuvering it, all the while trying to make sure that her children develop autonomy and independent skills.

One mother, Ellen, who, with her partner, Diane, is raising three adopted children, made an analogy that beautifully describes this maternal state of mind.

I worked in an ICU as a nurse at one point. You can be talking to people, but there is a hyper-alertness to beeps and sounds in the background and you can immediately hear when something is not right. And I think of that in terms of being a mother for these kids—that you run your life, but there is something behind at all times sort of locating them in your mind, and where they are, and what they're doing, and how they are doing things. And so any little thing sort of snaps you forward. I don't know how to describe it any more than that, but it was—you know. . . . Before kids . . . it was not there. There was no need for it.[5]

The bits of adrenaline or panic mothers feel when a child is briefly unlocatable or ill, or barely escapes an accident remind mothers what can happen if they slip up. It sets the agenda. Just as the buzzers and bells, monitors and screens, in the intensive care unit guide the nurses, this constellation of core maternal feelings informs—directly and indirectly—maternal behavior. As Cathy described it, raising children shifts priorities so much that what was once "number ten is really number one" for a mother.[6]

Anyone who has been a child knows that mothers' protective actions and admonitions can be unbearable. Walking around a semifrozen pond one sunny winter day, I hear a woman scold in a hard voice a child of about three, whom I take to be her daughter, "*You* don't need to throw that stone. *Why* do you need to throw it?" the mother demands. The little girl is carefully dressed in a pretty coat, tights, and Mary Janes. She holds a pebble in one hand. She wants to throw it. But that would mean leaving the asphalt path and approaching the water along a muddy bank. The mother adds, "*Don't* go near the water." My ire rises. The prohibition grates. I recall the particular pleasure of skidding stones across ice, the delight of hurling things.

A moment later I recall my own irritated exhaustion sometimes when my kids were little. They'd wake up too early, need too much surveillance, ricochet around the house like a dozen squirrels on speed. (I remember a neighbor with older children who walked by one day right after our second son was born, and, laughing in warm commiseration, shouted out, "Yup, three more years and you'll be able to sit long enough to finish a cup of coffee.") I know the mother's tired bark, or worse, the way the duty of protection sometimes becomes a cloak for meanness. No mother likes herself much at the end of such days. Weary, guilty, we believe our worst reviews. And in spite of what some advice givers push for, the work of keeping children safe should not be confused with auditioning for sainthood.

In many ways, loving a child toughens women, matures us, lets us attempt things on behalf of, or in the name of, children we might not take on otherwise. Often we come into our own as mothers, become more confident people, find new strength, and feel more able. However, I am trying to trace out one central, very powerful response mothers have when they feel that children are endangered, and to indicate the extent of its effects, and its many personal and cultural ramifications. The sense of alarm is simply so powerful that at moments it brings women, however strong, to their knees. My hope is, as with so much else that is initially preconscious or unconscious, that naming it, exploring it, and understanding it better will help mothers free ourselves from some of its more oppressive dimensions, and will let us better comprehend some of the ways it has typically been manipulated to sustain inequality across societies.

When we try to understand why women have continually been closed out of so much political and economic power, why the fight for social equality is historically recent, and why mothers are so sensitive to, so ever-hungry for, advice—however demeaning or inaccurate—about child-rearing, one key, overlooked piece of the puzzle has been the terrorizing effectiveness of the mother's warning system. In comprehending its power, one has to take into account not only the basic alarm, but all the ways mothers respond to it and to its endless echoes, and all the ways societies have repeatedly overlaid it with impossible criteria and undue rationalizations for unsupported maternal responsibility.

I learned an unexpected lesson working with economically strapped women in a housing project. In spite of the way they had been publicly portrayed, the mothers I came to know did not have problems because they lacked a sense of responsibility. In truth, their circumstances were too hard. Yet, as often as not, they blamed themselves, as the larger nation blamed them. And their despair at falling short made them lose hope. They took too much responsibility and felt terrible shame. They knew the scrubbed and polished magazine and television images of mothers as well as anyone. Why couldn't they manage to offer their kids *that* life? In turn, their children suffered the dual perils of the surrounding world's indifference and their mother's shame, depression, and rage. I came to understand that the stereotypical image of the apathetic welfare mother is a large lie. Portrayed as lazy, she is often resourceful; yet she is also frequently glazed with trauma, having battered her head so many times against an impossible situation, her reality invalidated and unwitnessed, that she is left feeling defeated; harmed, too, by false hope, like a bird stunned after flying into glass.

The majority of American women and families are freed from the worst poverty and have viable if not good family incomes. Some are wealthy, and many are extraordinarily well off when compared to the three billion world citizens who attempt to survive on two dollars a day or less. (In truth, the poorest Americans, the Nobelist Amartya Sen points out, often African American or Hispanic, are as badly off in terms of health and life expectancy as the poor in countries like Bangladesh.)[7] Relative wealth, child health, and real safety offer enormous benefits, but they have not brought contemporary mothers peace. The vulnerability remains, and is repeatedly prodded and poked.

One mother described her essential feeling about mothering: "I think that you are stripped naked and raw when you have kids—in a way that you just never experience if you don't have kids, because you know that if something happens to your kids, it doesn't just happen to your kids. It happens to you." However relatively benign our situations, however plentiful our material lives, our guts, and perhaps our primordial minds behave like night watchmen blowing whistles, warning us that the world is not safe, that to protect our children we must remain awake and highly vigilant.[8]

My younger son's daycare provider years later reminded me how, as a five-month-old infant starting daycare, for several weeks he refused to take a bottle even as he cried from hunger. Resourcefully, this wonderful woman, distressed by his distress, would dress him in his snowsuit, set him in a stroller, take him out into the raw New England weather, and walk with him until the motion, relative solitude, and cold air soothed him so he would drink as they strolled. I, in turn, was relieved to be working outside the home and yet struggling to tolerate the half-day separations. Breastfeeding, I would start to feel a frantic letdown reflex even as I was stuck in traffic miles and minutes from him. Sometimes, I would feel undone by my sense of urgency. The stronger it became, the more time and traffic slowed into an inescapable quagmire. I had to get to him, I had to have him in my arms, right away, or one of us would die.

And that's the point. The passion we feel toward infants, children, adolescents, the way they are by turns innocents, lovers, and enemies, angels and incubi, tempests and the whole universe, defies reason—and every imposed idea about how it ought to be. One mother I interviewed described the depth of feeling awakened in her by her child, and its consequences: "There is nothing that is the same for me," she offered. "This has opened up great dilemmas, not just wonderful experiences. I am fundamentally not the same person, and the fallout from that is that it has shaken up other parts of my life." She added later, "If I could, I'd seal [my son] in bubble wrap. That being impractical, I just buy super-duper crash helmets and make him wear them all the time" to keep her active son safe while he is bicycling, ice skating, or skateboarding.[9]

When we feel comfortable with the substitute care—whether a loving person or a good school—those of us who work outside the home may most days assume our kids are fine and think little about them while we labor. We often do not talk about children when we're at work. But if another conversation pauses, or heightened trust opens a lane to the personal, the tone changes, and you hear that a woman's heart is at that moment aching or content depending on how she feels her offspring are faring. As one mother put it, "I would never have expected this, but I find I'm only ever as happy as the one of my children who's feeling or doing least well."

Underneath the gratification and joy, the nagging, the neighborhood chatter, arguments about bedtime, homework, and television, the thoughts of cookie baking, fights, or high times, and entangled in the love, this raw nakedness is what it means to be a mother. Whether you are poor or rich, working outside the home or in, the final helplessness of unbearably strong sentiment, the urgency to provide for and protect children (albeit sometimes from one's own failings) is finally transcendent. In a way, this core feeling of attached mothers is so obvious that it is invisible, so much a given of the landscape that it rarely becomes an object of focus. Every mother does not love every child, certainly not "optimally." But given any help, environmental support, money and other resources, space between pregnancies, the feeling of being valued herself—or given a glimpse of the suckling's winning grimace that lets her milk flow—she will find herself attached, and quietly apprehensive.

And the secret, the obvious yet often overlooked point, is that the vulnerability and the love are inseparable. Mothers are told that they "worry too much." Relative to the actual risks of a given moment, this statement can be true. But to tell a mother to stop fretting is to tell her to stop loving her child. In a discussion of the physiology of love in her book *Woman,* Natalie Angier writes, "What's interesting is that arousal, stress, and anxiety may be not merely antecedent to but instrumental in the creation of deep love and attachment." Stress "tenderizes the brain," Angier states, making it readier for love. And, I would add, love creates fear of loss, which then, almost perversely, helps sustain, even deepen the attachment.[10] Yet the resulting vigilance that works so effectively to keep children alive is alternately undervalued, obscured in sentimentality, patronized—or pathologized in psychiatry books.

Typical descriptions of mothering also gloss over mothers' ongoing work of responding to the needs they observe as they seek to keep children safe. Lisa, a young, single mother of a three-year-old and an infant, recounted for me one sequence of the tiny minute-by-minute decisions she made to balance demands within her family and to keep her children from feeling stressed. (I had asked her to choose a small part of the preceding day and tell me about it.) She described visiting with the father of her baby, but leaving early because the baby became fussy and she felt it was unfair to him to linger. She drove to pick up her older son, who had been with his grandparents, hoping then to run an errand and buy him some socks. But he was cranky, and she sensed that neither child could manage the shopping at that point, so she drove home. She put the baby down to nap and took the older child outside; she knew he badly wanted to play with a neighborhood friend who was also outside. Trying to prepare him for their limited time, she warned him that when the baby woke up they would need to go inside because it would be the baby's time to play.[11]

Asked the same question, Jean Marie, a married mother of ten children, told this story:

Now, yesterday for example, I was boiling eggs for lunch because I have a good friend who comes often for lunch . . . I was watching the clock because I always am and I had a quick errand to do. One daughter was sunbathing, she just looked too comfortable to even ask her to listen for the timer. So I said to my daughter who's fourteen, "Listen for the timer. When it rings, drain these eggs and put some cold water in [the pot]." I get in the car and I'm no sooner halfway down the street when I said, "That's a dangerous situation, the water is too hot, she's only fourteen and she doesn't always realize that the steam from the water can come back."

Rather than doing her errand, Jean Marie decided, "I have to go back to the house. I came back in the house to drain the eggs just as she is draining them. I said, 'Stop! I'm doing it!' "12

Both of these stories were casually told. Neither mother would have thought for a minute that what she did was in any way significant. But both anecdotes capture perfectly the endless planning, anticipating, and thought-filled concern we take for granted as everyday mothering. Lisa's story reveals how she calculated each action according to what she felt her kids needed and could tolerate. One needed rest; the other needed social time with a peer. She juggled and forfeited her own desires to socialize, do errands, or relax in order to attend to them smoothly. Jean Marie described her aborted outing: she allowed one child to sunbathe undisturbed and put off running her brief errand in order to make sure another child was not hurt.

Jean Marie told me about a woman who lived across the street from her. "This girl had four kids, and she's just a dynamite mother." One day she had a cranky morning getting them ready for school and had yelled at them. Then off they went. Later in the day, there was some disaster reported on the news, something like the *Challenger* explosion or the Oklahoma City bombing. The mother "went out of her mind" with panic. She called the school. She had to see each child. She had yelled at them, and now she had to know they were okay. "She went right up to school and she said, 'I want to see every one of my kids!' "13

Some would quickly suggest that Lisa could have managed errands, Jean Marie didn't need to return home, the neighbor could have waited for school to end. Indeed, I might have disrupted the sunbather, or made the fourteen-year-old deal with the eggs. On the other hand, on the morning of September 11, 2001, I did find myself, dazed, wandering toward my younger son's school, and I did find myself locating and hugging him and my husband, who teaches there, before I turned around and walked home to telephone my older son. But such personal reflections are not the larger point. What's important is that these mothers were doing what they felt they needed to do to keep their children safe and well. Subsumed under a mantle of "That's motherhood," their immense, intense work is allowed mostly to disappear. Yes, it is very satisfying; yes, it is love answered by love; but it is also committed, constant, consuming labor that makes an enormous, chronically undervalued, social contribution.

At one moment in our interview, Jean Marie wept. When I asked her what had caused her tears, she said she thought it was a combination of years of sleep deprivation and also the feeling that she'd managed to be "a great mother." Of the dozen mothers I interviewed and countless others I talked with informally, she was the only one who risked even a momentary positive self-assessment. And I think she felt safe making it because her devotion had been extraordinary—absolute. She had defeated the lurking bad-mother goblin by going to the mat; she had gradually arranged her life so that she was exclusively focused on her ten children. For twenty-five years she had done nothing but attend to them, anticipating the dangers of steam from a boiling pot and everything else: "I was at a pool . . . with my friend who had two kids, and I brought four and I would count [to make sure all six kids were safe in the water] . . . and then two more minutes I would be counting again. So it's like, they're all there, they're all there." (Jean Marie did not work outside the home; she worked eighteen or so hours a day at home; she allowed herself a week a year to visit her own family alone and a couple of hours one evening each week to sing in the church choir. Her husband worked long hours at a job but participated actively with the children on evenings and weekends.)[14]

Few American families have ten children. Nevertheless, Jean Marie offers a vivid example of an internal experience—and the actions that come from it—described by all the mothers with whom I spoke. Chances are that each of her children received no more than—say—the single child of a single working mom. But because she gave herself completely, exclusively, and to the point of utter exhaustion, she was fairly certain that she had given enough.

A neighbor who first led me to Jean Marie told me about helping her one night to sort a week's worth of clean socks. I imagined a huge game of Memory, not unlike the one I play when I fold the family laundry, but grander—as the sorters tried to recall where they'd just seen each of a hundred socks' missing mates. There is still plenty of physical work in child-rearing. But too often rendered invisible, blotted out, is the emotional and cognitive labor: the thought, the planning, the mindfulness of meeting children's needs, keeping sons and daughters alive through sheer concentration—matching and pairing, placing and re-placing each event in the day together with the larger schema in the mother's brain.

When our younger son was not quite sixteen, he attended a big outside afternoon rock concert in Boston on a day we were many hours away. The plans were elaborate; I was apprehensive. He was to telephone us by eight in the evening to confirm that he had arrived safely home. At nine, when we had heard nothing, my anxiety revved. I felt completely miserable. When, at ten, he called to say he had been delayed by crowds, then stuck on the subway, my chest uncrushed. Seeing my relief, a friend, an experienced mother and grandmother, sighed, and said, "I've been concentrating all evening on getting him home safely, and it appears to have worked." We laughed. I had thought that it was my own stupendous mental effort that had done the trick.

The real safety of children has improved. If child mortality in the United States is radically lower than it once was, why don't mothers feel at ease? Answering that question requires spelling out how conditions in contemporary America have changed expectations placed on mothers, and how they continually jostle and press our alarms.

Once again, there is the matter of psychology's doctrines of correct love: nurse "like a gipsy"—and other contradictory stipulations. As the requirements for mother love and the definition of what is desirable have become more rarefied—optimally attuned love, correctly attached love, not selfish love or anxious love or passionate love or critical love—the criteria seem almost to depart from reality. However hard all adults must work to subdue and domesticate the wilderness within, contemporary advice givers have focused a bizarre perfect-love demand upon mothers. The impossibility of satisfying such a mandate makes many mothers feel unsure and inadequate.

Along with the quality of love, the pressure to demonstrate it continually has grown in ways that might make our foremothers spin in their graves. Printed on my breakfast cereal box is a section called "The Nurturing Corner," in which I am advised on "Five Great Ways to Show Your Kids You Care." ("Celebrate their accomplishments, big and small" and "Plant something with them in the garden.") Not only is the boundary between sales tactics and advice giving appallingly confused, but the whole do-more-for-your-children reminder is over the top. Imagine for a moment that the Puritans pontificated on cereal boxes. They would direct their advice at children, and counsel them on ways to show parents respect and duty and on how to perform their own household labors more proficiently. No better perhaps, but the perspective gives one pause. My point is that overtones everywhere, so prevalent that we don't notice the saturation, escalate expectations and massage mothers to give more—and to feel unsatisfied with themselves whatever they do.

A second reason some mothers feel uneasy is that even though the majority of contemporary women are active outside the home, we live with the gnawing sense that maybe we shouldn't be. It might be fine many days, but if a child is faltering in any way, it could signify that we are bad for how we chose, no matter what the real cause of her difficulties. Each child is a universe of possibility, not to mention a huge economic investment; a mother must focus on helping her realize every aspect of herself. Denied the partial relief of overwhelming survival concerns, middle-class mothers' internal expectations have caught the cultural breeze (and vice versa) and become limitless.

And although no American law prohibits a woman from going into the work world, and the majority of American mothers now work to support or help support households, braying pundits continue to claim that by doing so she alone is depriving her children and harming society. In 2001, Richard Lowry published a diatribe entitled "Nasty, Brutish, and Short: Children in Day Care—and the Mothers Who Put Them There" in the *National Review*. "[T]he fact is," he proclaimed, "that working moms are at the very center of a variety of cultural ills. Maybe a little stigma is exactly what they deserve." A page later he added, "Work has, in post-feminist America, become central to the identity of women (and child-rearing doesn't count)."[15] However idiotic such statements, they inevitably distort reality and at the same time heighten self-doubt and guilt for mothers when children struggle.

Ironically, one cannot but wonder if the working mother's escalated guilt, stirred up by the likes of Lowry, negatively affects children more than her time away from home. For example, when a mother tells a child to go to bed at night but then feels guilty if the child protests (*I am neglectful and bad for being away during the day; he is right to object*), the child, feeling her hesitation, may capitalize upon it not only by hardening his refusals, but by coming to believe that he has indeed been deprived. Children are brilliant at sensing parental uncertainty, self-doubt, or ambivalence. And while all parents make bad decisions, which they must temper, apologize for, or undo, the heightened guilt some mothers feel thanks to endless media cues and the urgent wish to be perceived as adequately giving according to their culture's lights, can cause them to back away from useful limits that would in fact relieve their offspring. In turn, without some quiet evening time to regroup, the same mother may come to feel depleted, deprived, and angry, and the whole family suffers.

To grasp the escalation of demands upon mothers more fully, I want to try once more to capture the difference between the current expectations of mothers in America, and in the world as it mostly is and has long been. J. M. Synge's play *Riders to the Sea,* set in the late nineteenth century on an island off the coast of Ireland, is about a mother, Maurya, whose husband and six fishermen sons are one by one tragically drowned. The opening stage directions describe their simple cottage, where Cathleen, a twenty-year-old daughter in the family, "finishes kneading cake, and puts it down in the pot-oven by the fire; then wipes her hands, and begins to spin at the wheel."[16] This image is classic. It captures the labor of survival and arguably the way many, maybe a majority, of women have lived for centuries.

Having learned her work in childhood from her mother and other female kin, Cathleen will do it until she dies or wears herself out and her daughters take over from her. No one would have offered her much formal education. Was she even taught to read? No one would have spoken to her about opportunities, life choices, talents, professional training.

In turn, while Maurya's love and suffering over child loss are the center of the play, it would surprise me if anyone would have suggested she was responsible to do more than feed and clothe her daughters, send them to church, keep them marriageable, teach them the skills entailed in hard daily labor and communal life. Cathleen's younger sister, Nora, realizes that the wet clothes from a drowned man are indeed those of her missing brother by counting the stitches in a sock and recognizing her own knitting pattern.[17]

Their world, from our perspective, is circumscribed, and no doubt oversimplified by Synge's portrayal. When I visualize Cathleen's or Maurya's life, I am delighted to have vastly increased opportunity and safety. At the same time, I wonder what to make of the strange new demands for what should constitute maternal care which have accompanied the extraordinary contemporary economic and societal upheavals. Are they necessary for the well-being of children—or at least partially framed as updated justification for excluding mothers from the power centers of the public world? Yes, adults must teach children the ways and work of a much more complex world, however unclear the correct curriculum. And yes, small villages no doubt performed a kind of collective parenting, which has now largely disappeared, the absence of which burdens individual parents (and children) more. (A recent musical exploring life on a Maine island features teenage boys singing about how every mother on the island watches them as if they were her own children. No matter what they do, where they go, they humorously gripe, they're always under maternal surveillance.)

What we call modern or postmodern life represents a shift in fulcrum between replication of culture and innovation, or at least a large confusion about how the two fit together. With it have come demands on mothers both to fill the gaps between what is no longer communally offered, and also to raise children able to function within this great new chaos and complexity. Rather than urging this new world to care better for children, it seems more efficient to pressure mothers.

Contemporary demographics are a third reason that improved child survival has brought mothers little peace. Jean Marie is an exception. Most American families have few children. The current American "total fertility rate" for all women is just over two live births per woman per lifetime, not quite enough to achieve what is called "replacement level"—"the rate at which a given generation can exactly replace itself."[18] Consequently, parents sense they have "all their eggs" in one basket, or two. Often now couples have waited to bear children and perhaps have had to seek medical fertility help to conceive them. Birth control has changed heterosexual women's lives radically. And the reality that ever more children are born by choice probably heightens the sense of conscious hope and concomitant emotional liability. Parents cannot finesse their wishes; children are no longer the inevitable byproduct of sex. Vulnerability is upped at the outset. Conscious intention makes each child represent a large emotional investment, usually before it has entered the world.

Furthermore, children are often born to parents who know nothing about infants. Rarely have they grown up with enough younger siblings around to familiarize themselves confidently with the ways of small creatures. Arlene Eisenberg, who wrote *What to Expect When You're Expecting,* observed how young women (she didn't mention young men) simply no longer know about babies. " 'It used to be you could get all the good information about raising your kids from your mother,' " she said in an interview with the *New York Times* in 1999. " 'But it's all changed. Most young women have never held, never even seen, a newborn baby. It's really a shock.' "[19]

This historically extraordinary lack of hands-on experience adds to the sense of generational discontinuity. The possibility of a son or daughter learning to parent at his or her parents' side, taking care of younger children—in other words participating in mastering a craft through observation, practice, and talk with a knowledgeable mentor—is lost. Thus the adult children grow up only with the experience of having received, not given, child care. This imbalance distorts the way as parents they approach the infant, and it raises anxiety. I can remember standing with my husband over our newborn's bassinet, helping him breathe in, and breathe out. A funny noise, and our hearts would stop. What creature was before us?

Furthermore, because children are more likely to survive in this century than in years past, there is less open communal expectation of child loss, and less support for enduring it. At the same time, like a puppet backlit behind a curtain, its shadow expands to fill space. And its danger is real. When I think of the women I know, a number have faced pregnancy losses or stillborn infants. Others have mourned unexpected infertility. Still others have had children brought to the brink of death—and held there for long periods of time—by illness or accident. And a few have had children die. For all these women, grief is heightened by their sense of being singled out. Why did this happen to my child while so many others prosper?

Is there a more wrenching sorrow? Some of the loneliest women I meet are those who have recently had an infant stillborn, a failed insemination attempt, a miscarriage, or an adoption that fell through. They feel terrible, consumed by loss; and few around them adequately understand the depth and tenacity of their suffering. At least in the past families in which children died had company in almost every other dwelling in their village or neighborhood. And, as we have seen exemplified in the extreme by the Puritans, people often had communally shared and relatively cohesive religious practices that, however high the price, offered some form of collective solace.

Writing about child death among gentry families in eighteenth-century England, Amanda Vickery notes, "Contemporaries feared the thundering force of parental grief, and maternal anguish in particular was recognized as a 'species of savage despair.'" Yet Vickery also spells out the "vocabulary of Christian endurance," the way words like *fortitude* and *trial* were used to help people summon courage to bear their *travail.* To the extent that such a vocabulary remains today, it is often sequestered within religious sects and is less coherently available to the wider American society. The contemporary woman whose child dies is denied the comfort of being encircled by fellow sufferers.[20]

This deprivation of comfort alludes to an even larger dilemma of feeling. My impression is that we have lost not only a vocabulary, but a whole *mentalité* of survival. Death was often so prevalent in the past that the pain of enduring it was more at the center of collective everyday experience. Moreover, because death is less constantly present, and because life for many Americans is now physically and materially easier, people perhaps find psychic pain even more discordant. We take it personally, view it as aberration rather than accepting it as a normal part of life. So, too, personal sacrifice gains its purpose and dignity when survival is at stake, and becomes abashed, sometimes even the object of ridicule, when its collective necessity is less apparent.

Mothers' alarm systems are continually bombarded by contradictory media messages about child safety, and this phenomenon is crucial to understanding levels of fearfulness. On the one hand, the tone of the news is that this is the twenty-first century: We have modern medicine, rescue helicopters, and air bags. Don't worry. Pregnancy isn't illness. Childbirth is "natural." The major lethal childhood illnesses have been "conquered." On the other, the media ply parents with endless stories—gathered from all over the world—of violence, loss, disease, and disaster involving children. There are no boundaries on the universe a mother must monitor, no limits upon the new information tossed in her direction; she is never able to rest assured that she has adequately surveyed the territory; she is always being covertly warned of impending disaster, being reminded to stay on high alert.

The result is that mothers have their fears continually freshened. On a Sunday morning, driving to the next town to walk with a friend, I turned on A.M. radio for a weather report and caught the news headlines. The lead story? An anonymous car accident in South Africa, where eight people were killed, "including three children." All the news in the whole world, and the station led with a child-killing car crash over ten thousand miles away on another continent? While, obviously, all deaths deserve witness, most don't get it. Usually, in fact, in African countries many thousands of people can die before the media tunes in. So the relative prominence of this story is difficult to explain, except as it grips parents' hearts. You hear it and you cringe, you hold the wheel harder, worry about children in cars. Because you're a little upset, your own chemicals flow, and I suspect you pull your kids closer. You get the impression that if you don't attend, something will surprise you with harm. Newsmakers know that family tragedies sell because listeners (viewers, readers) immediately identify. But this phenomenon often becomes the basis for cynical, profit-seeking transactions. And, from what mothers spontaneously and consistently related in interviews, it has the effect of upping anxiety and maternal discomfort.

I recall an awful story from a woman's magazine I read in a waiting room a couple of years ago describing the injury lap belts did to the writer's daughter in a car accident, and the multiple surgeries the injured girl had to endure. Why did the editors print it? Perhaps they felt it was important to inform their readers of a concern, and attempt to rouse a push for reform. And they knew it would be read. Perhaps the mother implored them to tell her story. Why did I read it? Well, could I, as a mother trying to take responsible care of my children not at least skim an article that warned me about the dangers of seat belts? What if I ignored the piece and then they got hurt, and I could have spared them? I contend that many mothers think like this all the time. I hope that the net result of the story is that the car industry has modified belts. But, more likely, I suspect that I and probably a million other mothers have simply added gruesome images of seat-belt-induced injuries to our mental lists of perils.

Women's magazines regularly carry similar stories, and often their theme is of salvation, thanks to totally dedicated mothering. In a *Good Housekeeping* (2002) story entitled "Beating the Odds," a young woman describes her mother's lifesaving devotion. "Two years ago, I received five new organs in a rare transplant operation. The doctors didn't expect me to make it . . . but my mom never let me stop fighting . . . Unable to move my arms and legs, and silenced by the breathing tube inserted in my trachea, I looked at my mother. Painfully, I mouthed the words: 'I want to die.' 'No, Kathryn, you can't give up,' Mom said, reading my lips." The daughter continues, "Nobody really knew what kept me going. But I imagine my mom had something to do with it. Having given up her job teaching high-school biology and left my dad, sister and brother at home, she was by my side every day, arriving early and leaving late, nursing me, waiting."[21]

Kathryn is describing the most intense variant of the maternal behavior I've been documenting throughout the book. And I, perhaps all of us, know mothers who have sat in ICUs with children exactly as Kathryn's mother did. In truth, I cannot think of anyone I've met who would not attempt to do the same thing for her child in the face of such extraordinary misfortune. Nevertheless, the story is also oppressive. It sensationalizes child danger; like a forearm banging a keyboard, it presses octaves of alarm keys. And, once again, it does so in the service of valorizing maternal sacrifice. At the same time, it does not describe what really is entailed for the mother, nor does it consider how the rest of the society could and should participate to match her contribution. Why did Kathryn's mother's feel she had to trade work seniority, income, and pension plan to care for her child? How would it have been if she and the father took turns? A mother is glorified for giving up everything to save her child; the rest of the picture is left undrawn. I know both as a therapist and as a friend what such heroism costs mothers emotionally for years after: the nightmares, physical and psychological pain, the real suffering undescribed in the story, however overjoyed the woman is to have a living child.

When you gather dangers from the whole world, when you add together all the possibilities of harm in our complex contemporary world, the varieties of threatening possibility are endless—even when stories are less sensational. Take for example the premature publicity frequently given to incomplete or simply incorrect research about child development—the "if you don't bond immediately, you'll never bond at all" type of narrative. Any that manage to settle on one side or another of a current cultural hot spot get much too much attention. They have destructive, if brief, influence until the more careful, and often underpublicized, refutations come along.

When in 2001, the psychologist Jay Belsky published research suggesting that some children who spent more than thirty hours a week in daycare were more aggressive than those who didn't, the *New York Times* covered the story extensively. *Time* magazine ran a big piece. Meanwhile, the European press, Katha Pollitt pointed out in her column in *The Nation*, reflecting the experience of countries that have long taken good, group child care for granted, recognized that the report was premature and not terribly newsworthy. And, in the midst of the bad outcome noise, where was the article suggesting that if employers paid mothers equal wages and society subsidized daycare, parents would have to work fewer hours to pay the basic bills while children could benefit from higher quality care? Where was the essay exploring, if indeed the aggression finding was both accurate and undesirable, how to restructure daycare settings for different age groups?[22]

While mothers feel altered and vulnerable, finally stripped naked by child love, the outside world, filtered and partly defined now by how the media portrays it, relentlessly plays upon these feelings. Children everywhere, it continually signals, are endangered. Mothers I spoke with made spontaneous reference to current news stories about recently harmed or rescued children. I asked the mother of a teenage daughter, "What is most psychologically different for you now from before you were a mother?" Typical of the women I interviewed, she answered, "I guess I would have to say thinking constantly about the well-being of another human being." In the years after her child was born, Pam was surprised to discover how much she felt her daughter's feelings, particularly her pain. "The first time they fall down and get a boo-boo, you feel it as well." Then, referring to the day's television news, she added, "You feel it not only for your own child but for other children . . . Just before I was leaving the house they found a little boy who was missing in Waterville Valley overnight . . . He was conscious and alive . . . And the *feeling* that goes through you, though you don't know who he is . . . but he is somebody's child. And whatever it is . . . that cluster of emotion, you feel it at a very, very basic level."[23]

A week or so after a sixteen-year-old girl, abducted from her lifeguard job, had received much attention in the local media, I interviewed two mothers. Both referred to the tragedy and described how strongly it had affected them. Each said that after watching the news story, she became more worried and cautious. Lisa observed, "I mean that once you have kids, you just think, Oh my God, if that was my kid, what would I do? I wouldn't be able to survive without them . . . Me, I think I just worry all the time. I am so afraid to let them do anything. [Yet] I don't want to hold them back." Jean Marie offered, "That [story] is enough to make your heart stop. In fact, right after that . . . my daughter who is fourteen said, 'I am going to walk Jennifer down the street,' and I immediately said, 'No, no you're not.'" But then she thought better of her first response. It was about 9:30 at night in a safe neighborhood. Jean Marie told her daughter when she expected her back and carefully watched the clock. The daughter was a little late. "I became basically paralyzed. And again, not wanting to give in to it and live like that, I said, 'This makes no sense.'"[24]

After the news and television dramas heighten maternal fear, entrepreneurs of all stripes offer products to lower it. For example, a Boston newspaper article (2000) reported how digital surveillance cameras are being installed in daycare centers to relieve parental unease. Working parents who cannot be with their children during the day can watch them (but, oddly, not hear them) on their laptop screens. Of interest is the anxiety that motivates parents to pay the higher cost for such equipment and to desire the service at all, as well as the way the news story is presented. The reporter writes, "For parents who are only too familiar with the heart-wrenching details of the death of 8-month-old Matthew Eappen while in the care of Louise Woodward as well as the sexual molestation conviction at the Fells Acres Day School, these video cameras can seem like a godsend, judging by the early reaction."[25]

Both the Louise Woodward trial (she was found guilty of involuntary manslaughter) and the Fells Acres Day School convictions are stories familiar to most Bostonians and many Americans. The infant Matthew Eappen was killed by Woodward, his teenage au pair, who in 1997 shook him much too hard while she was alone taking care of him. The Fells Acres Day School accusations, of rape and sexual abuse by three adults, were made in 1984, and the suspects were convicted in 1986, a full fourteen years before this recent surveillance-camera piece appeared.

Both events are horrid. One's heart goes out to the children, the parents and extended families, and to the many loving people devoted to providing professional child care who, "by association," have to endure elevated suspicions. All the same, the newspaper article shows—and itself perpetuates—how the events have taken on the quality of boogie-monster scare stories. Not only are they being used in this instance to rationalize surveillance cameras, but, in a larger sense, they remind parents to feel frightened. Is hyping fear a good idea? Some cautionary tales are useful; knowing where real dangers lie is invaluable. And certainly it sells both news and cameras. But what else does it accomplish? Like the television and radio, such journalistic efforts repeatedly overcue hypervigilance.

Furthermore, the stories have a more insidious, though perhaps consciously unintended, effect as well. They whisper, "Mom, stop working outside the home . . . it's dangerous." Each time mention is made of child death or harm in the hands of non-kin care providers, a certain number of mothers reach their breaking point. They quit paid work, cut hours, take a less demanding position, or stay home. Furthermore, what became painfully apparent in the case of Matthew Eappen was that his mother's job, the fact that she was a professional, and affluent enough (in some people's minds) to stay home, became a lightning rod. She was mercilessly assaulted with accusations of selfish ambition and irresponsibility.

Staying home full-time with children is great for those who desire it, tolerate it well, and can somehow manage to afford it. It can also make a real contribution to the well-being of a whole neighborhood or community. But, as a guilt- and fear-induced choice, or an imposed notion of optimal motherhood, it leaves much to be desired. The reflex of personal concern successfully diverts attention from the pressing social needs to pay adequate wages to care providers, to support economically mothers who stay home, to build a society in which child-rearing is indeed thought about carefully.

Working mothers are not loved. In fact, they draw a lot of the current bad-mom publicity. Consider the popularity of First Lady Laura Bush, who is portrayed as private, family-oriented, devoted to her husband, and a reluctant participant in the public world, versus the image of Hillary Clinton, who as First Lady was portrayed as a pushy feminist lawyer meddling in her husband's domain.

The fact is that go-to-work/stay-at-home decisions are economically and ideologically driven, institutionally based, and very personal. A wide variety of choices deserve full support (much more than they get) and produce fine kids. I think it would be terrific if society subsidized (for example by means of living wages, one- or two-year-long paid parental leaves, fair promotion and good benefits for people in part-time jobs, universal health care, work-force re-entry assistance, and pension or higher social security payments for stay-at-home parents) mothers or fathers to be home at least part-time for their child-rearing years. But the real goal is to create many options and many forms of good care for children—to support equally the factory worker parent and the executive, the parent who works part-time or full-time and the one who stays at home—not to manipulate people or heighten their mutual enmity through fear.

In 1983, I cofounded, staffed, and helped guide the daycare center where I sent my sons while I went to work. It is still going today and is annually attended by about forty children. Not only does daycare replicate the small-group "habitat" that I believe is natural to kids for at least part of their day, but it offers a mix of privacy and public observation that functions well to protect children from the isolated fatigue and frustration of single caregivers, be they kin or professionals. The providers have one another for company, support, and mutual checking. During the years I was involved, parents in our center helped hire the teachers and got to know them through all kinds of contact. They observed the care by coming in and out to drop off and pick up children. In some centers, parents regularly volunteer and spend time with the teachers and children together. The interaction between parents and providers is a healthy thing, preferable to one-way cameras. (What if the daycare workers had the fair and equal right to train cameras on the family homes? According to the statistics of abuse, that would make much more sense.) An added benefit for me was that when I felt at a loss with one of my children, I sought advice from the daycare staff and learned from them.[26]

There's something wrong-headed about turning cameras on daycare as a means of preventing harm to children. Not that bad things can't happen. They can and do. But technological surveillance finesses the important questions: How much should society change in order to make work situations that honor the needs of parents and children? (When are we going to face the obligation to make care for all citizens as compelling a value as it deserves to be, and back it with resources?) If some children need more proximity to parents, shouldn't this come from emotional closeness, longer paid leaves, or care centers located at work so parents and children can see, smell, touch, hold, and talk to each other during the day? Why not have it come from more flexible work hours, shorter workdays and weeks, fairer benefits, and better sickness policies? Not only does the camera expose people in weird and impersonal ways; it also drains energy from defining and implementing important social changes that will genuinely improve family life.

But the point I started with and the one to which I want to return is the way these terrible but mostly exceptional tragedies are turned into frightening pageants, ghostly floats, cautionary tales to be wheeled out and paraded before parents. In these scenarios, harm to children from life, largely social injustice, violence, indifference, or unreasonable workplace demands, hard to track in its specifics, is conveniently blamed on low-paid laborers who take care of children while parents work, and indirectly on working mothers. Are you worried about your child? Take a job with "mother's hours." It pays less and lacks benefits, but with it you can return home when the school bus arrives. What if you're not home, and a stranger meets the bus and takes your child . . . it happened in . . . I heard it on the news.

*   *   *

We talk glibly about mothers loving children. It is a great national cliché—routinely intoned by political candidates, pondered on television commercials—every child "deserves love." Adults will sometimes say longingly, "I wish that my mother/father had hugged me, had told me that she/he loved me." Sweetness, tenderness, warm touch, encouragement, are all expressions of love for which people hunger. Yet the whole of love—love that has not been neutered by platitudes, gelded for domestic employment—is so much more than its blander expressions. The great engine of mother love, the iron horse, the steaming, churning, driving locomotive, ferocious and gentle—overlooked by casual invocations, diminished by sentimental coercion—is a passionate machine. And with it, attached, crucial as the coal car on an old train, comes the willingness to let your mind and heart be taken over— thinking and worrying about how to do right by a child, how to keep her alive and safe, how to help her prosper. Mother love is the agreement to live in this always dangerous world paradoxically: ever-vigilant to threat, aware that life is completely fragile, yet with your emotions intimately touching, wheel to rail, your children, fully in contact, your soul given freely, even foolishly—handed over—as if children were as immortal as the sky—and you could afford the risk.

12

Putting Children First

MOTHERS I spoke with almost always spontaneously stated that they *put their children first*. And they placed this philosophy at the heart of mothering. Their actions differed depending on their circumstances and expectations. For one mother, an example of putting her child first meant working full-time as a doctor, yet forsaking professional trips that would have kept her away from home too much: "I should be traveling now. I turn down every invitation to speak, attend, and participate." For a second, divorced mother, it similarly meant leaving a lucrative bank job that required travel: "I really feel I need to stay put." For a third, it meant cutting way back on paid work when her first son was born, although by doing so she had to accept living with less money. She felt gratified devoting herself to her two children, yet sad and frustrated about her professional sacrifice and tight finances: "When they were younger, I made a choice to be with them more than not."[1]

For one mother at home, putting children first meant making the day's decisions according to her kids' schedules, their needs for rides to school and activities, her sense that she should be present whenever they appeared. For another woman, it meant staying married through the rocky times when she otherwise might have left. For a divorced mother, it meant not dating much, not bringing boyfriends into family life. For a married woman working outside the home, it meant giving up most time alone with her husband, although she knew it would restore them both. Their priority, after work demands were met, was time with children.

I was caught by surprise as I listened. Putting children first. I hadn't expected the phrase to be ubiquitous. The expression itself initially sounds saccharine. Certainly it is easy prey to sentimental notions of motherhood. But construing it that way patronizes the women who described making difficult choices based on their sense of their families' needs. They quietly experienced their behavior for what it was: a core, ethical commitment, a profound sense of responsibility for having brought new lives into the world, a just effort on their children's behalf. Because of varied interpretations—the different actions entailed for each woman—it didn't imply that children received the same amount of attention, or care that an expert—or other mothers—would necessarily view as optimal or "good." Rather, each mother would look at what was at hand—what she thought was possible within *her* context—and then make accommodations. She would attempt to be the insulation, the shock absorber between the world around her (external demands embodied, for example, in employment, economic, marital, neighborhood, and church matters) and her children's needs as she perceived them.

Studies bear out the individual mothers' comments and suggest part of the price they pay by putting children first. Researchers at the University of Maryland found that "today's mothers spend just as much time with their children as mothers did in 1965." Even though three-quarters of mothers with children under eighteen now work outside of the home, contemporary mothers are managing to find 5.8 hours a day to be with their children, as opposed to 5.6 in 1965, when few mothers worked outside the home. When asked how this could be true, the sociologist Suzanne Bianchi observed that working mothers sacrificed sleep.[2]

The compromises described by the women I interviewed also reflect larger economic patterns. Jane Waldfogel, an economist at Columbia University, has demonstrated that "childbearing exerts enormous downward pressure on women's wages. Using data from the National Longitudinal Surveys, Waldfogel compared the earning power of mothers and nonmothers across occupations—controlling for age, education, and experience—and found that childless women now earn 90 percent of what their male counterparts earn, while mothers earn only 73 percent."[3] Mothers not only do most of the work of child-rearing, they disproportionately absorb its costs.

I gradually came to understand that putting children first was not only an act of love, but a marker of the priority that mothers had established; it was a primary assumption and, simultaneously, an adaptive effort. If you find yourself both filled with love and loony with worry, as new mothers do, one way to translate the feelings into useful action is to pledge yourself to this ideal. Besides its central purpose of protecting children and helping them prosper, the commitment functions as a kind of talisman, a cryptic message to your soul that you are shouldering your uncontainable responsibility to the utmost. "You know," a mother said to me, "if something bad happens, I have to believe that I've done everything I can."

Living out the commitment requires endless compromises. And while each one may be small, mothers' acceptance of inequality for the sake of child protection increases with each new sacrifice. I asked one mother to tell me about the jobs she'd had since her children were born. Before then, she had "started up the ladder" at work. She possessed advanced degrees, talent, and many opportunities. After, she described a series of decisions calculated to allow her to work according to her husband's and young sons' needs and schedules, rather than with her own career in mind. When I inquired about her thinking, she allowed that she had made the choices—continually forsaking promotions—without recognizing at the time what she was doing, though the pattern was retrospectively clear to her. Still, she felt guilty that she had been home less than her own mother, a full-time homemaker: "I have always measured myself against my mother . . . There were five of us, but she was a stay-at-home mom, and she always cooked everything from scratch and nothing came out of a box or can or anything like that . . . There was no chaos, there was no talking back. To me she was the perfect mother. And so she was the person whom I measured myself against, and I don't find that I measure up to her because I'm in a different place."[4]

Similarly, a *New York Times* (1999) account, typical of many newspaper stories during the past few years, described how Lois Beard, a mother of three and an accomplished senior army officer, seemed to be on her way to becoming the first woman army general with children. But she "called it quits and retired. After holding every job and attending every school required to be selected as general, she decided she could no longer be both a mother and a commander." Mrs. Beard's husband was also in the military. Her sixteen-year-old daughter, Rachel, described how, while she missed both parents when they were away, "she saved her ire for her mother, not her father." She felt angry at her mother for not being present, and punished her by not talking to her when she returned home. Mrs. Beard resigned because she feared "she was taking herself out of her children's lives." She added, "I don't have the resilience I used to have. I need sleep."[5]

In the same vein, the *Boston Globe* (2000) carried an article and large photo spread about Liz Walker, a single parent and Boston television newscaster, who gave up her prestigious night anchor position to spend more time with her twelve-year-old son. "I'm 48. My son is 12. He's 5-feet-11-inches tall. He already looks me in the eye. Pretty soon, he'll be gone." Consistent with the sleep deprivation reported in the University of Maryland study, Walker observed that for twelve years, "I was always tired."[6]

Mothers I spoke with also put their children first because they wanted to convey to them how much they were valued. Jill, who teaches high school (work chosen in part to maintain a child-compatible schedule), told about her distress at missing her daughter's skating performance when it conflicted with a class she had to teach. "I want them to think that I believe that what they are doing is important. And that I support it and that I think it's very exciting." She worried that because she was unable to go "they will think I just don't care enough to change my plans to accommodate them." Jill did not want to disappoint her daughter; moreover, she did not want her to feel less valued for not being watched. Jill associated attending her children's performances—something her own parents had rarely managed for her—with building their self-worth.[7]

Putting her daughters' needs first, Jill observed, comes "somewhat with the territory." She reflected quietly, "I guess I wouldn't want her to feel that I was making a choice for myself at her expense." The women partly "put children first" based on circumstance, pressures, and values, but they were also influenced by their own recollections either of what they recalled their mothers doing for them, or what they wished for as children but felt they did not get. Both types of memories added to their requirements for themselves.[8] At bottom, putting children first often meant filtering each decision each mother made—from the small ones about when to run an errand during the day to large ones about where to live and work, or how to deal with a marriage—according to how she imagined it would affect her children.

I was struck while working in the housing project with how much families would sacrifice to provide name-brand sneakers for an infant or toddler. I know this image has become a commonplace, but I saw babies in expensive shoes they were sure to outgrow in a couple of months, and heard mothers explain their feelings. Through whatever tragicomic twists of fate, the amount of money spent on sneakers, and their relative status, became a testimony both to putting a child first and an urgent gesture to inoculate him against the impinging stigmatization of his circumstances. That such expenditures were impractical, often interfering with other urgent uses for the money, mattered little, because the effort to find a symbolic way to neutralize the poison gas of shame imposed upon the child by poverty and low status was all-important. What initially looks irrational reveals itself from another angle as logical and desperately loyal.

In his original and excellent book, *Three Seductive Ideas,* Jerome Kagan sheds additional light on the notion of putting children first. Kagan challenges a host of intellectual fallacies in the field of child development and criticizes the shallowness of the current popular attributions of human motivation: This simplistic, pop-psychology view claims that "our animal heritage imposes on us an irresistible need for power, fame, sex, and property and an easy access to anger." Furthermore, if evolution has created these motives, the view suggests, "they should be treated as acceptable." The problem Kagan rightly fingers is that this formulation not only distorts Darwin's ideas, but it "ignores the fact that humans are also equally capable of empathy, shame and guilt."[9]

Kagan continues his discussion of what constitutes humanness. He writes, "The concern with right and wrong, the control of guilt, and desire to feel virtuous, are, like the appearance of milk in mammalian mothers, a unique event that was discontinuous with what was prior . . . The continual desire to regard the self as good is a unique feature of *Homo sapiens*."[10]

Kagan's assertion offers us another way to understand the meaning of "putting children first." Because women have had—and continue to have—less political and economic power in almost every society, the question of what constitutes their virtue has both been writ large and narrowly imposed. (That is, it has been measured only in those areas that remain after one removes all those in which most women have had no access or rights—areas in which their very appearance signifies a departure from virtue.) In many societies female virtue is initially defined by virginity and chastity. However, once a woman is married and a mother, the predominant areas in which she has been given social sanction to "regard the self as good" have been homemaking, religious practice, and child care.

When mothers are criticized or held unduly accountable, one common response is to search harder for virtue. In this sense, mother blaming and misogyny can be understood, perversely, as quick and dirty ways for groups to maintain high, even disproportionate, levels of maternal sacrifice. It seems that mothers will forsake many goals if they believe that by pulling back they are better serving or protecting their children. Societies are adept, often without realizing it, at generating continual alarms and compelling rationalizations to encourage this behavior. For example, neither newspaper story about women resigning from ambitious jobs included any discussion of how the workplace might change to ease the mothers' double bind or better support or compensate mothers. Instead, the *Globe* story shamelessly focused on how Walker's son's teacher had said that she thought the boy was "very proud" that his mother was coming home, and ended by prodding Walker to express regret for having worked so hard when he was young![11]

I understand easily why mothers forgo certain promotions and choose work that allows them time with children; it's essentially the choice I made when my kids were little. My point is simply that mothers should have better options. With a few good laws and more generous attitudes, primary caretakers could take time out from jobs or work part-time without personally absorbing such high cost. Why not make a mother a part-time general until her children leave home? Or give her time out of the workforce, while maintaining her benefits, to care for children, and then let her come back in at the level at which she left? Or help arrange a part-time job for her husband so he can stay home more? Several women doctors I know stopped practicing in order to raise children. Now they feel that they can't return because new treatment techniques have outdated their training. Does any medical school or hospital offer a program to help midlife women return to doctoring? No one I spoke with had heard of one.

As family life has lost its basis in necessity, survival, and shared work, love has been pushed by social ideologues and advice givers who attempt to impose upon it very particular, narrow definitions of what maternal feelings and behaviors might be allowed to constitute virtue.

One result is that it has become unduly difficult for mothers to achieve a sturdy sense of goodness. Wherever they have turned, they have found social and economic inequality and, with it, criticisms and demands so diverse and contradictory as to make a Catch-22 seem straightforward by comparison. Mothers are left feeling off balance, uncertain, uneasy about themselves and how they are doing. In this context, putting children first additionally serves as a walking stick to steady themselves along a slippery path.

A symbolic example one mother humorously offers—to illustrate the sometimes ridiculous struggle one engages in to comply with current fashions of good mothering, and thus to momentarily achieve virtue—is her account of cupcake-baking for a child's school birthday party. In Susan Straight's short memoir "One Drip at a Time," the author, a divorced working mother of three, describes standing at the back of her van in the school parking lot, late for work, frosting cupcakes, and imagining the critical eyes of the stay-at-home moms upon her as she scrambles to finish the task. She is self-critical, believing she somehow *should* have managed better, and so, perhaps projecting her own concerns, perhaps not, fears that others will judge her an inadequate mother. "Other women passed behind me, and I thought I felt their glances, like a cold breeze, like pity or disdain, through the cotton of my shirt."[12]

Finally, she finishes the frosting, enters the school building, and describes her daughter's awkward mix of pride, loyalty, and embarrassment: "Closing up the van that day, the cupcakes cheerful with their handful of sprinkles, a dark fudge smear on my good khaki pants (of course), I headed over to the school to be a good mom. And I was. My oldest daughter said, 'Everybody loves the cupcakes. Especially the sprinkles. You're the best mom in the world.' Her eyes darted nervously. 'But you have chocolate on your pants.' "[13]

In a similar vein, a mother I interviewed talked about her unhappiness at having to make individual valentines for all the members of her three-year-old's daycare group. It took a lot of time and seemed excessive to her for children so young. Yet could she let her daughter be the only one with no valentines to offer others? That wouldn't be fair to the child. When, pursuing love, virtue, and relief from guilt, some parents try to do more, those who don't want to participate in a particular trend find themselves worrying that they've placed a child at a disadvantage or deprived her.[14]

In truth, mothers sometimes give up too much of themselves, baking cupcakes, gluing valentines, picking up dirty socks or wet towels off bedroom floors, standing beside frigid hockey rinks, supervising homework, staying home when they might go to night school or for an evening with workmates. Messages from the culture encourage mothers to feel bad, and, in turn, they may believe that their only route to parenting virtue is to do until they overdo. In the face of idealized views and criticisms, mothers may feel their only route to safety and happiness is to seek the feeling too intently.

These speculations suggest a broader question: What maternal behavior, according to today's advice givers, actually signifies virtue? I spent several hours one morning perusing the online bookseller Amazon.com to fig-ure out which one among thirty or so childcare books was selling best. An almost seven-hundred-page tome, *The Baby Book* (1993) by William Sears, M.D., and Martha Sears, R.N., led the pack. Though new to me (my children are way past babyhood), the Searses dominate a big piece of the advice market and have published many volumes. (Several days later, our younger teenage son turned slightly pale upon seeing *The Baby Book* on my desk, and was visibly relieved to learn the purchase was professional. "A lot of baby-butt showing," he added solicitously, refer-ring to the four multicultural and discretely naked little creatures on the cover.)

On first opening *The Baby Book,* I recovered a pleasant feeling from when I began mothering. Looking into such books then was like peer-ing through windows into a strange new world and glimpsing the inner workings, the very gears, of the miraculous. So *that* is how you sponge a newborn. I remember loving the illustrations that showed infants of different ages; and I eagerly took in the proffered information. The thrill and fear of having *my own* baby mixed with the books' contents. At their best, these experts became touchstones in the face of my un-certainty. On each page, they offered gripping mini-tales of infancy. Philosophies were another matter. A friend recently reminded me how much, when our children were little, we used to grumble and feel chas-tised by the goody-goody pressure in the texts to function as full-time angels of mercy.

The Searses have capitalized brilliantly upon the new-mother state of mind. Seven hundred pages of *Baby Book* cover only the first two years of life; to call the scope encyclopedic is to understate. Reading through the section on ear infections—something that plagued both my sons as toddlers—I came away with a clear and helpful understanding of how they happen and how to treat them. (It reminded me that when the boys were afflicted I had asked their pediatric nurse if someone in the office would teach me to do an ear examination myself, so I could per-form a preliminary triage before coming in. She said no.)

At the same time, the underlying attitude of the text is troubling. In the section on preventing ear infections, the authors point out that babies who attend daycare catch colds more frequently. Apparently that is so. But will the next edition acknowledge that although toddlers in daycare catch twice as many colds, research suggests that the same children in elementary school get sick only a third as often as their home-raised peers? I don't think I would have reacted to this single observation had I not already come to feel that the book was skewed.[15]

Skimming *The Baby Book,* I did not find a single direct threat of death from bad mothering. Could it be that such admonitions have finally disappeared? Yes and no. They continue their protean transformations. The onslaught of information, the chosen topics, partly functioned—like the media stories—to overcue danger, to subliminally, but familiarly, summon the threat of harm. For example, here is a bulleted "Special Note" from page 662: "Take puncture wounds to the scalp seriously. Externally, these may look insignificant. But a nail, for example, may penetrate the scalp and skull and lead to a serious infection in the underlying brain. Notify your doctor."[16]

It is hard to imagine a mother who owns and reads such a book who would not on her own call the pediatrician *instantly* if her baby's skull were punctured—assuming the baby had access to medical care. (I wonder why the authors did not advocate for universal health coverage for children rather than highlight the dangers of puncture wounds?) What's more, statistically speaking, you cannot help but wonder what risk an infant faces of incurring a brain-infecting puncture. It seems excessive to mention such a concern in the text, even more so to bullet it. Let us suppose for a moment that the writers' and publisher's rationale is something like, "If it saves even one life, it's worth it." Additionally, let us grant that the positive psychological function of this tidbit is that is makes mothers feel prepared: "Okay, I know what to do when the nail comes." Both these notions seem plausible. Nevertheless, I think that this interpretation misses the way a subliminal warning of (unduly) elevated risk is persistently, almost bizarrely, instilled. (Do you know *anyone* to whom such an accident has happened? I'd like to see the annual numbers nationwide.) Your maternal vigilance must always be up. Turn your back for a moment, and your precious baby could have a brain-destroying nail in her head. Danger is everywhere—even in what looks insignificant. Stay close. Be cautious. Let go of separate strivings. Consult the doctor.

Beyond information, the Searses make a full-court press for the benefits of their method of achieving close attachment with newborns and infants; this "Attachment Parenting" is the ideological core of the book. In the context of all we've discussed, their argument and its meta-message are almost uncannily familiar. In truth, to this by now somewhat jaded reader, the central subtext—that you will mother best and your children will turn out best if you follow "Dr. Bill's" attachment instructions—approaches the oppressive. Yet apparently, many readers feel that the angle and clarity of his position are attractive. No doubt seductive as well is the inference that if you follow his advice (unspoken: if you manage to be like his wife, Martha, the attuned, loving mother of *eight* children, who lends personal anecdotes to the text), you *can* achieve a sense of virtue. And, ultimately, it is this covert offer that may provide the allure. *Here* is the right way to put children first. The threat—that you will fail their love standard and leave your children disadvantaged for the whole rest of their lives—is understated even as it looms.

Early on, Sears warns about the dangers . . . *of other experts' advice:* "We realize that love for your baby and the desire to be a good parent makes you susceptible to any baby-rearing advice. But children are too valuable and parents too vulnerable for any author to offer unresearched information . . . Every statement has been thoroughly researched and has stood the test of time." To say the least, these claims are large.[17]

Shortly thereafter, Dr. Bill makes his pitch about the right way to mother infants, which he then reiterates and elaborates throughout. His five points are succinctly listed in a little box: "1) Connect with your baby early. 2) Read and respond to your baby's cues. 3) Breastfeed your baby. 4) Wear your baby. 5) Share sleep with your baby."[18]

Are these bad ideas? I don't think so. In fact, they have appeal—depending on your means and your fancy. I've read that sleeping with infants can up the chance of suffocating them; I don't know; I am personally inclined to physical closeness. To the degree that new mothers need permission and encouragement to respond fully and warmly to their babies, Sears offers it. Additionally, I respect Sears's point that mothers employed outside the home who resist connecting deeply with infants—for fear of traumatizing themselves and the baby when they have to return to work—are probably acting on a misguided assumption that benefits neither party.

Unfortunately, observing the doctor develop his opinions and marshal data, one begins to sense a zealot. Underneath the benign pronouncements, the flexibility (do what suits you), and polite disclaimers, it seems there is only one truly right way: it is his; and it requires near total devotion. Breastfeeding is really the only way to go. The mother carrying the infant on her body is superior. Having the baby in bed is better for everyone. He repeatedly claims that research supports him. But his own opinions are loosely mixed with other studies, the sources of which are rarely cited. (The book includes neither notes nor bibliography.)

"True," Dr. Bill acknowledges, "this style of parenting takes tremendous amounts of patience and stamina, but it's worth it!"[19] He's got the fervor, but I'm not convinced he's got the facts—nor that what he advocates, while taxing, is indeed superior to other styles that might make an infant feel just as well cared for yet offer mothers more flexibility. All parenting takes tremendous patience and stamina. Why ask for more constricting maternal behavior than may be necessary?

In a boxed entry entitled "Early Attachment—Lifelong Memories," Sears implies that children will remember forever how available their mothers were during their infancy. *Where* is his evidence for a statement that inevitably induces guilt, fear, and perhaps needless self-sacrifice in new mothers? Without it, it seems we cross over—yet again—into the realm of fantasy and propaganda—costumed this time in pseudoneurological-psychological-plus-pediatric-and-paternal-experience piety. (If he is correct, why does he not suggest the need for federal laws to grant yearlong paid parental leaves?)[20]

To support his central argument, Sears claims, "Attachment parenting improves behavior, development and intelligence." These sweeping opinions come with little hard evidence. Elaborating on his claims about intelligence, Sears writes: "Many studies now show that the most powerful enhancers of brain development are the quality of the parent-infant attachment and the responses of the caregiving environment to the cues of the infant. I believe that attachment parenting promotes brain development by feeding the brain the right kind of information at a time in the child's life when the brain needs the most nourishment." I'd like to know just what studies he's talking about. In *The Myth of the First Three Years of Life* (1999), John T. Bruer examines the evidence and challenges the notion that infancy is the time in a child's life when brains need the most feeding or stimulation. Brains need hearty nourishment throughout life. Having reviewed the literature, Bruer writes, "currently there is no research linking early childhood attachment with brain development."[21]

Beyond the nourishment claim, the whole relationship of intelligence to secure attachment in infancy seems to be unresearched and unknown. In order to try to understand this question I turned to the *Handbook of Attachment* (1999), edited by Jude Cassidy and Phillip R. Shaver, an almost nine-hundred-page double-column small-print state-of-the-art volume filled with articles by psychologists and researchers who attempt to delineate what is and is not currently understood about human attachment. Of the books' many pages, only one (according to the index) discusses intelligence. And indeed the book states, "In general, there have been few associations between attachment classifications and contemporaneous or subsequent measures of intelligence."[22]

There currently is some evidence that what is called a "secure attachment" in infancy improves toddler-parent harmony, while the effects of infant attachment on behavior in later childhood are unclear. The "outcomes of attachment security appear to be more contingent and provisional than earlier expected. The most reliable outcome of a secure attachment in infancy is a more harmonious parent-child relationship in the immediate years to come." While having a basically harmonious toddler is a blessing, it is hardly defining. "Research examining the longer-term consequences of attachment for close relationships yielded a strikingly mixed picture, suggesting that intervening events (including changes in attachment security, family circumstances, social stress, and/ or the growth of the normative developmental capabilities) can alter the expected outcomes of attachment in infancy."[23]

In other words, William and Martha Sears are making inflated "re-search"-based, "time-tested" claims for attachment parenting that are unproven; the researchers, partisans of attachment theory themselves, are much more equivocal about what has so far been learned or demonstrated. Furthermore, to the degree that secure attachments are beneficial to children—and I am as in favor of loving relationships as anyone—there are likely many ways for interested caretakers to form them with their charges, and many significant social impediments that the authors of the best-selling *Baby Book* do not explore.

Perhaps the most contradictory section of *The Baby Book* is a chapter entitled "Working and Parenting." Sears's stated position is that employment is fine, that attachment is the issue, that it's a pity that the question of mothers working outside the home is divisive. At the same time, in each subsection of the chapter, he comes out in indirect and guilt-inducing ways against mothers working. For example, he emphasizes that employed mothers miss "milestones" and "teachable moments." Full-time mothering, he implies, is simply better for young children. What are the effects of the mother spending time away from the baby? "Basically, they are a lessening of the benefits of mother-infant attachment. In recent years, there has been a flurry of research validating, almost down to the cellular level, the importance of mother's presence." What instruments are being used to measure these effects? Do the cells reflect father's presence? How does this supposed cellular effect correlate with the next eighty years of life? And if proximity indeed eventually shows itself to be so important, what can society do about it besides continually pressuring mothers?

If staying home is an economic hardship, Sears recommends that a mother figure out the costs of returning to work (in his account, costs for care are to be subtracted exclusively from her salary) and that she then evaluate her priorities. She should try hard to stay home for two or three years. Once again, none of these admonitions are for the spouse, workplace, or society. It's all on the mother. And the vaunted evidence that her sacrifice will yield something superior is exaggerated, at the very least.[24]

In fact, based on Ann Crittenden's well-researched assessment in

The Price of Motherhood of the economic consequences for contemporary mothers who take leaves of absence from the workplace or stay home permanently, and their trickle-down effect upon children, evidence appears to be building in just the opposite direction from what Sears suggests. Whatever gains a child might get from a mother leaving work to stay with her are often outweighed by effects on most mothers and children of the resulting economic and social costs. Crittenden writes, "Studies conducted on five continents have found that children are distinctly better off when the mother possesses enough income and authority in the family to make investing in children a priority." Later in the chapter, she concludes, "The emergence of women as independent economic actors is not depriving children of vital support; it is giving them more powerful defenders. Depriving mothers of an income and influence of their own is harmful to children and a recipe for economic backwardness."[25]

Society needs to change, not mothers. I completely support a parent who wishes to stay home two or three years, or forever; just as I completely support one who wishes to—or must—work for income. For some women and children—or men and children—staying at home is wonderful. For others it's an impossible dream, and for still others it's simply the wrong way to parent. Mothers need economic, social, and legal backing to pursue varied options. Babies and older children will benefit most from having parents who feel sustained in the path they have chosen, who feel that they have options. Maternal equality, choice, and autonomy matter more to children's well-being across childhood than how many hours a day women carry their babies in Snuglis or how many nights they share a bed.

In *The Baby Book,* the threat of harm and loss of virtue are forcefully connected to distorted applications of attachment theory that focus too exclusively on individual relationships while obscuring the more important social issues. From one angle, the book is a well-intentioned effort, packed with useful information for new mothers. From another, it is part of a preconscious or semiconscious scare culture holding out specters of damage for young children whose mothers seek to give care, pursue equality, and assert themselves in the larger world.

Jerome Kagan is also skeptical of the current overemphasis on attachment theory and of the whole larger gestalt of infant determinism that it reflects. He feels it is particularly popular in the United States because it "ignores the power of social class membership" and "minimizes the role of chance." Kagan writes, "It would be pleasing if a mother's care of her infant in the first two years set the child's future in a significant way. But I am afraid that, like Copernicus's beautifully circular orbits, this emotionally satisfying hypothesis strays too far from the facts."[26]

To the degree that good attachments promote everyday harmony in families, to the degree that they provide well-being and even psychological health, of course they are beneficial. But left out of such a simplistic version of events is the whole recursive nature of external realities and relationships. Sears's use of attachment theory attempts to simplify the extraordinarily complex feat of raising a child, to reduce infinite social and personal variables, yet again, to "good" mothering. The book offers a familiar, superficially clear path that promises a way to find virtue through sacrifice and thus fend off internal and external declarations of harm. "Wear" the infant, quit your job, keep a vigilant eye out for brain punctures, and one authority figure will say you have put your baby first.

So why not just ignore advice we don't favor? Whether we want to or not, we absorb the often toxic child-rearing philosophies that make up our cultural atmosphere, especially when they reach a certain density. A person is always free to say "I don't believe that." But, in truth, the presence of a "that" in which you must aggressively disbelieve, itself defines something about the territory in which you find yourself. Furthermore, surrounded by others who believe a set of ideas, no matter how preposterous, it is hard for a dissenting mind to escape unscathed. You are always free to disagree, but until your own position finds fellow travelers, it can be exhausting to hold. Considerable psychic energy is required to stand even slightly apart from the pack—especially on issues having to do with mothering—where the threat of failing a child looms so large. There is enormous pressure on mothers to comply with norms.

An old memory provides an illustration of just how intense and up close the socialization process can be. When I was maybe seven or eight, I was playing dolls with my neighbors. At one point, doll in hand, I went running off to get something. An older neighbor girl, the most powerful member of our little group, loudly said to another, "Look what a bad mother she is. She's dangling her baby, not cradling her." Stopped in my tracks, I blushed and said nothing. I remember urgently wanting to redo the moment to satisfy her silly standard. For months after, I carefully cradled dolls and gingerly transported them. Now, too many years later, I can retrieve the 1950s scene. But *what* was it all about?

Most relevantly it is about the way the psyche and culture together use shame to create group compliance and inculcate behaviors. I wanted the older girl's approval. She, a queen bee of sorts, had been granted power by the rest of us—though I can no longer say just why. Perhaps because she was almost a teenager, opinionated, popular. I liked her. I wanted her to confirm me and my maternal instincts. Such are the ways of children. And through exchanges like this one, larger cultural biases get intimately transcribed. Ten years later, supported by broader ideas and affiliations, I might have known enough to laugh, or to take her comments lightly; but at that moment, I felt skewered.

A similar incident is recounted in a magazine piece (2000) critiquing Dr. Laura Schlessinger. (Hers is said to be the most listened-to radio advice program in America.) Schlessinger appeared as a guest on a syndicated news and call-in program. The phone lines reportedly "got screwed up," so a female cohost filled the silence by telling "Dr. Laura" of her own conflicted feelings about leaving her children in daycare while she worked. According to the journalist, "Dr. Laura icily replied, 'The choice is simple, it's either you or your kids. Your kids come first and then your career. Period.'" The host was so mortified and "discombobulated" that she cut immediately to a commercial, apparently in an attempt to regain composure. The exchange is an adult version of what I experienced as a child. A person with power, in this case "an expert," defined another woman's behavior as unacceptable mothering, and she did it in front of an audience so that public shaming and stripping away of virtue heightened the effect.[27]

Since there is much impetus to keep mothers in check, and metaphorically "at home" if not physically, the temptation, whether willful or unconscious, to construct social philosophies and publish advice books that reinforce the creed, is enormous. While one would like to believe that the best interests of children are at the fore, this assumption seems dubious. And however much one would like to imagine women united in support of one another, that, too, is far from the total reality.

Contemporary prophets, like their predecessors, have a wide variety of agendas. Since so often their opinions about what is good for children overreach their knowledge, overreach anything that is in fact known, it is hard not to question underlying motives. Schlessinger's harm comes not from her assertion that one might put children first, but from her presumption that she knows what that means, that the woman she is talking to does not, and that she is entitled to denigrate sincere conflict.

What if Schlessinger had said, "Children must come first some of the time, but it is the whole family's and nation's responsibility as well as yours. Furthermore, how that admonition translates into practice is very complicated. Little wonder you feel conflicted and worried. You, in spite of relative privilege, are struggling with inadequate support in the workplace, a dearth of quality child care, and perhaps less help than you need at home as well. Your husband or partner may also have less flexibility than is ideal or fair. Remember, though, children thrive in many circumstances; and they benefit from having a mother who is both deeply engaged in the world and holding them in her mind—as you so clearly are." I know this is labored, but you get the point.

In truth, most mothers put children first so consistently that their thoroughness creates a Little Red Hen phenomenon. Everyone else can say "Not I." What if employers, the makers of everything from unsafe car tires to sugary soft drinks; the manufacturers of cigarettes, asbestos, and lead paint; legislators who set the minimum wage way too low and inadequately fund daycare, education, health care, and affordable housing; the importers of street drugs; slum landlords; drunk drivers; pedophiles and perpetrators of incest and all those who cover for them; recruiters of child soldiers and child prostitutes; worldwide exploiters of child labor; makers of nuclear weapons and creators of land mines;

"entrepreneurs" attempting privately to buy up the world's fresh water supply; and the reckless despoilers of our shared physical environment were as genuinely interested in putting children first as, albeit imperfect, human, and inevitably flawed mothers are?

Women I spoke with initially expressed a slight sense of surprise when I asked them to ponder what the society might do to better support their caretaking work. It struck me as we talked that they were realistic—and thus inclined to see themselves as responsible to fit into the world, not the other way around. "I will do what it takes to keep my baby alive" becomes an axis around which all else rotates. Many applaud this stance. "Individual responsibility" is held in high esteem. "You chose to have children; it's up to you to take care of them" is a common rejoinder. But lost in such constructions is the way in which the overemphasis on individual responsibility, the pressure to be a good mother right now, obscures how American (and international) law and social policy are inadequately supportive of mothers' family situations, even as many public voices declare that a loving family life is the moral center of the country. (Played out to their furthest point, the unarticulated nasty implication of these simplistic constructions is that our poorest citizens should practice a kind of self-genocide—with all its immense attendant losses. To be "responsible" in these terms—to care for children in a "middle-class" fashion without social help—would force most to give up having children at all.)

Another reason many mothers initially hesitate to think about how the world might change is that their sense of virtue comes more readily from sacrifice than protest. The Puritan mothers in Boston in 1649 considered the imminent threat to their midwife, Alice Tilly, so urgent that they were willing to risk public wrath for speaking out. So too a group of mothers might feel "entitled" to protest a kindergarten teacher who mistreats children but are more hesitant to ask schools to better accommodate their commuting and work needs. In the first instance, they can feel confident that they are being "good" mothers; in the second, their standing is less clear to themselves as well as others.

*　　*　　*

A mother can function most successfully when society supports her work fully, but neither side assumes the centrality of such a proposition. The United States benefits richly because mothers dedicate themselves to children, yet the country as a whole fails to recognize that children will be well served only when they are put first in other ways too, when society organizes itself to better meet their needs. Instead, many social factors reinforce mothers' instincts to seek virtue by making disproportionate private compromises, to put children first and attempt to bear the consequences themselves. One woman, Joan, described how she was trying to reconcile the professional-career-child-rearing crunch.

> In our culture, people say when they meet someone they haven't met — they ask, "What do you do?" That's one of the first things that they ask. And there's a lot of emphasis on productivity, having a career and this sort of thing, which has led, I think, in part, a lot of women in my generation to have aspirations. And to feel like they have a place in the world and in the professional world. And then they have children. It turns everything up in the air because once you have kids, there is also the expectation that the mother is the primary caregiver . . . and that has made it very difficult to play multiple roles.[28]

A new mother quickly hits a wall. No matter how long she's trained in school, no matter how highly skilled she's become or what her professional accomplishments, once she has a baby she's squeezed. The cultural representations of the good mother loom. Because she feels intensely about her infant, she wants to meet these expectations, to fulfill — even surpass — the conventions that are her only safety. She wants — expansively — to give her child the world. And she doesn't want to lose him. So she is delectably ripe, perfect for plucking, by a standard that says "It really is all on you."

If she works outside the home, she is continually reminded — directly and indirectly — that a truly good worker — especially a good professional in the contemporary workplace — is completely available, from the moment of waking to the moment of sleep, to respond to the demands of her job. Caught between these ideals, how can she find a sense of virtue? Better simply to sacrifice professional advancement, social security accrual, pension vestment, and long-term earning power. There is no doubt that some employers have made some accommodations with flextime and on-site daycare, but, in truth, these concessions only scratch the surface.

Chatting with a young medical student in the cafeteria at the hospital where I work, I asked her what specialties interested her. She would like to study surgery, she offered, but she probably won't. "Why not?" I asked. The field, she explained, is still completely male-dominated. Any surgeon who works fewer than eighty hours a week is considered second-rate. There's no way a woman can practice and raise a family. Her resignation makes me sad. It would be easy enough, were people committed to the effort, to design schedules that let women operate and mother. Or to leave the workforce and return. The unspoken rules succeed brilliantly, if covertly, both at keeping women out of a challenging, lucrative realm of medicine and at reinforcing the fallacy that fathers can absent themselves so completely without causing harm. (What's more, we might ask if it's good for us as patients to be someone's eightieth hour of surgery in a week?)

Women are told that they are not present enough to do the most demanding jobs. They are split between home and work. They skip out to take care of a sick child or attend a performance at school. But we must wonder how the work world ever managed to put across the expectation that a good worker—"an ideal worker" in the words of feminist legal theorist Joan Williams—is someone virtually owned by the workplace, someone who constantly puts *work* first?[29] The standard of how many hours a day an excellent worker labors could in truth be set anywhere: four, six, eight, and so forth. Many of the great labor battles of the nineteenth and twentieth centuries were in fact fought not simply for wages, but for working conditions: to cut hours enough so that employees could have lives. These standards have been among the decencies eroded in recent years as real wages for many laborers have gone down, the cost of living has gone up, desirable consumer items have multiplied, and international competitive pressures have been seen as excusing new time demands and new "standards" of productivity.

In the simplest sense, if American society values family life, it can either continue to pressure mothers "to choose" to give up pursuing economic and political equality, to leave the workforce, or at least to cut back and abandon the more ambitious and better-paying jobs, or it can change its notion of what constitutes an "ideal worker" and so increase possibilities for men and women. An ideal worker could become someone who sometimes puts work first and sometimes puts family first, and has the wisdom to know when to do each.

As Williams intelligently spells out in her book *Unbending Gender,* the current standard of what is ideal is defined by how much a healthy male — without competing family commitments — can work. She writes, "We need to end the marginalization of caregivers by changing the definition of the ideal worker so that it reflects the norm of parental care." In other words, if we broaden our idea of good workers to include the premise that most adults naturally have responsibilities at home to care for children, aging parents, and other loved ones, that giving care is one of the great human attributes, to be cherished, and that it takes time, then we could go a long way to resolving our current conflicts.[30]

If, like Joan or the medical student, a woman has worked hard to pursue professional opportunities, she might reasonably expect to continue in her career and also to have time to raise her children. Such a wish is not universal. Many women whose jobs are dangerous, inflexible, low-paying, and overly taxing may long to get out of the workforce when their kids are small but be unable to afford it. And some mothers may simply choose homemaking as their exclusive priority. But the desire to integrate family work and equally paid employment is important because it represents an effort that might fully open the public world to women, and thus increase their well-being and that of their children, arguably even that of their spouse or partner.

According to Williams, "Roughly ninety percent of American women will become mothers at some point during their work lives." Sixty-three percent of mothers with children under three years old are currently in the workforce. It is time to collectively respect the legitimate demands of caretaking and translate the improved attitude into better family policies, greater economic parity, and job security and benefits for women and men who do take significant time at home.[31]

The urgent wish to protect children, the fear of putting them at risk, the pleasure of raising them, repeatedly inclines mothers to let go of or unnecessarily curtail separate strivings. To be a good mother, *not* to be a bad mother, *not* to make oneself vulnerable to the charge (psychic, communal, or societal) of having harmed children through inadequate selflessness, are such deep and defining feelings for mothers that we almost inevitably make the first questions personal: What can *I* do differently? How can *I* rearrange myself to make things work out? How can *I* put my children first? I suggest that one novel and spectacular way to put children first is for mothers to talk back to the imposed ideals and to our endlessly triggered alarm systems so that instead of taking so much upon ourselves, we make successfully rearing children everybody's baby.

Epilogue
Solomon's Wisdom

AS I WAS WORKING on this book, I gradually realized that my subject spooked me. I felt superstitious, scared of writing about the possibility of child loss, irrationally worried that I was putting my children at risk. No wonder little has been written directly about this core maternal fear. And yet, my apprehension enriched my understanding. My private feelings, it turned out, were a narrow lane opening onto a crowded piazza. Mothers dread the bereft desolation of child death, and the story I have been telling is both common and old—even as every generation of mothers, every mother, makes it new.

Almost three thousand years ago, by comprehending just how much mothers will sacrifice to protect their children, King Solomon earned his fame as a wise man. You may remember the story. Two women, disreputable "harlots" according to the biblical text, were staying alone in a house when, within a few days of each other, each gave birth. One newborn died, the other lived. Both mothers claimed the living child and asked Solomon to resolve their dispute. Whether they turned to him themselves or were taken to him by others is unclear.

In a passage in Kings, one of the mothers speaks to Solomon: "'Then on the third day after I was delivered, this woman also gave birth; and we were alone . . . And this woman's son died in the night, because she lay on it. And she arose at midnight, and took my son from beside me . . . and laid it in her bosom, and laid her dead son in my bosom." The words of the ancient biblical text are still easy to follow, immediate, and her account exact. She continues: "When I arose in the morning to nurse my child, behold, it was dead; but when I looked at it closely in the morning, behold, it was not the child that I had borne. But the other woman said, 'No, the living child is mine, and the dead child is yours.'"[1]

Both women claim one infant, and there are no witnesses. Whose is it? To find out, King Solomon calls for his sword. "Divide the living child in two," he orders. A bloody half will go to each petitioner. Horrified, one mother backs away. "Oh, my lord, give her the living child, and by no means slay it," she implores. Solomon awards the infant to this woman, who has sought to preserve her child at her own expense. The biblical passage continues, "And all Israel heard of the judgment which the king had rendered; and they stood in awe of the king because they perceived that the wisdom of God was in him to render justice."[2]

The fact that Solomon has comprehended maternal feeling accurately wins him extraordinary renown. An underlying, more cryptic message is that Solomon is a great, wise king because he has understood the secret mechanism at the heart of patriarchal power: gender hierarchy is most easily maintained by subduing a woman through her child love. In this reading, the raised sword represents the man's greater strength and willingness to kill; the threat reminds mothers, women, of their protective priorities and of their place. Even harlots, the story suggests, once they have children they value, are governable within such a system.

Meanwhile, the mother's willingness to part from her child to save its life is dismissed in the laudatory public retelling of the story as something like instinct, as the irrational thing true mothers do. A nameless woman gets her baby back thanks to the wise king. But that "award" is the end of her story, while it is only the beginning of his.

Solomon's famous decision offers a perfect tableau of a larger phenomenon: Mothers possess and are made vulnerable by such powerful protective feelings that they are often quickly willing to make sacrifices for their children. Yet the complexity and moral worth of the mother's love is rendered invisible in the public world, reduced to dumb animal reflex, or sentimentalized, or dissected and criticized, or simply taken for granted, its large social contribution obscured while the story focuses on the man's prowess.

Men are represented as singularly endowed with higher reason. The mother is reliant upon the king's beneficence: lucky for her men are so wise. In truth, the narrative sets the harlots up as props for the king. Sexually spoiled and powerless, foolish, they come in handy for demonstrating his skill. Furthermore, the story hides their histories: how they became prostitutes; which men, upstanding in their public lives, bought back-street sex, or fathered their babies, or decreed laws that made it impossible for them, once "spoiled," to marry, or to support themselves in other ways. By neglecting this background, the story particularly hides patriarchy's great moral omission: how the urgent imperative of sexuality also sometimes makes wise men act unwisely and then conceal those actions. Finally, the legend of the wise king glorifies a large fallacy by suggesting that one sex alone can create and deliver a system of justice that serves both.

For an alternative narrative about protection, let us return to Persephone and her mother, Demeter. Recall that Demeter stalled the world in winter to force Hades to return her daughter. Significantly, it is *only* because Demeter has autonomy and independent resources that she can protect Persephone. Demeter controls the harvest and fertility, so she is able to resist Zeus and stand up to Hades. Demeter is not dependent upon Zeus's single-sexed notion of justice.

The safety of children rests in the freedom of mothers, who must have equal stature and the ability to create a family and social system of checks and balances, a conversation.

We can also read the myth of Demeter and Persephone as a reminder of the way adult love pulls grown daughters away from their mothers, children away from their parents. And how, whatever the relative weight of old and new love, violence and desire, eating the pomegranate seed as Persephone does with Hades, and thus, symbolically, taking in the man's seed, forever divides the daughter's loyalty. She may return to her family home, but once sexually initiated, she is changed.

Pushed a little further, the story warns how, unchecked by male imperative and desire, Demeter can become a too powerful mother, one who will not let her daughter mature sexually, nor give up her own primacy, nor bear the loss of a child who has grown up and must leave. She cannot tolerate the human "seasons" of youth and age, of loving and losing. Instead, she attempts to stop time, and so to deny the waning of her vital role as the dependent child's beloved. The barrenness of the protracted winter she imposes symbolizes the prohibition against the daughter's transition into full sexuality and fertility—and ultimately it attempts to deny necessary death.

A final relevant aspect of both Solomon's story and Demeter's is the way they reilluminate the mix of fears—between men and women, parents and children (illustrated also in *Bacchae*). Apprehensions coexist, tangle, merge, become confused, appear disguised in one another's clothing. What harm is done by the mother's physical strength relative to the child's? What by her psychological hold? So, too, the father's? Psyches are complex; the interplay of their force with political and social power is difficult to address. Perhaps it has been easier to place false hope in simpler ideas, to believe that Solomon's wisdom justifies men's greater status, or that Demeter can adequately protect Persephone with love alone.

In the advice books and psychology texts that we looked at, men and women offered ideas about what mothers ought to do to keep children safe and what they might have done wrong to endanger them. The experts did their best to be useful; yet they also issued threats that played pointedly upon maternal vulnerability. Almost always, the mother deemed bad was one who sought to follow her own inclinations or to participate in the larger "men's" realm. Little wonder contemporary women so often feel blamed as they attempt to move into the public world. Not only has rapid social change and diaspora unsettled society—disrupted its intergenerational continuity and simultaneously asked so much more of mothers—but many women now find themselves increasingly engaged in the kinds of activities that have long brought sanction.

Yet, accept a work promotion, and *you* alone are harming *your* child, or so the current scare story goes. As the women who spoke on these pages articulate and demonstrate, that accusation and all its diverse historic antecedents have been thrown at mothers for centuries—probably not, we must conclude, simply to promote thoughtful care for children. It seems that the mother's willingness to act altruistically on behalf of her children is typically so strong that it can be manipulated quickly, effectively, and repeatedly by creating public admonitions—through sermons, expert opinions, art, medicine, psychology, and so on—that too singularly put the responsibility for children on mothers, and that link maternal autonomy with child danger or damage.

Advice books tell about their times. It doesn't matter if a woman read or believed every word of Flavel's *Token for Mourners.* The text allows us to witness what one popular minister said to women and men about child death in seventeenth-century England. And it reveals something about the larger social atmosphere that mothers breathe—as does the current advice offered by Martha and William Sears. The heightened vulnerability created by the mother's attachment has drawn continual responses from others, some empathic, some useful, some violent. Many seem to seek to control her behavior in exchange for a certification of virtue and a semblance of safe passage for her offspring.

One warning that stands out—because it is so constantly repeated in the texts we've examined—is the threat that a few mistakes early on, and the mother has ruined the child for life (if she hasn't killed it). Buchan asserts this notion, as do Key, Watson, and Winnicott. How much is such a statement a bid to capture the reading mother's attention and scare her into greater duty? How much is it a partially accurate observation about the unique pliability and early fragility of infants? How much is it a statement about the way, essentially, whoever raises us wounds us for life, as we in turn wound those to whom we give birth and love? Achilles can be killed only at the spot where his mother, Thetis, grasping his infant heel, held onto him to keep him from falling too far into the flames as she burned him to make him immortal. Her own imprint did the damage. *Gently,* one wants to caution. Let us stop claiming, spuriously and at the expense of mothers, what we do not know.

In turn, the real well-being of children has not necessarily had much to do with the particular rules and sanctions of experts. (Buchan's prohibitions about overmedicating and his concern about child labor are among the exceptions.) While, often, powerful emotions or incorrect behaviors in mothers were named as the source of children's woe, in fact, children arguably have been most harmed either by natural, political, and economic events beyond the mother's individual control, or by the way these forces typically have heightened mothers' social powerlessness.

There is also no doubt that violence, as well as threat, has consistently been used to reinforce maternal submission. Saint Augustine, writing in the fourth century, describes how his father beat his mother. Today, such intimate violence remains epidemic all over the world. Yet, it is difficult to understand how its terror functions so effectively to oppress until you factor in the priority women give to offspring. If you put children first, then enduring violence rather than letting them starve or suffer deprivation is the tradeoff. In most places and times, there has been nowhere to turn. Life, including emotional life, has been—and still mostly is—local. The different world beyond the village has been hard to know and almost impossible to reach. Very few women have had independent means, certainly not during the years they were raising children.[3]

When the culture devalues and enslaves the mother, how can she be like Demeter and protect her daughter? This is the question Clytemnestra asks in Euripides' play *Electra*. How can Agamemnon, in whose care her own father had placed her, sacrifice their daughter, Iphigenia, to help bring him victory in Troy? How can someone who was supposed to "protect" her and their children kill the daughter whom she "bore and loved"?[4]

At this moment in America we are experimenting with an alternative arrangement. It's messy, confusing, exhilarating, and hard. Yet, here we are as mothers—virtually for the first time in history, often able to control conception, to work at a variety of jobs, to pursue education, to earn money and keep bank accounts, to own property, to marry (but, sadly, only if heterosexual) according to personal inclination, to raise children outside of marriage, to take legal recourse against sexual violence, to divorce, to vote, to hold office and participate in the public world. American mothers (especially if white and living away from the worst violence) are able to anticipate that children will usually live and sometimes prosper.

These transitions are extraordinary. And they may be more fragile than we'd like to believe. Most of the past and much of the contemporary world favor arrangements that keep mothers in some kind of bondage. But anyone who attempts to minimize the remarkable nature of our tentative social changes is making a mistake. There are new possibilities.

Whereas many in the media claim that women have achieved their aims, are adequately equal, it is much more accurate to suggest that recent social changes have created a small island within a huge ocean. Will the land mass grow? Will the waters rise? The answer rests upon the political and social resolve of women and men to continue working at a labor only lately begun. Equality will not be achieved until women can become mothers without suffering disproportionate burdens and undue blame. The physiological and emotional transformations that occur when women become mothers, and the profound commitment entailed in "putting children first," need to be honored and supported with resources, not exploited.

The myth that mother love will make a better world is a complex one and ultimately deceptive. There is no doubt that love is infinitely better for children's psyches than its absence, or than terror. But it is unwise to let experts legislate maternal feeling to serve social agendas. Of course we want adults to nurture the young and to contain their own violence. The truth is, though, a woman raises her children to survive in the world she knows. And often, harshness mirrors one's own perceptions and experiences of hardship. We prefer to see children as reflections of mothers' capacities to nurture, rather than admitting that mothers' behavior and feelings often reflect society's choices.

But there is a deeper problem that I want to return to one last time. Love is not meant to run within narrow channels, neatly to rise and fall in response to the levering of locks. Intimate love is sometimes calm, even parched, but it is also like a rapids, roaring and crashing, awesome when it catches the light, too vital to be simply pretty. The closer relationships are, the more emotions are pushed to reveal their complexities. Like the same river but now flooding, filled with silt, strayed waterfowl, wrecked boats, and uprooted trees, love carries bits and legacies of all that it has floated past. Better not to keep coercing mothers to control it more exactly, dam it more completely, more perfectly; better not to base too much social hope upon taming what will stay beyond our reach.

One night, toward the end of last summer, my husband and I sat at the dining room table. It was late in the evening, and we had made a moment to talk and drink a glass of wine together. Our older son was about to start college. We both brimmed with sadness. This wonderful child, funny, irreverent, incisive, kind, so lately it seemed come into our lives, was leaving. However often he'd return, even take up residence again, it would not be the same. After we had witnessed his growing up day by day, sometimes moment by moment, he was departing from view. His guitar playing, pronouncements, exchanges with friends—all the tiny, daily ways love gains texture and lives itself out, would suddenly disappear—another sleight of hand by the cosmic magician. Now he's with us, now he's gone. Time passing. We laughed a little about various of his foibles . . . and ours. And then we both found ourselves crying quietly.

"I keep seeing him just born," my husband allowed. "What about you?" I paused for a moment, making my voice steadier, gathering the large feelings into words. "I am just grateful that somehow we lived in the right place and time . . . so that he lived. I am grateful that we have been able to raise him safely."

NOTES

BIBLIOGRAPHY

INDEX

Notes

I have omitted the names of all the interviewees, or have given them as initials, to protect privacy. As well as interviewing twelve women, I also e-mailed questions to other mothers, and I talked informally with many more.

Introduction

1. Interview 8, April 6, 2000.
2. Personal communication: S.G., October 2001.
3. Jean-Jacques Rousseau, *Emile*, pp. 324, 325, 330.

1. Twice Vulnerable

1. Personal communication: P.C., June 2001.
2. Op. cit., S.G.
3. Adrienne Rich, *Of Woman Born*, p. 22.
4. Hugh Cunningham, *Children and Childhood in Western Society Since 1500*, p. 21. Steven Ozment, *Ancestors*, p. 67.
5. Richard Weissbourd, "Distancing Dad," *American Prospect*, December 9, 1999, p. 33.
6. Robert Frost, *The Complete Poems of Robert Frost*, p. 70.
7. Ibid., p. 71.
8. Ibid., p. 73.

2. Night Walks

1. Personal communication: A.S., May 2000.

2. Jeff Bingaman and Jon S. Corzine, "Health of the Mother," *New York Times,* February 7, 2002, p. A23.

3. Interview 3, February 11, 2000.

4. Personal communication: M.J., October 2001.

5. Personal communication: S.M., May 2001.

6. Anne Lamott, *Operating Instructions,* p.22.

7. bell hooks, *Where We Stand,* p. 161; Lindsay Griffiths (Reuters), "Hardships Plague Women Worldwide, UN Report Says," *Boston Globe,* September 21, 2000, p. A14; (Reuters) "UN Finds Burden Unfair for Women," *Boston Globe,* October 16, 1998, p. A13.

8. Paula Michaels, "The Doctor Says the Baby's Fine but in Your Gut You Know Something's Not Right," *Reader's Digest,* January 2002, p. 131 (reprinted from *Parenting*).

9. William and Martha Sears, *The Baby Book,* p. 372.

10. *Parenting,* December/January 2002, pp. 32, 33, 95; *Parents Magazine,* December 2001, pp. 87, 96, 78, 70, 163.

11. Ibid., *Parents Magazine,* p. 130; op. cit., *Parenting,* cover headline.

12. Op. cit., *Parents Magazine,* p. 163.

13. Richard S. Kissam, M.D., *The Nurse's Manual, and Young Mother's Guide,* p. 90.

14. Michael R. Haines, "Mortality in Nineteenth-Century America: Estimates from New York and Pennsylvania Census Data, 1865 and 1900," *Demography,* August 1977, pp. 311–12 (with thanks to Ms. Lucretia McClure, reference librarian, Countway Library, Harvard Medical School).

3. *"My Son Who Died"*

1. James Joyce, *Ulysses,* p. 388.

2. Conor McPherson, *The Weir,* p.38.

3. Ibid., p 39.

4. Ibid., p 40.

5. Mary Shelley, *Maurice, or the Fisher's Cot,* pp. 103, 104, 105, 110–11.

4. *Giotto's Tears*

1. Hannah Green, *Little Saint,* pp. 156–57.

2. Ibid.

3. Steven Ozment, *Ancestors,* p. 100.

4. Elizabeth Wayland Barber, *Women's Work,* pp. 29, 30.

5. Cynthia Eller, *The Myth of Matriarchal Prehistory,* pp. 180–81.

6. Hugh Cunningham, *Children and Childhood in Western Society Since 1500,* pp. 40, 52.

7. Robert Baldock, quoted in Emily Eakin, "Did Cradles Always Rock? Or Did Mom Once Not Care?" *New York Times,* June 30, 2001, pp. A15–17.

8. Frances D'Emilio (Associated Press), "Cleaning of Giotto Paintings Bares Rift," *Boston Globe*, March 19, 2002, p. A10.

9. Linda Pollock, *A Lasting Relationship*, pp. 114–15.

10. Euripides, *The Trojan Women*, pp. 153, 154; Sophocles, *Oedipus Rex*, p. 11; Homer, *Odyssey*, Book XI, lines 220–27, p. 179.

11. Seneca, "On Consolation" in Mary R. Lefkowitz and Maureen B. Fant, *Women in Greece and Rome*, pp. 114–15.

12. Euripides, *Ion*, pp. 224–25, 246–47.

13. John Boswell, *The Kindness of Strangers*, pp. 76, 101.

14. David I. Kertzer, *Sacrificed for Honor*, p. 13.

15. Ibid., pp. 10, 123–53.

16. Op. cit., Boswell, pp. 3, 75, 101, 112, 132, note 154.

17. Personal communication, Judith Himber, Ph.D.

18. Janna Malamud Smith, *Private Matters*, p. 210.

5. Semele Remembered

1. Edith Hamilton, *Mythology*, pp. 52, 53.

2. Sigmund Freud, *The Interpretation of Dreams*, p. 262; see also Jonathan Lear's marvelous essay "On Killing Freud (Again)" in *Open Minded*, pp. 16–33.

3. Cynthia Eller, *The Myth of Matriarchal Prehistory*, pp. 106, 107.

4. See Edith Hall, "Introduction" in *Euripides: Iphigenia Among the Taurians; Bacchae; Iphigenia at Aulis; Rhesus*, pp. xxx, xxxix.

5. Euripides, *Iphigenia in Aulis* in *The Complete Greek Tragedies: Euripides IV*, pp. 245, 253.

6. Ibid, pp. 276–77.

7. Ibid., pp. 275, 263, 277.

8. Ibid., pp. 278–79.

9. Ibid., pp. 266, 293.

10. Sue Blundell, *Women in Ancient Greece*, pp. 66, 67.

11. Euripides, *Hecuba*, p. 18.

12. Op. cit., *Iphigenia*, p. 254.

13. Euripides, *Ion*, p. 194.

14. Personal communication: Roger Sorkin, 2001.

15. Euripides, *Bacchae* in *The Bacchae and Other Plays*, p. 191. (I have altered Agaüe to Agave—as some other translations do—for ease of reading.)

16. Robert Graves, *The Greek Myths*, pp. 103–11.

17. Simone de Beauvoir, quoted in Adrienne Rich, *Of Woman Born*, p. 68.

18. Op. cit., *Bacchae*, p. 199.

19. Mary Anne Weaver, "A Reporter at Large," *The New Yorker*, January 10, 2000, p. 51.

20. Sophocles, *Oedipus Rex, The Oedipus Cycle*, p. 40, quoted by Sheila Murnaghan, "Maternity and Mortality in Homeric Poetry," *Classical Antiquity*, pp. 241–64.

21. Op. cit., *Bacchae,* p. 193.

22. Sigmund Freud, *Civilization and Its Discontents,* p. 75; E. R. Dodds, *The Greeks and the Irrational,* pp. 76–77.

23. Op. cit., Blundell, citing scholarship of F. I. Zetlin, p. 169; op. cit., *Bacchae,* p. 196.

24. Ibid., *Bacchae,* p. 203.

25. Ibid., p. 225.

26. Ibid., p. 232.

27. Ibid.

28. Ibid., p. 234.

29. Ibid., p. 238.

30. Ibid., p. 236.

31. D. W. Winnicott, "Hate in the Countertransference" in *Through Paediatrics to Psycho-Analysis,* p. 202.

6. *John Flavel's* Token for Mourners

1. John Flavel, *A Token for Mourners,* p. 3.

2. Charles Evans, *American Bibliography,* p. x.

3. George Emery Littlefield, *Early Boston Booksellers 1642–1711,* pp. 204–5; Peter Gregg Slater, *Children in the New England Mind,* p. 16. (Cotton Mather married three times, and produced nine children with his first wife, Abigail Phillips, before she died; and six with his second, Elizabeth Hubbard, before she died.)

4. Thomas Goddard Wright, *Literary Culture in Early New England 1620–1730,* pp. 187–88, 224–28, 234; op. cit., Littlefield, p. 189; op. cit., Slater, p. 16.

5. Victor Neuburg, "Chapbooks in America" in Cathy N. Davidson, ed., *Reading in America,* p. 89; William J. Gilmore, *Reading Becomes a Necessity of Life,* pp. 62, 64.

6. Kevin J. Hayes, *A Colonial Woman's Bookshelf,* p. 56; E. Jennifer Monaghan, "Literacy Instruction and Gender in Colonial New England" in *Reading in America,* p. 64. Bradstreet is quoted by Monaghan, p. 65.

7. "The Life of the Late Rev. Mr. John Flavel, Minister of Dartmouth" in *The Whole Works of the Rev. Mr. John Flavel,* pp. v, vii, viii, ix.

8. Ibid., pp. viii–ix.

9. Mary Beth Norton, *Founding Mothers and Fathers,* pp. 45, 48, 51, 54, 329, 338; Philip Greven, *Spare the Child;* Judith Lewis Herman, *Trauma and Recovery.*

10. Darrett B. Rutman, *Winthrop's Boston,* pp. 27, 36.

11. See Laurel Thatcher Ulrich, *Good Wives,* pp. 154–55; Samuel X. Radbill, M.D., Foreword to Thomas E. Cone, Jr., M.D., *History of American Pediatrics,* p. viii: "It is hard for us today to realize the omnipresence of worms." Also, it is important to recall that European women were able to settle in New England because of the extraordinary sixteenth-century epidemics of death that native peoples suffered, depopulating New England in the previous century. See Charles C. Mann, "1491" in *The Atlantic Monthly,* pp. 41–53.

12. Elizabeth Reis, *Damned Women,* pp. 1, 13, 14, 32, 35.

13. Op. cit., Flavel, p. 7.

14. Ibid., pp. 5–6.

15. Ibid., pp 7–8.

16. Ibid., pp. 31, 35, 37.

17. Ibid., p. 19.

18. Ibid., pp. 8–9, 13.

19. Ibid., pp. 48, 67, 124.

20. Ibid., pp. 94, 96.

21. George Bernard Shaw, *Saint Joan*, p. 158.

22. Increase Mather, *A Sermon Concerning Obedience & Resignation to the Will of God in Every Thing*, pp. 36–37. I first read a reference to this sermon in Laurel Thatcher Ulrich, "Vertuous Woman Found: New England Ministerial Literature, 1668–1735" in *Puritan New England*, pp. 215–31.

23. Ibid., Mather, pp. 34–35.

24. Daniel J. Boorstin, *The Americans*, p. 10; op. cit., Reis, pp. 119, 123.

25. Op. cit., Norton, pp. 102, 104.

26. Op. cit., Slater, p. 46; J. C. Furnas, *The Americans*, pp. 72, 33; op. cit., Reis., p. 124.

27. M. J. Lewis, "Anne Hutchinson" in *Portraits of American Women from Settlement to the Present*, pp. 39, 41.

28. "Anne Hutchinson" in Edward T. James, ed., *Notable American Women*, p. 247; op. cit., Norton, p. 223; Amy Shrager Lang, *Prophetic Woman*, pp. 41, 55–68.

29. Ibid., Lang, pp. 56–57, 44.

30. Anne Bradstreet, *The Works of Anne Bradstreet*, p. 237. See also Ann Stanford, "Anne Bradstreet: Dogmatist and Rebel" in Alden T. Vaughan and Francis J. Buemer, eds., *Puritan New England*, pp. 287–98.

31. Mary Beth Norton, "The Ablest Midwife That Wee Knowe in the Land," *William and Mary Quarterly*, January 1998, pp. 119, 128, 111; op. cit., Rutman, p. 231.

32. Ibid., Norton, pp. 105, 121.

33. Ibid., p. 117.

34. Ibid., p. 122.

35. Ibid., pp. 121–22.

36. Ibid., p. 125.

37. Ibid., p. 114.

38. Op. cit., Slater, p. 28; Michael Wigglesworth, *The Day of Doom*, p. 60.

39. Ibid., Wigglesworth, pp. 50, 54, 59.

40. Edward Taylor, "A Funerall Poem Upon the Death of my ever Endeared, and Tender Wife Mrs. Elizabeth Taylor, Who fell asleep in Christ the 7th day of July at night about two hours after Sun setting 1689 and in the 39 yeare of her Life" in *The Poems of Edward Taylor*, pp. 472, 476.

41. David E. Stannard, "Death and the Puritan Child" in *Puritan New England*, pp. 241–44.

42. James Janeway, *A Token for Children*, pp. 93, 94.

43. Ibid., p. 43.

44. Ibid., p. 65.

45. Op. cit., Reis, p. 113. Reis notes that more women than men were accusers and accused in the Salem witch trials of 1692, and it seems possible that the psychological pressures upon women manifested themselves in the frenzy. With female behavior under so many strictures, little wonder women were agitated. And it was safer to act against women than to rebel against male authority. Part of the collective insanity may have come from women's unconscious wishes to create scapegoat repositories on which to project their own unbearable feelings of badness. The common accusatory testimony describes the "witches" suckling satanic imps. These creatures could symbolize many forbidden feelings—from weariness with the endless demands of sucking infants to illicit pleasure in female sexuality. The imps do also resemble babies long dead. Perhaps they signified intruding residues of traumatic loss. A supposed witch, later hanged in spite of endless professions of innocence, Bridget Bishop was said to have "puled out her brest and the black man gave her a thing like a blake pig it had no haire on it and shee put it to her brest and gave it suck."

7. William Buchan's Advice to Mothers

1. Jan Lewis and Kenneth A. Lockridge, "'Sally Has Been Sick': Pregnancy and Family Limitation among Virginia Gentry Women, 1780–1850" in Rima D. Apple and Janet Golden, eds., *Mothers & Motherhood,* p. 198; Catherine Scholten, *Childbearing in American Society,* p. 73.

2. Victor Neuberg, "Chapbooks in America" in Cathy N. Davidson, ed., *Reading in America,* pp. 83–84.

3. James Janeway, *A Token for Children,* pp. 63, 77, 78, 80, 81.

4. Charles E. Rosenberg, *The Care of Strangers,* p. 159; Laurel Thatcher Ulrich, "The Living Mother of a Living Child," *William and Mary Quarterly,* January 1989, p. 31; Lewis Thomas, *The Youngest Science,* p. 13.

5. Elizabeth Cady Stanton, *Eighty Years & More,* p. 119.

6. Ibid., pp. 119, 120.

7. Alice Judson Ryerson, "Medical Advice on Child Rearing," *Harvard Education Review,* Summer 1961, p. 318.

8. John Locke, *Some Thoughts Concerning Education,* p. 96.

9. Jean-Jacques Rousseau, *Emile,* pp. 93, 118.

10. John Stevens Cabot Abbott, *The Mother at Home,* p. 155.

11. Linda Kerber, *Women of the Republic,* pp. 233–64; William Gilmore, *Reading Becomes a Necessity of Life,* pp. 120, 121.

12. Kevin J. Hayes, *A Colonial Woman's Bookshelf,* pp. 88, 89, 94–96. On a lighter note, and perhaps illustrative of an aspect of the medical and religious tensions of the day, Hayes also found that in the early 1700s the famous minister Jonathan Edwards became concerned about his teenage male congregants reading midwifery books for prurient reasons. He conducted an investigation and wrote

an unpublished manuscript entitled "Papers concerning young men's reading mid-wives books," in which he documented the dangerous pornographic possibilities of the texts!

13. See Mary Beth Norton, *Liberty's Daughters*, and Linda Kerber, *Women of the Republic;* Hugh Cunningham, *Children and Childhood in Western Society Since 1500*, p. 62.

14. Op. cit., Gilmore, pp. 6, 117.

15. Op. cit., Abbott, pp. 10–11; James Thomas Flexner, *Washington*, pp. 222–23 (with thanks to Dick Ryerson); op. cit., Scholten, p. 80.

16. Op. cit., Kerber, p. 239.

17. Ibid., p. 241.

18. Sir Leslie Stephen and Sir Sidney Lee, eds., *The Dictionary of National Biography*, vol. III, pp. 180–81. For more on Buchan and bathing, and the comparison between Buchan and Benjamin Spock, M.D., see www.countway.med.harvard.edu /bml/highlights/bml-buchan2.html.

19. William Buchan, M.D., *Advice to Mothers*, p. 33, v; op. cit., Scholten, p. 71.

20. Ibid., Buchan, p. v.

21. Ibid.

22. Ibid.

23. Ibid.

24. Ibid.

25. Ibid., p. vi.

26. Ibid., pp. 7–8.

27. Ibid., pp. 9, 26.

28. Ibid., p. 22; Richard W. and Dorothy C. Wertz, cited in Ulrich, "The Living Mother of a Living Child," p. 27.

29. Op. cit., Buchan, p. 8.

30. Ibid., p. 10.

31. Marylynn Salmon, "The Cultural Significance of Breast-Feeding and Infant Care in Early Modern England and America" in Rima D. Apple and Janet Golden, eds., *Mothers & Motherhood*, p. 5.

32. Op. cit., Buchan, pp. 30–31.

33. Valerie Fildes, "Child Abandonment and Neglect, 1550–1800" in Valerie Fildes, ed., *Women as Mothers in Pre-Industrial England*, p. 161.

34. Op cit., Buchan, p. 60.

35. Ibid., pp. 60–61.

36. Ibid., pp. 10–11.

37. Ibid., pp. 11, 13.

38. Ibid., pp. 13–14.

39. Ibid., p. 19.

40. Ibid., pp. 20, 23, 28.

41. Adrian Wilson, "The Ceremony of Childbirth and Its Interpretation" in Valerie Fildes, ed., *Women as Mothers in Pre-Industrial England*, pp. 68–75; op. cit., Buchan, p. 28.

42. Buchan, pp. 33, 34–35, 41, 52–53; op. cit., Cunningham, p. 113, citing Boswell, *The Kindness of Strangers,* pp. 415–16.

43. Op. cit., Boswell, pp. 421–24; op. cit., Buchan, p. 54.

44. Ibid., Buchan, p. 97.

45. Ibid., Buchan, pp. 85, 81. (Buchan may have taken his material on chimney sweeps from the social reformer Joseph Hanley.)

46. Op. cit., Scholten, p. 83.

47. Op. cit., Buchan, p. 25.

48. Ibid., p. 69.

49. Ibid., pp. 101, 102.

50. Ibid., pp. 73, 74.

51. Ibid., pp. 83–84.

52. Sigmund Freud, *Civilization and Its Discontents,* pp. 91–92.

8. From Medicine to Psychology

1. Michael R. Haines, "Mortality in Nineteenth-Century America," *Demography,* August 1977, pp. 311–12 (with thanks to Lucretia McLure, reference librarian, Countway Library, Harvard Medical School).

2. Charles D. Meigs, M.D., *Woman,* p. 57.

3. Ibid., 55–58.

4. Ibid., pp. 605, 470, 412, 298.

5. Ibid., pp. 299, 144.

6. Ibid., pp. 682–83.

7. Ibid., pp. 75–76.

8. Seton needle: kindly described to me by Jack Eckert, Countway reference librarian, Harvard Medical School, May 2, 2000.

9. Robert K. Massie, *Nicholas and Alexandra,* p. 189.

10. Shirley Hazzard, *The Bay of Noon,* p. 38.

11. Nancy F. Cott, *The Bonds of Womanhood,* pp. 57–58.

12. Molly Ladd-Taylor and Lauri Umansky, eds., *"Bad" Mothers,* pp. 8–9; Harriet Jacobs, *Incidents in the Life of a Slave Girl Written by Herself;* Arlie Russell Hochchild, "The Nanny Chain" in *The American Prospect,* January 3, 2000, pp. 32–36.

13. Ann Hulbert, "The Century of the Child" in *The Wilson Quarterly,* p. 24.

14. Ibid., p. 21.

15. Rima D. Apple, "Constructing Mothers" in Rima D. Apple and Janet Golden, eds., *Mothers & Motherhood,* p. 91.

16. Unsigned, "The Life of Ellen Key," *Harper's Weekly,* January 3, 1914, p. 23; Arthur Ruhl, "A Talk with Ellen Key," *Collier's,* July 22, 1916, p. 19; Madeleine Z. Doty, "Women of the Future: In Sweden, the Genius," *Good Housekeeping,* August 1918, p. 108 (with thanks to Joan Campbell, Clapp Library, Wellesley College). I first read mention of Ellen Key in Ann Hulbert's piece, and found articles by Ellen Key about mothering in *The Atlantic Monthly* and *Harper's Weekly,* and pieces

about her in many contemporary magazines, including *Collier's, Good Housekeeping, The Nation,* and *The New Republic.*

17. *New York Times,* March 6, 1909, cited in *Book Review Digest,* December 1909; Rebecca West, "Eroto-Priggery," *The New Republic,* March 13, 1915, p. 150.

18. Ellen Key, *The Century of the Child,* p. 183.

19. Ibid., pp. 36, 46; Volker Roelcke, M.D., "Healing and Annihilation," *Psychiatry Grand Rounds,* Cambridge Health Alliance, April 11, 2001.

20. Ibid., Key, pp. 37, 44, 104–5.

21. Ibid., pp. 101–2.

22. Ibid., p. 84.

23. Ibid., pp. 114, 316–17.

24. Ibid., pp. 76–82, 132, 275, 284.

25. Half a century later, in *The Feminine Mystique* (1963), Betty Friedan brilliantly and convincingly traced out the *reductio ad absurdum* consequences of views like Key's, as they were articulated by university professors, social scientists, and others who unself-consciously taught as fact highly polarized and rigid notions of femininity. Even though they had likely never heard of Ellen Key (and Friedan doesn't mention her), the young college women Friedan interviewed had drunk from the Swedish prophetess's fountain. They believed that only marriage and motherhood mattered; college was a place to meet a man, and they valued their education simply for its ability to improve their homemaking skills. (Ellen Key actually valued romantic love over marriage—and thus was seen in some circles as a radical free-love advocate.) Friedan quotes a college senior in 1959: "Our parents expect us to go to college. Everybody goes . . . But a girl who got serious about anything she studied—like wanting to go on and do research—would be peculiar, unfeminine. I guess everybody wants to graduate with a diamond ring on her finger. That's the important thing" (p. 153).

26. Op. cit., Haines, p. 12. See Ehrenreich and English, *For Her Own Good,* p. 185.

27. David Cohen, *J. B. Watson,* pp. 157, 257, 179.

28. John B. Watson, Ph.D., *Psychological Care of Infant and Child,* p. 3.

29. Ibid., p. 4.

30. Ibid., pp. 9, 12.

31. Ibid., p. 87.

32. L. Emmett Holt, M.D., LL.D., *The Care and Feeding of Children,* p. 13.

33. Ibid., p. 131.

34. As Nancy Chodorow and Susan Contratto observed in their now classic paper "*The Fantasy of the Perfect Mother*" (1982), idealization and blame of mothers constitute two sides of the same coin. See Chodorow and Contratto, p. 65.

35. Renee Romano, "'Immoral Conduct': White Women, Racial Transgressions, and Custody Disputes" in Ladd-Taylor and Umansky, eds., *"Bad" Mothers,* pp. 230–51; Ruth Feldstein, "Antiracism and Maternal Failure in the 1940s and 1950s" in Ladd-Taylor and Umansky, p. 152.

36. Op. cit., Holt, p. 39.

9. The Psychoanalytic Searchlight

1. Interview 6, February 2000.

2. Peggy Orenstein, *Flux*, p. 112.

3. See Janna Malamud Smith, "Mothers," *New York Times Magazine*, June 10, 1990. See also Judith Grunebaum and Janna Malamud Smith, "Women in Context(s)," in Betsy DeChant, ed., *Women and Group Psychotherapy.*

4. Interview 1, January 2000.

5. Ibid., p. 8.

6. Interview 3, February 2000.

7. Stephen A. Mitchell, *Relationality*, p. x.

8. Margaret Mahler, Fred Pine, and Anni Bergman, *The Psychological Birth of the Human Infant*, p. 233.

9. Ibid., p. 77.

10. Ibid., p. 79.

11. Ibid., p. 80.

12. Ibid., pp. 81–82.

13. Elizabeth Wayland Barber, *Women's Work*, p. 85.

14. Cathy N. Davidson, *Revolution and the Word*, p. 41.

15. D. W. Winnicott, "Mind and Its Relation to the Psyche-Soma" in *Through Pediatrics to Psycho-Analysis*, p. 245; Winnicott, "Ego Integration in Child Development" in *The Maturational Processes and the Facilitating Environment*, p. 57. In the same volume, see also, Winnicott, "Ego Distortion in Terms of True and False Self," p. 145.

16. D. W. Winnicott, "Primary Maternal Preoccupation" in *Through Paediatrics to Psycho-Analysis*, pp. 302, 303.

17. Op. cit., Winnicott, "Ego Integration," pp. 58–59.

18. D. W. Winnicott, "Infant Feeding" in *The Child, the Family and the Outside World*, p. 33.

19. D. W. Winnicott, "Close-up of Mother Feeding Baby" in *The Child, the Family and the Outside World*, p. 48.

20. Op. cit., Winnicott, "Infant Feeding," pp. 30–31.

21. D. W. Winnicott, "Breast Feeding" in *The Child, the Family and the Outside World*, p. 51.

22. Ibid., p. 50.

23. Erich Auerbach, *Mimesis*, p. 404. (Italics added.)

24. Robert Desjarlais, et al., eds., "Women" *in World Mental Health*, p. 186.

25. Ibid., p. 179.

10. The Free Mother

1. Charles Taylor, *Sources of the Self*, pp. 64–65.

2. Stendhal, *The Red and the Black*, p. 49. For a discussion of love and psychological growth, see Jonathan Lear, *Love and Its Place in Nature.*

3. Jerome Kagan, *Three Seductive Ideas*, p. 94.

4. Kevin Bales, *Disposable People,* p. 40.

5. "4.5 Prevalence of Violence against Women by an Intimate Partner," *Progress of the World's Women 2000,* World Health Organization: www.unifem.undp.org/progressww/2000/charts.html; Barbara Crossette, "Unicef Reports on Violence Facing Women," *New York Times,* June 1, 2000, p. A13.

6. Sarah Buel, "What Clinicians Need to Know about Family Violence," *Women,* Cambridge Hospital, May 5–6, 1995, audiotape.

7. Tina Howe, *Pride's Crossing,* pp. 69, 116.

8. Ibid., p. 68.

9. See Janna Malamud Smith, *Private Matters,* pp. 53–72; Nancy Scheper-Hughes, *Death Without Weeping,* p. 277.

10. Erica Goode, "When Women Find Love Is Fatal," *New York Times,* February 15, 2000, pp. D1, D6. The psychologist quoted is Donald Dutton, University of British Columbia.

11. Alice Munro, "The Children Stay," *The New Yorker,* December 22 and 29, 1997, p. 99.

12. Ibid., p. 103.

13. Ibid.

14. Ibid.

15. Ibid.

16. Associated Press, "Afghan Death by Stoning," *New York Times,* May 2, 2000, p. A4.

17. See Janna Malamud Smith, "Where Have All the Fathers Gone?" in *Tikkun,* March/April 2000, pp. 73–75.

18. Amy Finnerty, "What Do You Do All Day?" *New York Times Magazine,* March 5, 2000, p. 55.

19. Among the poorer mothers I worked with in a housing project clinic, the unsteady jobs, relational oppression, and frequent physical violence often made marriage undesirable; the women favored boyfriends, who could be more easily sent away when they became mean or broke. In her research on why poor women often don't marry or remarry, Kathryn Edin cites similar reasons and further emphasizes how deeply the women distrust that the men will care for their children. Many of Edin's subjects felt that when they became pregnant, their men became much more violent. The men wondered if the children were theirs. But I suspect they also felt diminished and doubted their ability to help provide. In turn, during hard times the mothers experienced the men as liabilities, taking food from children's mouths: Kathryn Edin, "Few Good Men," *American Prospect,* January 3, 2000, pp. 26–31.

20. Rebecca Mead, "Comment: Psychobabble's Out, Biobabble's In," *The New Yorker,* November 15, 1999, pp. 39, 40; Courtney Weaver, "Heartburn," *New York Times Book Review,* February 13, 2000, p. 16.

21. Sarah Blaffer Hrdy, *Mother Nature,* pp. xii, 485–510.

22. R. C. Lewontin, *Biology as Ideology,* p. 87; Erica Goode, "Human Nature," *New York Times,* March 14, 2000, pp. D1, D9.

23. Jerome Bruner, "Tot Thought," *New York Review of Books,* March 9, 2000, p. 28.

24. Ibid.

11. *Worrying Mothers*

1. John Bowlby, *Attachment,* pp. 48, 189.

2. Interview 10, July 7, 2000.

3. See Sara Ruddick, *Maternal Thinking.* Ruddick is the first person I know of who wrote in detail about the way that mothers think about their work. Quotation is from Interview 8, April 2000.

4. Interview 1, January 2000.

5. Interview 9, July 4, 2000.

6. Interview 8, April 6, 2000.

7. Amartya Sen, *Development as Freedom,* p. 23; also Janna Malamud Smith, "Psychotherapy with Low-Income Women" in Leston Havens and Alex Sabo, eds., *Real World Psychotherapy.*

8. Interview 3, February 11, 2000.

9. Interview 7, March 10, 2000.

10. Natalie Angier, *Woman,* p. 307.

11. Interview 11, July 17, 2000.

12. Interview 12, July 21, 2000.

13. Ibid.

14. Ibid.

15. Richard Lowry, "Nasty, Brutish, and Short," *National Review,* May 28, 2001, pp. 36, 38 (with thanks to Lois Ames).

16. John M. Synge, *Riders to the Sea* in *The Complete Plays,* p. 83.

17. Ibid., p. 90.

18. Stephanie J. Ventura, et al., "Births: Final Data for 1998," *National Vital Statistics Reports,* vol. 48, no. 3, March 28, 2000, National Center for Health Statistics.

19. "Arlene Eisenberg, 66, Author of 'What to Expect' Guides," obituary in *New York Times,* February 10, 2001, p. A11.

20. Amanda Vickery, *The Gentleman's Daughter,* p. 125.

21. Kathryn Smith as told to Leslie Chess Feller, "Beating the Odds," *Good Housekeeping,* January 2002, pp. 118, 120.

22. Sheryl Gay Stolberg, "Researchers Find a Link Between Behavioral Problems and Time in Child Care," *New York Times,* April 19, 2001, p. A18; Sheryl Gay Stolberg, "Another Academic Salvo from a 'Mommy Wars' Veteran," *New York Times,* April 21, 2001, p. A7; Sheryl Gay Stolberg, "Ideas and Trends: Science, Studies and Motherhood," *New York Times,* April 22, 2001, p. 3; Nancy Gibbs, "What Kids (Really) Need," *Time,* April 30, 2001, pp. 48–49; Katha Pollitt, "Subject to Debate: Childcare Scare," *The Nation,* May 14, 2001, p. 10. Pollitt cites Deborah Vandrell at the University of Wisconsin about the European press.

23. Interview 4, February 21, 2000.

24. Interviews 11 and 12: July 17, 2000, and July 21, 2000.

25. Patricia Wen, "Where Children Are Seen, Not Heard," *Boston Globe,* June 5, 2000, pp. A1, B12.

26. I discussed this surveillance dilemma in Janna Malamud Smith, *Private Matters,* p. 238.

12. Putting Children First

1. Interviews 7, 4, and 6: March 10, 2000; February 21, 2000; and February 29, 2000.

2. Jacqueline L. Salmon, "Study Says Time Mothers Spend with Children Has Not Changed," *Boston Globe,* March 28, 2000, p. A3.

3. Sylvia Ann Hewlett, "Have a Child, and Experience the Wage Gap," *New York Times,* May 16, 2000, p. A31.

4. Interview 10, July 7, 2000.

5. Elizabeth Becker, "Army Mothers Find Obstacle on Route to General's Office," *New York Times,* November 29, 1999, pp. A1, A16.

6. Nathan Cobb, "Walker Downshifts," *Boston Globe,* April 17, 2000, p. C1.

7. Interview 5, February 21, 2000.

8. Ibid.

9. Jerome Kagan, *Three Seductive Ideas,* p. 186.

10. Ibid., p. 190.

11. Op. cit., Cobb.

12. Susan Straight, "One Drip at a Time," Camille Peri and Kate Moses, eds., *Mothers Who Think,* p. 46.

13. Ibid., p. 58.

14. Interview 2, February 2000.

15. William Sears and Martha Sears, *The Baby Book,* p. 621; "Day Care Builds Immunity to Colds," *New York Times,* February 15, 2002, p. A17.

16. Ibid., p. 662.

17. Ibid., p. xiii.

18. Ibid., p. 5.

19. Ibid., p. 9.

20. Ibid.

21. Ibid., pp. 11, 12; John T. Bruer, *The Myth of the First Three Years,* p. 53.

22. Ross A. Thompson, "Early Attachment and Later Development" in *Handbook of Attachment,* Jude Cassidy and Phillip R. Shaver, eds., p. 279.

23. Ibid., pp. 280, 281.

24. Op. cit., Sears and Sears, pp. 373, 374.

25. Ann Crittenden, *The Price of Motherhood,* pp. 120, 130.

26. Op. cit., Kagan, p. 147.

27. Bill Berkowitz, "Talk Radio's Laura Schlessinger," *Z Magazine,* January 2000, pp. 50–52.

28. Interview 1, January 2000.

29. Joan Williams, *Unbending Gender,* p. 4.

30. Ibid., p. 55.

31. Ibid., p. 9; Laura Pappano, "Running Out of Time," *Boston Globe Magazine,* June 25, 2000.

13. Solomon's Wisdom

1. 1 Kings 3 in *The Oxford Annotated Bible: Revised Standard Version of the Holy Bible,* Herbert G. May and Bruce M. Metzger, eds. New York: Oxford University Press, 1962, p. 419 (with thanks to Judith Himber, Ph.D.).

2. Ibid., pp. 419, 420.

3. Patricia Clark, "Women, Slaves, and the Hierarchies of Domestic Violence: The Family of St. Augustine" in Sandra R. Joshel and Sheila Murnaghan, eds., *Women and Slaves in Greco-Roman Culture,* pp. 116–20.

4. Euripides, *Electra* in David Grene and Richmond Lattimore, eds., *The Complete Greek Tragedies: Euripides V,* p. 53.

BIBLIOGRAPHY

Abbott, John Stevens Cabot. *The Mother at Home; or, the Principles of Maternal Duty familiarly Illustrated.* New York: American Tract Society, 1833. Micropublished in "History of Women," reel 152, no. 957. New Haven, Conn.: Research Publications, Inc., 1975.

Amory, Hugh. "Under the Exchange: The Unprofitable Business of Michael Perry, a Seventeenth-century Boston Bookseller," *Proceedings of the American Antiquarian Society,* vol. 103. Worcester, Mass.: American Antiquarian Society, 1993.

Angier, Natalie. *Woman: An Intimate Geography.* Boston: Houghton Mifflin, 1999.

Anonymous. *A Domestic Guide to Mothers in India. Particular Instructions on the Management of Themselves and Their Children by a medical Practitioner of several years experience in India.* T Graham and C. Burjorjce, printers. Bombay: American Mission Press, 1836.

Anonymous. *Mrs. Barwell's Infant Treatment with Directions to Mothers for Self-Management Before, during and after pregnancy.* Revised enlarged and adapted to habits and climate of the United States. By a physician of New York, under the approval and recommendation of Valentine Mott, MD. New York: James Mowatt, 1844.

Apple, Rima D. "Constructing Mothers: Scientific Motherhood in the Nineteenth and Twentieth Centuries." In *Mothers and Motherhood: Readings in American History,* edited by Rima D. Apple and Janet Golden. Columbus: Ohio State University Press, 1997.

Aries, Phillipe. *Centuries of Childhood: A Social History of Family Life.* New York: Vintage, 1962.

Auerbach, Erich. *Mimesis: The Representation of Reality in Western Literature.* Translated by Willard R. Trask. Princeton, New Jersey: Princeton University Press, 1953.

Austin, J. L. *How to Do Things with Words.* Cambridge, Mass.: Harvard University Press, 1962/1994.

Bales, Kevin. *Disposable People: New Slavery in the Global Economy.* Berkeley: University of California Press, 1999.

Balzac, Honoré de. *Pére Goriot.* Translated by A. J. Krailsheimer. Oxford: Oxford University Press, 1991.

Barber, Benjamin R. *Jihad vs. McWorld: How Globalism and Tribalism Are Reshaping the World.* New York: Ballantine, 1995/1996.

Barber, Elizabeth Wayland. *Women's Work: The First 20,000 Years: Women, Cloth and Society in Early Times.* New York: Norton, 1994.

Becker, Elizabeth. "Army Mothers Find Obstacles on Route to General's Office," *New York Times,* November 29, 1999.

Beebe, Beatrice, and Frank M. Lachmann, "The Contribution of Mother-Infant Mutual Influence to the Origins of Self- and Object Representations." In *Relational Perspectives in Psychoanalysis,* edited by Neil J. Skolnick and Susan C. Warshaw. Hillsdale, N.J., and London: Analytic Press, 1992.

Belsky, Jay. "Interactional and Contextual Determinants of Attachment Security." In *Handbook of Attachment: Theory, Research, and Clinical Applications,* edited by Jude Cassidy and Phillip R. Shaver. New York and London: Guilford Press, 1999.

Benjamin, Jessica. *The Bonds of Love: Psychoanalysis, Feminism, and the Problem of Domination.* New York: Pantheon, 1988.

Berkowitz, Bill. "Talk Radio's Laura Schlessinger," *Z Magazine,* vol. 13, no. 1, January 2000.

Bernard, Jessie. *The Future of Motherhood.* New York: Dial Press, 1974.

Bingaman, Jeff, and Jon S. Corzine, "Health of the Mother," *New York Times,* February 7, 2002.

Blackwell, Marilyn S. "The Republican Vision of Mary Palmer Tyler." In *Mothers & Motherhood: Readings in American History,* edited by Rima D. Apple and Janet Golden. Columbus: Ohio State University Press, 1997.

Blundell, Sue. *Women in Ancient Greece.* Cambridge, Mass.: Harvard University Press, 1995.

Boo, Katherine. "A Reporter at Large: After Welfare," *The New Yorker,* April 9, 2001.

Boorstin, Daniel J. *The Americans: The Colonial Experience.* New York: Vintage, 1958.

Boswell, John. *The Kindness of Strangers: Abandonment of Children in Western Europe from Late Antiquity to the Renaissance.* London: Allen Lane/Penguin Press, 1988.

Bowlby, John. *Attachment.* Second Edition. New York: Basic/Harper Torchbooks, 1982.

Boydston, Jeanne. *Home & Work: Housework, Wages, and the Ideology of Labor in the Early Republic.* New York: Oxford University Press, 1990.

Brandt, Allan M. *No Magic Bullet: A Social History of Venereal Disease in the United States Since 1880.* New York, Oxford: Oxford University Press, 1987.

Brown, Keith Michael. *Sacred Bond: Black Men and Their Mothers.* Boston and New York: Little, Brown, 1998.

Bruer, John T. *The Myth of the First Three Years: A New Understanding of Early Brain Development and Lifelong Learning.* New York: Free Press, 1999.

Bruner, Jerome. "Tot Thought," *New York Review of Books,* vol. XLVII, March 9, 2000.

Buchan, William, M.D. *Advice to Mothers on the Subject of their own health, and on the means of promoting the Health, Strength, and Beauty of their Offspring.* New York: Richard Scott, 1815/1804.

Buel, Sarah. "What Clinicians Need to Know about Family Violence," *Women: Contemporary Treatment Issues.* Cambridge, Mass.: Cambridge Hospital, May 5–6, 1995, audiotape.

Chodorow, Nancy. *The Reproduction of Mothering: Psychoanalysis and the Sociology of Gender.* Berkeley: University of California Press, 1978.

Chodorow, Nancy, and Susan Contratto, "The Fantasy of the Perfect Mother." In *Rethinking the Family: Some Feminist Questions,* edited by Barrie Thorne and Marilyn Yalom. New York and London: Longman, 1982.

Clark, Patricia, "Women, Slaves, and the Hierarchies of Domestic Violence: The Family of St. Augustine." In *Women and Slaves in Greco-Roman Culture: Differential Equations,* edited by Sandra R. Joshel and Sheila Murnaghan. London and New York: Routledge, 1998.

Cobb, Nathan. "Walker Downshifts," *Boston Globe,* April 17, 2000.

Cohen, David. *J. B. Watson: The Founder of Behaviorism.* London, Boston, and Henley: Routledge and Kegan Paul, 1979.

Cone, Thomas E., Jr., M.D. *History of American Pediatrics.* Boston: Little, Brown, 1979.

Conroy, Peter V., Jr. *Jean-Jacques Rousseau.* New York: Twayne Publishers, 1998.

Cott, Nancy F. *The Bonds of Womanhood: "Woman's Sphere." In New England, 1780–1835.* New Haven and London: Yale University Press, 1977.

Crawford, Cristina. *Mommie Dearest: A True Story.* New York: Morrow, 1978.

Crawford, Michael J. *Seasons of Grace: Colonial New England's Revival Tradition in Its British Context.* New York and Oxford: Oxford University Press, 1991.

Crittenden, Ann. *The Price of Motherhood: Why the Most Important Job in the World Is Still the Least Valued.* New York: Metropolitan Books, 2001.

Crossette, Barbara. "Unicef Reports on Violence Facing Women," *New York Times,* June 1, 2000.

Cunningham, Hugh. *Children and Childhood in Western Society Since 1500.* London and New York: Longman, 1995.

Damasio, Antonio. *The Feeling of What Happens: Body and Emotion in the Making of Consciousness.* New York: Harcourt Brace, 1999.

Darnton, Robert. *The Great Cat Massacre: And Other Episodes in French Cultural History.* New York: Vintage, 1985.

Davidson, Cathy N. *Revolution and the Word: The Rise of the Novel in America.* New York and Oxford: Oxford University Press, 1986.

Deetz, James, and Patricia Scott Deetz. *The Times of Their Lives: Life, Love, and Death in Plymouth Colony.* New York: W. H. Freeman, 2000.

Demos, John. "Underlying Themes in the Witchcraft of Seventeenth-century New England." In *Puritan New England: Essays on Religion, Society and Culture,* edited by Alden T. Vaughan and Francis J. Buemer. New York: St. Martin's Press, 1977.

Desjarlais, Robert, Leon Eisenberg, Byron Good, and Arthur Kleinman, eds. "Women" in *World Mental Health: Problems and Priorities in Low-Income Countries.* New York and Oxford: Oxford University Press, 1995.

Dodds, E. R. *The Greeks and the Irrational.* Berkeley and Los Angeles: University of California Press, 1951/1973.

———. "Introduction and Commentary to the Bacchae." In *The Plays of Euripides,* Bacchae, Second Edition. London: Oxford University Press.

Doty, Madeleine Z. "Women of the Future: In Sweden, the Genius." *Good Housekeeping,* vol. 67, August 1918.

Douglas, Ann. *The Feminization of American Culture.* New York: Avon, 1978.

———. *Terrible Honesty: Mongrel Manhattan in the 1920s.* New York: Farrar, Straus and Giroux, 1995.

Drachman, Virginia G. *Hospital with a Heart: Women Doctors and the Paradox of Separatism at the New England Hospital, 1862–1969.* Ithaca and London: Cornell University Press, 1984.

Edin, Kathryn. "Few Good Men: Why Poor Mothers Stay Single." In *The American Prospect,* vol. 11, no. 4. January 3, 2000.

Eggers, David. *A Heartbreaking Work of Staggering Genius.* New York: Simon and Schuster, 2000.

Ehrenreich, Barbara. *Fear of Falling: The Inner Life of the Middle Class.* New York: Pantheon, 1989.

Ehrenreich, Barbara, and Deirdre English. *For Her Own Good: 150 Years of the Experts' Advice to Women.* New York: Doubleday/Anchor, 1978.

Ellenberger, Henri. *The Discovery of the Unconscious: The History and Evolution of Dynamic Psychiatry.* New York: Basic Books, 1970.

Eller, Cynthia. *The Myth of Matriarchal Prehistory: Why an Invented Past Won't Give Women a Future.* Boston: Beacon Press, 2000.

Estrich, Susan. *Sex & Power.* New York: Riverhead Books/Penguin Putnam, 2000.

Euripides. *Andromache.* In *The Complete Greek Tragedies: Euripides III,* edited by David Grene and Richmond Lattimore. Translated by John Frederick Nims. Chicago and London: University of Chicago Press, 1947/1958.

———. *Bacchae.* In *The Bacchae and Other Plays.* Translated by Philip Vellacott. Penguin Books, 1954/1972.

———. *Electra.* In *The Complete Greek Tragedies: Euripides V,* edited by David Grene and Richmond Lattimore. Translated by Emily Townsend Vermeule. Chicago and London: University of Chicago Press, 1959.

———. *Hecuba.* In *The Complete Greek Tragedies: Euripides III,* edited by David Grene and Richmond Lattimore. Translated by William Arrowsmith. Chicago and London: University of Chicago Press, 1947/1958.

———. *Ion.* In *The Complete Greek Tragedies: Euripides III,* edited by David Grene and Richmond Lattimore. Translated by Ronald Frederick-Willette. Chicago and London: University of Chicago Press, 1947/1958.

———. *Iphigenia in Aulis.* In *The Complete Greek Tragedies: Euripides IV,* edited by David Grene and Richmond Lattimore. Translated by Charles R. Walker. Chicago and London: University of Chicago Press, 1958/1963.

———. *The Medea.* In *The Complete Greek Tragedies: Euripides I,* edited by David Grene and Richmond Lattimore. Translated by Red Warner. Chicago and London: University of Chicago Press, 1955, p. 55–108.

———. *The Trojan Women.* In *The Complete Greek Tragedies: Euripides III,* edited by David Grene and Richmond Lattimore. Translated by Richmond Lattimore. Chicago: University of Chicago Press, 1958, pp. 121–75.

Evans, Charles. *American Bibliography: A Chronological Dictionary of all Books Pamphlets and Periodical Publications Printed in the United States of America from the Genesis of Printing in 1639 to and Including the year 1820.* New York: Peter Smith, 1941.

Eyer, Diane. *Motherguilt: How Our Culture Blames Mothers for What's Wrong with Society.* New York: Times Books/Random House, 1996.

Fadiman, Anne. *The Spirit Catches You and You Fall Down.* New York: Farrar, Straus and Giroux, 1997.

Faludi, Susan. *Stiffed: The Betrayal of the American Man.* New York: Morrow, 1999.

Feldstein, Ruth. "'I Wanted the Whole World to See': Race, Gender, and Constructions of Motherhood in the Death of Emmett Till." In *Mothers & Motherhood: Readings in American History,* edited by Rima D. Apple and Janet Golden. Columbus: Ohio State University Press, 1997.

Fildes, Valerie, ed. *Women as Mothers in Pre-Industrial England: Essays in Memory of Dorothy McLaren.* London and New York: Routledge, 1990.

Finnerty, Amy. "What Do You Do All Day?" *New York Times Magazine,* March 5, 2000.

Flavel, John. *A Token for Mourners: The advice of Christ to a distressed mother, bewailing the death of her Dear and Only son; wherein the Boundaries of Sorrow are duly fixed, excesses restrained, the common pleas answered, and divers rules for the support of God's afflicted ones prescribed.* Brattleborough, Vt.: William Fessenden, 1813.

Flexner, James Thomas. *Washington: The Indispensable Man.* Boston and Toronto: Little, Brown, 1969.

Fremont, Helen. *After Long Silence: A Memoir.* Delta, 1999.

Freud, Sigmund. *Civilization and Its Discontents,* vol. XXI. Translated by James Strachey. London: Hogarth Press and Institute of Psychoanalysis, 1978.

———. *The Interpretation of Dreams.* London: Hogarth Press, 1978.

Friedan, Betty. *The Feminine Mystique.* New York: Dell, 1963/1983.

Frost, Robert. *The Complete Poems of Robert Frost.* New York: Holt, Rinehart and Winston, 1949.

Furnas, J. C. *The Americans: A Social History of the United States 1587–1914.* New York: G. P. Putnam's Sons, 1969.

Garrows, David J. *Liberty and Sexuality: The Right of Privacy and the Making of Roe v. Wade.* New York: Macmillan, 1994.

Gibbs, Nancy. "What Kids (Really) Need," *Time,* April 30, 2001.

Gilje, Paul A. "Infant Abandonment in Early Nineteenth-Century New York City: Three Cases." In *Growing Up in America: Children in Historical Perspective,* edited by N. Ray Hiner and Joseph M. Hawes. Urbana and Chicago: University of Illinois Press, 1985.

Gilligan, James. *Violence.* New York: Vintage, 1997.

Gilmore, William. *Reading Becomes a Necessity of Life: Material and Cultural Life in Rural New England,* 1780–1835. Knoxville: University of Tennessee Press, 1989.

Golden, Janet. "The New Motherhood and the New View of Wet Nurses, 1780–1865." In *Mothers & Motherhood: Readings in American History,* edited by Rima D. Apple and Janet Golden. Columbus: Ohio State University Press, 1997.

Goode, Erica. "When Women Find Love Is Fatal," *New York Times,* February 15, 2001.

Gopnik, Adam. *Paris to the Moon.* New York: Random House, 2000.

Gordon, Linda. "Voluntary Motherhood: The Beginnings of Feminist Birth Control Ideas in the United States." In *Mothers & Motherhood: Readings in American History,* edited by Rima D. Apple and Janet Golden. Columbus: Ohio State University Press, 1997.

Graves, Robert. *The Greek Myths,* vol. 1. New York: George Braziller, 1957.

Green, Hannah. *Little Saint.* New York: Random House, 2000.

Greven, Philip. *Spare the Child: The Religious Roots of Punishment and the Psychological Impact of Physical Abuse.* New York: Knopf, 1991.

Griffiths, Lindsay, "Hardships Plague Women Worldwide, UN Report Says," *Boston Globe,* September 21, 2000.

Grunebaum, Judith, and Janna Malamud Smith, "Women in Context(s): The Social Subtext of Group Psychotherapy." In *Women and Group Psychotherapy,* edited by Betsy DeChant. New York and London: Guilford Press, 1996.

Haines, Michael R. "Mortality in Nineteenth-Century America: Estimates from New York and Pennsylvania Census Data, 1865 and 1900." In *Demography,* vol. 14, no. 3, August 1977.

Hal, Edith. "Introduction." In *Euripides: Iphigenia among the Taurians; Bacchae; Iphigenia at Aulis; Rhesus.* Translated with Explanatory Notes by James Morwood. Oxford: Oxford University Press, 1999.

Hamilton, Edith. *Mythology: Timeless Tales of Gods and Heroes.* New York and Toronto: New American Library, 1940/1942.

Harris, Judith Rich. *The Nurture Assumption.* New York: Free Press, 1998.

Havens, Leston, *A Safe Place.* New York: Ballantine, 1989.

Hayes, Kevin J. *A Colonial Woman's Bookshelf.* Knoxville: University of Tennessee Press, 1996.

Hazzard, Shirley. *The Bay of Noon.* New York and London: Penguin Books, 1970/1988.

Hensley, Jeannine, ed. *The Works of Anne Bradstreet.* The John Harvard Library.

Foreword by Adrienne Rich. Cambridge, Mass.: Belknap Press of Harvard University Press, 1967.

Herman, Judith Lewis. *Trauma and Recovery: The Aftermath of Violence—From Domestic Abuse to Political Terror.* New York: Basic Books, 1992.

Hewlett, Sylvia Ann. "Have a Child, and Experience the Wage Gap," *New York Times,* May 16, 2000.

Hochschild, Arlie Russell. "The Nanny Chain," *The American Prospect,* vol. 11, no. 4, January 3, 2000.

Hochschild, Arlie Russell, with Anne Machung, *The Second Shift.* New York: Avon, 1989/1997.

Holt, L. Emmett. *The Care and Feeding of Children: A Catechism for the Use of Mothers and Children's Nurses,* Third Edition. New York and London: D. Appleton, 1903/1894.

Homer. *Odyssey.* Translated by Robert Fitzgerald. New York: Farrar, Straus and Giroux, 1998.

hooks, bell. *Talking Back: Thinking Feminist, Thinking Black.* Boston: South End Press, 1989.

———. *Where We Stand: Class Matters.* New York and London: Routledge, 2000.

Howe, Tina. *Pride's Crossing.* New York: Samuel French, 1998.

Hrdy, Sarah Blaffer. *Mother Nature: A History of Mothers, Infants, and Natural Selection.* New York: Pantheon, 1999.

Hulbert, Ann. "The Century of the Child." In the *Wilson Quarterly,* vol. XXIII, no. 1, Winter 1999.

Jacobs, Harriet. *Incidents in the Life of a Slave Girl Written by Herself,* edited by Jean Fagan Yellin. Cambridge, Mass.: Harvard University Press, 1987.

James, Edward T., ed. "Anne Hutchinson," *Notable American Women: A Bibliographical Dictionary,* vol. II. Cambridge, Mass.: Belknap Press of Harvard University Press, 1971/1975.

Janeway, James. *A Token for Children; being an account of the Conversion, Holy and Exemplary Lives, and Joyful Deaths of Several Young Children.* London: Printed for Francis Westley, 1825/1671.

Johnson, Barbara. *The Feminist Difference.* Cambridge, Mass., and London: Harvard University Press, 1998.

Jones, Kathleen W. *Taming the Troublesome Child.* Cambridge, Mass., and London: Harvard University Press, 1999.

Joyce, James. *Ulysses.* New York: Vintage/Random House, 1961.

Kagan, Jerome. *Three Seductive Ideas.* Cambridge, Mass.: Harvard University Press, 1998.

Kenison, Katrina, and Kathleen Hirsch, eds. *Mothers: Twenty Stories of Contemporary Motherhood.* New York: North Point Press, 1995.

Kerber, Linda. *Women of the Republic: Intellect and Ideology in Revolutionary America.* Chapel Hill: University of North Carolina Press, 1980.

Kernberg, Otto F., M.D. "Sadomasochism, Sexual Excitement, and Perversion." In *Journal of the American Psychoanalytic Association,* vol. 39, 1991.

Kertzer, David I. *Sacrificed for Honor: Italian Infant Abandonment and the Politics of Reproductive Control.* Boston: Beacon Press, 1993.

Key, Ellen. *The Century of the Child.* New York and London: G. P. Putnam's Sons/ Knickerbocher Press, 1911/1909.

Kimmel, Michael. *Manhood in America: A Cultural History.* New York: Free Press, 1996.

Kingsolver, Barbara. *Holding the Line: Women in the Great Arizona Mine Strike of 1983.* Ithaca and London: ILR Press/Cornell University Press, 1989/1996.

Kirschner, Suzanne R. *The Religious and Romantic Origins of Psychoanalysis: Individuation and Integration in Post-Freudian Theory.* New York: Cambridge University Press, 1996.

Kissam, Richard S., M.D. *The Nurse's Manual, and Young Mother's Guide: Containing Advice on the Management of Infants, and Conduct to Be Observed by the Mothers Before and After Childbirth.* Hartford: Cooke, 1834.

Ladd-Taylor, Molly, and Lauri Umansky, eds. *"Bad" Mothers: The Politics of Blame in Twentieth-Century America.* New York and London: New York University Press, 1998.

Lamott, Anne. *Operating Instructions: A Journal of My Son's First Year.* New York: Fawcett/Colombine, 1993.

Lang, Amy Shrager. *Prophetic Woman: Anne Hutchinson and the Problem of Dissent in the Literature of New England.* Berkeley: University of California Press, 1987.

Lasch, Christopher. *Haven in a Heartless World.* New York: Basic Books, 1977/ 1979.

Layton, Lynne. *Who's That Girl? Who's That Boy?: Clinical Practice Meets Postmodern Gender Theory.* Northvale, N.J., and London: Jacob Aronson, 1998.

Lazarre, Jane. *Beyond the Whiteness of Whiteness: Memoir of a White Mother of Black Sons.* Durham and London: Duke University Press, 1996.

———. *The Mother Knot.* New York: McGraw-Hill, 1976.

Lear, Jonathan. *Love and Its Place in Nature.* New York: Farrar, Straus and Giroux, 1990.

———. *Open Minded: Working Out the Logic of the Soul.* Cambridge, Mass., and London: Harvard University Press, 1998.

Leavitt, Judith Walzer. "Birthing and Anesthesia: The Debate over Twilight Sleep." In *Mothers and Motherhood: Readings in American History,* edited by Rima D. Apple and Janet Golden. Columbus: Ohio State University Press, 1997.

Lefkowitz, Mary R., and Maureen B. Fant. *Women in Greece and Rome.* Toronto and Sarasota: Samuel-Stevens, 1977.

Lewis, Jan. "Mother's Love: The Construction of an Emotion in Nineteenth-Century America." In *Mothers & Motherhood: Readings in American History,* edited by Rima D. Apple and Janet Golden. Columbus: Ohio State University Press, 1997.

Lewis, Jan, and Kenneth A. Lockridge, "'Sally Has Been Sick': Pregnancy and Family Limitation among Virginia Gentry Women, 1780–1850." In *Mothers and Motherhood: Readings in American History,* edited by Rima D. Apple and Janet Golden. Columbus: Ohio State University Press, 1997.

Lewis, M. J. "Anne Hutchinson." In *Portraits of American Women from Settlement to the Present,* edited by G. J. Barker-Benfield and Catherine Clinton. New York and Oxford: Oxford University Press, 1998.

Lewontin, R. C. *Biology as Ideology: The Doctrine of DNA.* New York: Harper Perennial, 1991/1993.

"The Life of Ellen Key," *Harper's Weekly,* vol. 58, January 3, 1914.

Littlefield, George Emery. *Early Boston Booksellers 1642–1711.* Boston: Club of Odd Volumes, 1900.

Locke, John. *Some Thoughts Concerning Education,* edited by John W. and Jean S. Yolton. Oxford: Clarendon Press, 1989.

Lowry, Richard. "Nasty, Brutish, and Short: Children in Day Care—and the Mothers Who Put Them There," *National Review,* May 28, 2001.

Lyden, Jacki. *Daughter of the Queen of Sheba.* New York: Penguin, 1998.

Mahler, Margaret, Fred Pine, and Anni Bergman. *The Psychological Birth of the Human Infant: Symbiosis and Individuation.* New York: Basic Books, 1975.

Mann, Charles C. "1491," *The Atlantic Monthly,* vol. 289, no. 3, March 2002.

Markham, Beryl. *West with the Night.* New York: North Point Press/Farrar, Straus and Giroux, 1942/1983.

Massie, Robert K. *Nicholas and Alexandra.* New York: Atheneum, 1967.

Mather, Increase. *A Sermon Concerning Obedience & Resignation to the Will of God in Every Thing.* Boston: Timothy Green, 1714.

Matthee, Rudi. "Exotic Substances: The Introduction and Global Spread of Tobacco, Coffee, Cocoa, Tea, and Distilled Liquor, Sixteenth to Eighteenth Centuries." In *Drugs and Narcotics in History,* edited by Roy Porter and Mikulas Teich. Cambridge, England: Cambridge University Press, 1995.

McPherson, Conor. *The Weir,* London: Royal Court Theatre Productions, 1997/1998.

Mead, Rebecca. "Comment: Psychobabble's Out, Biobabble's In," *The New Yorker,* November 15, 1999.

Mechling, Jay. "Advice to Historians on Advice to Mothers," *Journal of Social History,* no. 1, Fall 1975.

Meigs, Charles D., M.D., *Woman: Her Diseases and Remedies.* Fourth Edition, Revised and Enlarged. Philadelphia: Blanchard and Lea, 1859.

Menand, Louis. *The Metaphysical Club.* New York: Farrar, Straus and Giroux, 2001.

Mernissi, Fatima. *Dreams of Trespass: Tales of a Harem Girlhood.* Reading, Mass.: Addison-Wesley, 1994.

Michaels, Paula. "The Doctor Says the Baby's Fine but in Your Gut You Know Something's Not Right," *Readers Digest,* January 2002 (reprinted from *Parenting*).

Miller, Jean Baker. *Toward a New Psychology of Women.* Boston: Beacon Press, 1976.

Mitchell, Stephen A. *Relationality: From Attachment to Intersubjectivity.* Hillsdale, N.J., and London: Analytic Press, 2000.

Monaghan, E. Jennifer. "Literacy Instruction and Gender in Colonial New England." In *Reading in America,* edited by Cathy N. Davidson. Baltimore and London: Johns Hopkins University Press, 1989.

Moore, Lorrie. *Birds of America.* New York: Knopf, 1998.

Morrison, Toni. *Beloved.* New York: Knopf, 1987.

Munro, Alice. "The Children Stay," *The New Yorker,* December 22 and 29, 1997.

———. *The Progress of Love.* Toronto: Penguin Books, 1986/1995.

Murnaghan, Sheila. "Maternity and Mortality in Homeric Poetry." *Classical Antiquity,* vol. 11, no. 2, October 1992.

Neuburg, Victor. "Chapbooks in America, Deconstructing the Popular Reading in Early America." In *Reading in America,* edited by Cathy N. Davidson. Baltimore and London: Johns Hopkins University Press, 1989.

New York Times, March 6, 1909. Cited in *Book Review Digest,* vol. 5, no. 12, December 1909. Minneapolis: H. W. Wilson.

Norton, Mary Beth. "'The Ablest Midwife That Wee Knowe in the Land': Mistress Alice Tilly and the Women of Boston and Dorchester, 1649–1650," Notes and Documents, *William and Mary Quarterly,* 3d. series, vol. LV, no. 1, January 1998.

———. *Founding Mothers and Fathers: Gendered Power and the Forming of American Society.* New York: Knopf, 1996.

———. *Liberty's Daughters: The Revolutionary Experience of American Women, 1750–1800.* Ithaca and London: Cornell University Press, 1996/1980.

Novick, Kelly, and Jack Novick, Ph.D. "The Essence of Masochism," *Psychoanalytic Study of the Child,* vol. 42 (1987): pp. 353–84.

Nuland, Sherman B. *Leonardo da Vinci.* New York: Viking, 2000.

Nystrom-Hamilton, Louise. *Ellen Key: Her Life and Her Work.* Translated by A.E.B. Fries, with an introduction by Havelock Ellis. New York and London: G. P. Putnam's Sons/Knickerbocker Press, 1913 (microfilm).

Orenstein, Peggy. *Flux: Women on Sex, Work, Love, Kids and Life in a Half-Changed World.* New York: Doubleday, 2000.

Ozment, Steven. *Ancestors: The Loving Family in Old Europe.* Cambridge, Mass., and London: Harvard University Press, 2001.

Pappano, Laura. "Running Out of Time," *Boston Globe Magazine,* June 25, 2000.

Peri, Camille, and Kate Moses, eds. *Mothers Who Think.* New York: Villard, 1999.

Peters, Joan K. *When Mothers Work.* Reading, Mass.: Addison-Wesley, 1997.

Pinker, Steven. *How the Mind Works.* New York: Norton, 1997.

Pipher, Mary, Ph.D. *Another Country: Navigating the Emotional Terrain of Our Elders.* New York: Riverhead Books, 1999.

Pollitt, Katha. "Subject to Debate: Childcare Scare," *The Nation,* May 14, 2001.

Pollock, Linda. *A Lasting Relationship: Parents and Children over Three Centuries.* Hanover and London: University Press of New England, 1987.

Rabinowitz, Nancy Sorkin. "Slaves with Slaves: Women and Class in Euripidean Tragedy." In *Women and Slaves in Greco-Roman Culture: Differential Equations,* edited by Sandra R. Joshel and Sheila Murnaghan. London and New York: Routledge, 1998.

Reis, Elizabeth. *Damned Women: Sinners and Witches in Puritan New England.* Ithaca, N.Y., and London: Cornell University Press, 1997.

Rich, Adrienne. *Of Woman Born: Motherhood as Experience and Institution.* New York: Norton, 1976/1986.

Ridley, Matt. *Genome: The Autobiography of a Species in 23 Chapters.* New York: Perennial/Harper Collins, 1999/2000.

Roelcke, Volker, M.D. "Healing and Annihilation: Psychiatric Research and Practice in the Era of Nazi Eugenics," *Psychiatry Grand Rounds,* April 11, 2001. Cambridge, Mass.: Cambridge Health Alliance.

Rosen, Ruth. *The World Split Open: How the Modern Women's Movement Changed America.* New York: Viking/Penguin, 2000.

Rosenberg, Charles E. *The Care of Strangers: The Rise of America's Hospital System.* New York: Basic Books, 1987.

Ross, Loretta J. "African American Women and Abortion, 1800–1970." In *Mothers and Motherhood: Readings in American History,* edited by Rima D. Apple and Janet Golden. Columbus: Ohio State University Press, 1997.

Rothchild, Sylvia. *Family Stories for Every Generation.* Detroit: Wayne State University Press, 1989.

Rotundo, E. Anthony. *American Manhood: Transformations in Masculinity from the Revolution to the Modern Era.* New York: Basic Books/HarperCollins, 1993.

Rousseau, Jean-Jacques. *Emile.* Translated by Barbara Foxley, M.A., Everyman's Library. London: J. M. Dent and Sons; New York: E. P. Dutton, 1957/1762.

Ruddick, Sara. *Maternal Thinking: Towards a Politics of Peace.* Boston: Beacon Press, 1989.

Ruhl, Arthur. "A Talk with Ellen Key," *Collier's,* July 22, 1916.

Rutman, Darrett B. *Winthrop's Boston: Portrait of a Puritan Town 1630–1649.* Chapel Hill: University of North Carolina Press, 1965.

Ryerson, Alice Judson. "Medical Advice on Child Rearing, 1550–1900," *Harvard Education Review,* vol. 31, no. 3, Summer 1961.

Salmon, Jacqueline L. "Study Says Time Mothers Spend with Children Has Not Changed," *Boston Globe,* March 28, 2000.

Salmon, Marylynn. "The Cultural Significance of Breast-Feeding and Infant Care in Early Modern England and America." In *Mothers and Motherhood: Readings in American History,* edited by Rima D. Apple and Janet Golden. Columbus: Ohio State University Press, 1997.

Scarborough, John. "The Opium Poppy in Hellenistic and Roman Medicine." In *Drugs and Narcotics in History,* edited by Roy Porter and Mikulas Teich. Cambridge: Cambridge University Press, 1995.

Scheper-Hughes, Nancy. *Death Without Weeping: The Violence of Everyday Life in Brazil.* Berkeley: University of California Press, 1992.

Scholten, Catherine M. *Childbearing in American Society: 1650–1850.* New York and London: New York University Press, 1985.

Sears, William, and Martha Sears. *The Baby Book: Everything You Need to Know About Your Baby from Birth to Age Two.* Boston, New York, and London: Little, Brown, 1993.

Segal, Charles. *Dionysiac Poetics and Euripides' Bacchae.* Princeton, N.J.: Princeton University Press, 1982.

Sen, Amartya. *Development as Freedom.* New York: Knopf, 1999.

Shattuck, Roger. *Forbidden Knowledge: From Prometheus to Pornography.* New York: St. Martin's Press, 1996.

Shaw, George Bernard. *Saint Joan.* Baltimore: Penguin, 1966/1924.

Shaw, Stephanie J. "Mothering under Slavery in the Antebellum South." In *Mothers and Motherhood: Readings in American History,* edited by Rima D. Apple and Janet Golden. Columbus: Ohio State University Press, 1997.

Shelley, Mary. *Maurice, or the Fisher's Cot: A Tale.* Edited and with an introduction by Claire Tomalin. New York: Knopf, 1998.

Simon, Amy R. "Attitudes of Women Towards the Death of Their Children in Michigan and Massachusetts from 1830–1890." Unpublished Thesis. University of Michigan, 1987.

Simon, Bennett. *Mind and Madness in Ancient Greece: The Classical Roots of Modern Psychiatry.* Ithaca, N.Y., and London: Cornell University Press, 1978.

Simonds, Wendy. "Confessions of Loss: Maternal Grief in *True Story,* 1920–1985." In *Mothers and Motherhood: Readings in American History,* edited by Rima D. Apple and Janet Golden. Columbus: Ohio State University Press, 1997.

Slater, Peter Gregg. *Children in the New England Mind: In Death and in Life.* Hamden, Conn.: Archon Books, 1977.

Smith, Dinita. "At 102, a First Author Recalls Slave Relatives," *New York Times,* May 29, 2000.

Smith, Janna Malamud. "Mothers: Tired of Taking the Rap," *New York Times Magazine,* June 10, 1990.

———. *Private Matters: In Defense of the Personal Life.* Reading, Mass.: Addison-Wesley, 1997.

———. "Psychotherapy with People Stressed by Poverty." In *The Real World Guide to Psychotherapy Practice,* edited by Alex N. Sabo and Leston Havens. Cambridge, Mass.: Harvard University Press, 2000.

———. "Where Have All the Fathers Gone?" Book Review: *Stiffed: The Betrayal of the American Man* by Susan Faludi. In *Tikkun,* vol. 15, no. 2, March/April 2000.

Sommers, Christina Hoff. "The War Against Boys." *The Atlantic Monthly,* vol. 285, no. 5, May 2000.

Sophocles. *Oedipus Rex* in *The Oedipus Cycle.* Translated by Dudley Fitts and Robert Fitzgerald. New York: Harcourt Brace Jovanovich/Harvest, 1939/1977.

Stanford, Ann. "Anne Bradstreet: Dogmatist and Rebel." In *Puritan New England: Essays on Religion, Society and Culture,* edited by Alden T. Vaughan and Francis J. Buemer. New York: St. Martin's Press. 1977.

Stannard, David E. "Death and the Puritan Child." In *Puritan New England: Essays on Religion, Society and Culture,* edited by Alden T. Vaughan and Francis J. Buemer. New York: St. Martin's Press, 1977.

Stanton, Elizabeth Cady. *Eighty Years & More: Reminiscences 1815–1897.* New York: Schocken Books, 1971.

Stendhal. *The Red and the Black.* Translated by Catherine Slater. Oxford and New York: Oxford University Press, 1991.

Stephen, Sir Leslie, and Sir Sidney Lee, eds. *The Dictionary of National Biography.* London: Humphrey Milford, 1921–1922.

Stern, Daniel N. *The Interpersonal World of the Infant: A View from Psychoanalysis and Developmental Psychology.* New York: Basic Books, 1985.

Stolberg, Sheryl Gay. "Another Academic Salvo from a 'Mommy Wars' Veteran," *New York Times,* April 21, 2001.

———. "Ideas and Trends: Science, Studies and Motherhood," *New York Times,* April 22, 2001.

———. "Researchers Find a Link Between Behavioral Problems and Time in Child Care," *New York Times,* April 19, 2001.

Synge, John M. *Riders to the Sea.* In *The Complete Plays.* New York: Vintage, 1935.

Taylor, Charles. *Sources of the Self: The Making of the Modern Identity.* Cambridge, Mass.: Harvard University Press, 1989.

Taylor, Edward. "A Funerall Poem Upon the Death of my ever Endeared, and Tender Wife Mrs. Elizabeth Taylor, Who fell asleep in Christ the 7th day of July at night about two hours after Sun setting 1689 and in the 39 yeare of her Life." In *The Poems of Edward Taylor,* edited by Donald E. Stanford. New Haven: Yale University Press, 1960.

Thomas, Lewis. *The Youngest Science: Notes of a Medicine-watcher.* New York: Bantam Books, 1983.

Thompson, Ross A. "Early Attachment and Later Development." In *Handbook of Attachment: Theory, Research, and Clinical Applications,* edited by Jude Cassidy and Phillip R. Shaver. New York and London: Guilford Press, 1999.

Thurer, Shari L. *The Myths of Motherhood: How Culture Reinvents the Good Mother.* New York: Penguin, 1995/1994.

Trilling, Lionel. *Sincerity and Authenticity.* Cambridge, Mass.: Harvard University Press, 1971–1972.

Tyler, Mary Palmer. *The Maternal Physician: A Treatise on the Nurture and Management of Infants, from birth until two years old. Being the result of sixteen years' experience in the nursery.* New York, 1811.

Urlich, Laurel Thatcher. *The Age of Homespun: Objects and Stories in the Creation of an American Myth.* New York: Knopf, 2001.

———. *Good Wives: Image and Reality in the Lives of Women in Northern New England* 1650–1750. New York: Vintage/Random House, 1982/1991.

———. "The Living Mother of a Living Child: Midwifery and Mortality in Post-Revolutionary New England," *William and Mary Quarterly,* 3d series, vol. XLVI, no. 1, January 1989.

———. *A Midwife's Tale: The Life of Martha Ballard, Based in her Diary, 1785–1812.* New York: Vintage, 1990.

———. "Vertuous Woman Found: New England Ministerial Literature, 1668–1735." In *Puritan New England: Essays on Religion, Society and Culture,* edited by Alden T. Vaughan and Francis J. Buemer. New York: St. Martin's Press, 1977.

Valenze, Deborah. *The First Industrial Woman.* New York and Oxford: Oxford University Press, 1995.

Vickery, Amanda. *The Gentleman's Daughter: Women's Lives in Georgian England.* New Haven and London: Yale University Press, 1998.

Walsh, Elsa. *Divided Lives: The Public and Private Struggles of Three Accomplished Women.* New York: Simon and Schuster, 1995.

Warner, John Harley. *The Therapeutic Perspective: Medical Practice, Knowledge, and Identity in America, 1820–1885.* Cambridge, Mass.: Harvard University Press, 1986.

Watson, John B., Ph.D. *Psychological Care of Infant and Child.* New York: Norton, 1928.

Weaver, Courtney. "Heartburn: We Still Get Jealous and That's a Good Thing." Book Review: *Dangerous Passion* by David M. Buss, *New York Times Book Review,* February 13, 2000.

Weaver, Mary Anne. "A Reporter at Large: Gandhi's Daughters," *The New Yorker,* January 10, 2000.

Weingarten, Kathy. *The Mother's Voice: Strengthening Intimacy in Families.* New York and London: Guilford Press, 1994/1997.

Weissbourd, Richard. "Distancing Dad: How Society Keeps Fathers Away from Their Children," *American Prospect,* vol. 11, no. 2, December 9, 1999.

Wen, Patricia. "Where Children Are Seen, Not Heard: Web Cameras at Day-Care Centers Capture Parents' Attention, Spark Debate," *Boston Globe,* June 5, 2000.

West, Rebecca. "Eroto-priggery," *New Republic,* vol. 2, March 13, 1915.

Wiggins, David K. "The Play of Slave Children in the Plantation Communities of the Old South, 1820–1860." In *Growing Up in America: Children in Historical Perspective,* edited by N. Ray Hiner and Joseph M. Hawes. Urbana and Chicago: University of Illinois Press, 1985.

Wigglesworth, Michael. *The Day of Doom: Or a Poetical Description of the Great and Last Judgment with other poems.* Edited with an introduction by Kenneth B. Murdock. New York: Spiral Press, 1929.

Williams, Bernard. *Shame and Necessity.* Berkeley: University of California Press, 1993.

Williams, Joan. *Unbending Gender: Why Family and Work Conflict and What to Do about It.* New York and London: Oxford University Press, 2000.

Winnicott, D. W. *The Child, the Family, and the Outside World.* Baltimore: Penguin Books, 1964.

——. *The Maturational Processes and the Facilitating Environment: Studies in the Theory of Emotional Development.* London: Hogarth Press and Institute of Psycho-Analysis, 1965/1960.

——. "Hate in the Countertransference." In *Through Paediatrics to Psycho-Analysis.* New York: Basic Books, 1975.

Wright, Thomas Goddard. *Literary Culture in Early New England 1620–1730,* edited by his Wife. New Haven: Yale University Press, 1920.

Yalom, Marilyn. *A History of the Wife.* New York: HarperCollins, 2001.

INDEX